ENGLISH ⊞ HERITAGE

Book of
St Augustine's Abbey
Canterbury

Edited by Richard Gem

B. T. Batsford / English Heritage
London

© The authors 1997

First published 1997

All rights reserved. No part of this publication
may be reproduced, in any form or by any means,
without permission from the Publisher

Typeset by Bernard Cavender Design & Greenwood Graphics Publishing
Printed and bound in Great Britain
by Butler & Tanner Ltd, Frome and London

Published by B.T. Batsford Ltd
583 Fulham Road, London SW6 5BY

A CIP catalogue record for this book is
available from the British Library

ISBN 0 7134 8144 7

(Front cover) St Augustine's Abbey, view of the north aisle
wall; in the background is the central tower of the
Cathedral *(English Heritage).*

(Back cover) St Augustine preaching, from a stained glass
window of *c.* 1320 in Christ Church, Oxford *(National
Monuments Record, CVMA).*

Contents

Illustrations

Colour plates

Acknowledgements

The authors would like to record their gratitude to the following for their advice and assistance: Peter Atkinson, Jonathan Bailey, Paul Bennett, John Atherton Bowen, David Buckton, Richard Cross, Joan Denne, Christopher Harper-Bill, the late Jim Hobbs, Monica Kendall, Jonathan Kinghorn, Diana Phillips, Nigel Ramsey, Ian Riddler, Judith Roebuck, the late Dudley Snelgrove, Veronica Tatton-Brown and Jeffrey West.

Introduction

Richard Gem

597 is one of those key dates in English history that are known to many people, even if they have a less sure understanding of its precise significance other than that it was the year in which Augustine arrived in Kent to bring Christianity to the English. With all such key dates there is something symbolic about them; that is, they are only a shorthand for historical events that were more drawn out in reality. Yet, for all the symbolism of this particular date, it corresponds to a very real historical process that saw the establishment of the Christian religion as one of the principal bases for the development of English political, social and cultural life up to modern times and, fourteen centuries later, it is still regarded as worthy of national commemoration.

St Augustine's Abbey in Canterbury was a focus second to none in importance for the unfolding of the historical process begun by Augustine's mission. For its first century and a half the Abbey, in partnership with the Cathedral, helped to form the spiritual and cultural values of the whole English Church. Thereafter changing political and social circumstances assigned to it more of a regional than national role. But at the time of the Norman Conquest it rose again to particular prominence and forms a microcosm for the processes by which the English adapted to the changed order. Nearly a millennium after its foundation the Abbey was dissolved by Henry VIII, yet despite the dispersal of the monks and the demolition of the greater part of the buildings, the memory could not be effaced: all that it stood for was too integral a part of England's history.

Since the middle of the nineteenth century the site of the Abbey has been progressively recovered and explored, and this has gone hand in hand with research into its history. The culmination of this process was the designation of the Abbey by UNESCO in 1989 as a World Heritage Site; bringing with it the recognition that its cultural value was not merely national but universal. Following on from this, and with the 1400th anniversary of 597 occurring in 1997, English Heritage has undertaken the provision of a new museum display and the better presentation of the site as a whole.

The Abbey ruins, for all the interest they hold, will never succeed in revealing their full significance without the aid of a wider historical presentation. It is the aim of this book to contribute to the understanding of this wider context. The limits of space are such, however, that it has not been considered possible to write here a comprehensive history of St Augustine's Abbey. Rather the aim has been to focus on selected aspects that are of especial significance and interest: the early history of Augustine's foundation and its cultural attainments; the transformation of the Abbey in the eleventh century; its impact on the topography of the city of Canterbury and county of Kent; and the history of the site following the Dissolution.

In pursuing the several themes of the book, however, the reader is invited to bear in mind one overriding consideration: the Abbey was a complex institution sustained on a wide economic and social basis, yet it existed in order to pursue not secular but religious objectives –

the cultivation of the spiritual life as focused by the monastic rule. According to the *Rule of St Benedict* a monastery was to be 'a school of the Lord's service', in which the monk was to persevere in love and obedience until death, when he might look forward to becoming 'a dweller in the tabernacle of the Lord', that is, in the heavenly sanctuary. Meanwhile much of his life was spent in worship in the earthly sanctuary of the monastic church, while the remainder was devoted to study and the more mundane work necessary for sustaining the daily life of the monastic community and its visitors.

The monastic life was not, however, something that existed in some introverted isolation from society. King Wihtred of Kent made provision in a charter of 699, granting privileges to all the monasteries in his kingdom, that the monks were in return to honour and pray for the king. King Ine of Wessex put it even more explicitly in a charter of 704:

> without the impediment of secular affairs or the imposition of fiscal burdens, the monks with free minds are to serve God alone and, helped by Christ, are to practise the monastic training of the monastery according to the rule; and they are also to pour out their prayers worthily before the face of the divine Majesty for the state and prosperity of our kingdom; frequenting the churches, they are to strive to make intercession for our weakness with the office of their prayers.

Bede in a letter of 734 made a comparison between those sectors of society who received lands in return for military service to defend the community, and those who also received lands, but in return for religious service to the community. The monastery had an integral role within society, not outside it.

From Late Antiquity to the Middle Ages

Among the Benedictine abbeys of late medieval England, St Augustine's was one among others that had achieved wealth and status. But in terms of its history it was unique: none other (with the possible exception of Glastonbury) could trace back so long a development of monastic life: a development that started in the formative years of western monasticism as the ancient world was giving way to the medieval. That transition has been the subject of much historical research over recent years, and one conclusion of this has been that one cannot rigidly define the end of Antiquity, since it was a gradual process that affected different geographical regions and different areas of life at varying speeds. In England the transition is generally seen as coinciding with the abdication of responsibility by the central Roman authorities for the defence of Britain in 410, followed by the increasingly uncontrolled settlements in Britain of Saxons, Angles and Jutes from the area of modern north Germany and Denmark.

In western Britain, however, the native authorities managed to stabilize their position in the late fifth century and, as we know from archaeological evidence, were in continuing contact with the Mediterranean world until the middle of the sixth century. This was also the period in which the British Church was developing under leaders such as Illtud and David in the West, and Ninian and Kentigern in the North. The British Church was also in creative contact with the Irish Church through such figures as Finnian of Clonard, who in turn was a teacher of Columba. Columba was a contemporary of Augustine, emigrating from Ireland to Scotland and undertaking important missionary work there before dying at his monastery on Iona in 597 (Iona was later to become for a time a principal base for the conversion to Christianity of the north of England). A few years before this, *c.* 590, another Irish monk, Columbanus, had emigrated to the Continent where he founded monasteries in the Frankish and Lombard kingdoms (especially at Luxeuil, in eastern France, and Bobbio, north-east of Genoa), and had a major impact on the development of the religious life. He also corresponded with Gregory the Great and subsequent popes.

Gregory himself was still very much a figure belonging to the Late Antique Mediterranean world, although this was a world in continuing transition. The last Roman emperor in the West had been deposed in 476, but for nearly two centuries before this the emperors had not been resident in Rome, and for more than three centuries to come the 'emperor', as far as the papacy was concerned, was the ruler in Constantinople (whether or not there were also Gothic or Lombard kings in Italy). Gregory himself had been ambassador in Constantinople at one time, and relations between subsequent popes and Byzantine emperors remained critical to Church policy and even theology. As late as the middle of the seventh century a pope had been arrested and exiled because of his theological differences with the emperor; differences which a monk from Cilicia had helped articulate. The monk was Theodore of Tarsus, who in 668 was appointed archbishop of Canterbury. Theodore and his colleague Abbot Hadrian of St Augustine's, who was a native of the Byzantine province of North Africa, may be regarded as representatives of that Mediterranean culture that developed in continuity with Late Antiquity down to the middle of the seventh century, when it was significantly modified by the Islamic conquest of the Middle East and North Africa.

Whereas the Anglo-Saxon settlement of England may be seen as marking one important stage in this country's break with its Classical Roman past, against a larger canvas this event may be seen as only one part of the picture. Viewed either from the perspective of western and northern Britain, or from that of continental and Mediterranean Europe, matters were less clear. Around the time of Gregory's birth, *c.* 540, the Emperor Justinian had reconquered North Africa and Italy, reintegrating them into the empire. In a rather different way Gregory was concerned for the spiritual reintegration into the civilized Christian world of the barbarians who had settled in the former north-west provinces of the empire. It is a perspective which was even to reach down to the time of Bede. In summarizing Gregory's achievements in his *Ecclesiastical History of the English People* (II, 1), Bede writes that 'he converted our nation, that is the nation of the English, from the power of Satan to the faith of Christ ... our nation hitherto enslaved to idols he made into a church' (words reminiscent of 1 Peter 2: 9–10). Elsewhere (V, 21) he records a letter from the Pictish king Nechtan in which Nechtan recognized that 'the nation of the English had long ago established its religion following the example of the holy Roman and apostolic church', and he now promised that his people likewise would 'always follow the custom of the same church, insofar as they could learn this considering their remoteness from the Roman language and nation'. To Bede conversion to Christianity was essentially conversion to the religion of the Roman Church, with its customs and language. This was not the Rome of the remote past that he had in mind, but the continuing Rome centred on the papacy, in continuity with the apostolic past.

Against this background, St Augustine's Abbey in the first century and a half of its existence may be seen as an essential link in the cultural chain that reattached Anglo-Saxon England to a continental culture which had undergone a less interrupted development since the beginning of the fifth century and on into the seventh. The monastery thus formed a bridge not only for ideas in the field of monastic life and liturgy, but also in music, architecture, the arts, learning and education. The traffic over this bridge was not one way: what was received was enhanced and sent out in new directions, and Michael Lapidge has even felt able to write that it is 'legitimate to regard the seventh-century school of Canterbury as one of the high points, perhaps the acme, of intellectual culture in the early Middle Ages' – such were the achievements of Theodore and Hadrian.

Medieval monasticism and reform

The possibility of seeing the Abbey's links with a wider cultural milieu becomes more obscure in the centuries immediately following its first great flowering. This is certainly due in part to its changed political fortunes, but it must also be admitted that the historical sources are much less adequate following the death in 735 of Bede, who had incorporated into his *Ecclesiastical History* so much information given him by Abbot Albinus of Canterbury. By the middle of the eighth century the English Church was much less on the receiving end of missionary activity from abroad (though evangelization in the countryside was still seen as a priority), but was now an active participant in sending missionaries to the heathen peoples of Germany. As far as the Frankish rulers were concerned the conversion of Germany was seen largely as a political issue; but the missionaries themselves followed a path of non-violence and martyrdom. Of central importance was the West Saxon missionary Boniface, who was ordained bishop in Rome, and was in 732 appointed archbishop for Germany beyond the Rhine, where he later called on the English to send help to their kinsmen the Old Saxons. But Boniface was also a key figure, acting as papal legate, in seeking the reform of the Frankish Church in the 740s. One element in Boniface's programme was to work for a renewal of the monastic life, and in this he was assisted by the West Saxon monk Willibald, who had travelled through the east Mediterranean lands and had spent ten years at the monastery of Monte Cassino, south of Rome. The reform of the monastic life, and its clearer differentiation from the life of canons (those who were more engaged in pastoral work and less in contemplation), became one of the key elements in the religious policy of the Carolingian rulers of the Frankish state – rulers who, in the person of Charlemagne, were raised to the office of emperor by the pope in 800.

In 747 Boniface had written to Archbishop Cuthbert of Canterbury telling him about his reforms. Cuthbert responded by convening a council which issued a series of decrees, including ones calling for monks and nuns to continue leading a quiet life according to their rule, and for monasteries to live up to their name by being places of prayer and study, of silence and work for God. Boniface's ideas continued to bear fruit on the Continent in the religious policies of the Carolingian emperors of the early ninth century, and these in turn continued to influence England. Thus Archbishop Wulfred (805–32) pursued a vigorous policy for upholding and reforming standards in the religious life, which were threatened by secular encroachments on monasteries and their endowments. Wulfred carried through a reform of his own cathedral chapter at Canterbury, but we have no direct evidence for what was happening at St Augustine's. Yet it seems almost inconceivable that at this period the monastery was not following a truly monastic way of life.

Understanding the development of religious life in the ninth and early tenth centuries has to take account of documentary sources which paint a rather bleak picture. In the first place, Alfred the Great writing *c.* 890 laments the decay of learning in his day in contrast to the high standards that had once been found among church communities; while his biographer Asser complained that the monasteries in Wessex no longer maintained the monastic rule in any consistent way. This picture is sustained in the sources relating to the monastic reform movement which broke upon the English Church in the second half of the tenth century: in the views of the reformers there were really no authentic monks in England any longer, and the true spirit of the monastic life had to be reimported from the reformed religious houses of the Continent, such as at Ghent and Fleury. Yet occasionally we can see past this polemic, and may suspect that there were versions of the monastic life being practised, even if these did not meet the idealists' standards. Such was probably the case at Glastonbury, and perhaps at St Augustine's.

None the less it was as a result of the monastic reform movement of the second half of the tenth century, guided by the figures of Dunstan, Æthelwold and Oswald, and under the patronage of the West Saxon monarchy (which had by now created a united kingdom of England), that there emerged the form of Benedictine monasticism that was to characterize the remainder of the Middle Ages. The tenth-century movement was itself a return to the ideas of the Carolingian reformers of a century previous, especially Benedict of Aniane (not to be confused with the original Benedict), and it was a feature of the monasticism of the next two centuries that it was constantly trying to maintain its idealism by a return to the sources of monastic life. A new wave of enthusiasm came in the middle of the eleventh century, exemplified by the foundation in 1034 of the monastery of Bec in Normandy, where the future Archbishop Lanfranc became a monk. Another followed soon upon it, at the end of the eleventh century and early in the twelfth, with the foundation of the Cistercian order. St Augustine's Abbey was caught up in these currents by Canterbury's two great monastic archbishops of the period, first Dunstan and then, following the Norman Conquest, Lanfranc. The turbulence associated with the latter is discussed in detail later in this book; yet it must be recognized that these troubles were followed by over four centuries of stability, during which the Abbey settled into the dependable rhythm of the Benedictine life.

The changes associated with the Norman Conquest were, of course, far more sweeping in their impact than the reform of the religious life of monks. The Church itself was gripped by a mood of root and branch reform, which aimed at the elimination of perceived abuses by the reduction of lay power and the enhancement of ecclesiastical power, especially the power of the papacy. But, more generally, the whole culture of Europe was undergoing fundamental social and economic changes in the eleventh century, and one consequence of the Norman Conquest was

to link England more closely into these changes than might have been the case otherwise. This book is not the place to analyse this process in detail, but what is of concern here is that the cultural developments of this period in architecture, art and literature made it possible for the monastery of the eleventh and twelfth centuries to give new outward expression to the inner spirit of the monastic life. The rebuilt Abbey of the eleventh century and later, therefore, looked very different from anything that had preceded it in the previous 500 years.

From Dissolution to rediscovery

The late medieval Abbey had settled into the fabric of Canterbury and Kent, through its sharing in the life and physical structure of the city, and its management of its extensive agricultural estates in the countryside. It also played a role in the historical consciousness and affairs of the nation: it was the custodian of the tombs of the earliest archbishops of Canterbury and the first Christian princes; its abbot sat as a peer in Parliament. Yet this was all to be swept aside by Henry VIII's revolution in the sixteenth century. Traditional interests were a brake upon the crown's centralizing power; the lands of the monasteries could be used to secure the support of a new order. On 30 July 1538 the abbot and thirty monks surrendered to the crown St Augustine's Abbey and all its possessions. The ensuing demolition of the buildings and partial conversion into a royal lodging house are detailed below.

The suppression of the monasteries was the second act of the English Reformation, following on from the abolition of papal authority between 1531 and 1534. St Augustine's was perhaps more exposed than many other religious houses, because it represented and perpetuated the influence that the bishopric of Rome had on the foundation of the Church in England. But although the Dissolution may have been undertaken as an act of political expediency, the subsequent triumph of Reformation doctrine under Edward VI and

13

Elizabeth I justified the abolition of monasticism and confirmed that St Augustine's could not be refounded simply by a change in the political regime. Yet the end was not as final as sixteenth-century observers might have thought.

In the first place, Roman Catholicism and the influence of the papacy did not simply evaporate because the English crown and Parliament abolished their jurisdiction in England. Many English families remained Catholic, while English religious houses established themselves on the Continent awaiting the opportunity to return to England; it was to be a long wait, but emancipation eventually came in the nineteenth century, followed by the restoration of a Roman Catholic episcopate and the foundation of new monastic houses. The authority of Gregory and Augustine lying behind this current of resistance was not forgotten, and when a new metropolitan cathedral church was eventually built at Westminster, scenes from Augustine's mission were accorded a significant place in the decoration.

However, there was a second current that was equally important in keeping alive the memory, not so much of Gregory and Augustine, as of St Augustine's Abbey itself. The history of the contribution to this process of the antiquarians and topographical artists, then of the High Church Tractarian movement, and finally of the scientific archaeologists, is discussed later in this book.

The final word here should perhaps be to point out that these later centuries, no less than the earlier ones, belong to the history of St Augustine's Abbey, and help to make it a monument of the highest importance in the culture not only of the English nation but of the wider world. For that culture consists not only in the religious and artistic spirit, but also in the human urge to understand our past and to hand on that understanding to future generations.

1
St Augustine's life and legacy

David Farmer

The life and mission of St Augustine of Canterbury are not recorded in detail in any contemporary account, and our principal source is the rich but incomplete collection of the letters of Pope Gregory the Great (590–604). Gregory was the first mover of the conversion of the Anglo-Saxons and it was he who chose Augustine for the task. From the eighth century St Gregory rather than St Augustine was regarded as England's apostle. Bede's eloquent rhetoric illustrates the point:

> We can and should by rights call him our apostle, for though he held the most important see in the world and was head of churches which had long been converted to the true faith, yet he made our nation, till then enslaved to idols, into a church of Christ, so that we can use the Apostle's words about him: 'if he is not an apostle to others, yet at least he is to us, for we are the seal of his apostleship in the Lord'.
> (*Ecclesiastical History* II, 1)

Gregory's earliest biographer, an anonymous monk of Whitby, and also St Aldhelm of Malmesbury (639–709), used similar words. In 747 the synod of Clovesho decreed that the feast of 'our father Gregory' should be celebrated on 12 March.

In the following account an attempt will be made to present Gregory and Augustine in their own time. It will be necessary to question or correct works of monastic historians who wrote long afterwards. Their writings favoured the importance and antiquity of their own venerable institutions. It is often forgotten that Bede's narrative was written about 130 years after Augustine's arrival in England in 597. It was largely inspired by Albinus, abbot of the monastery of Sts Peter and Paul (later called St Augustine's) in Canterbury (*c.* 710–32), who was a product of the Canterbury school of Archbishop Theodore (669–90) and Abbot Hadrian (*c.* 669–*c.* 710). Naturally Bede as a good scholar made use of several of Gregory's letters as well as of the substantially authentic replies of Gregory to Augustine's questions. But he did not know (or failed to use) important letters like that to Queen Bertha, the wife of Æthelberht, king of Kent. Also his account of Augustine's supposed consecration in southern Gaul is inaccurate. Later medieval accounts were sometimes influenced by rivalry with the Cathedral priory of Christ Church, or by the archbishops' claims to primacy, or by manipulation of charter evidence to support claims of exemption from episcopal authority. Later still, Dom Clement Reyner in his *Apostolatus Benedictinorum in Anglia* (The Apostolate of the Benedictines in England) (1626) would claim that Gregory and Augustine were both Benedictines, and that the conversion of England was mainly due to the preaching of their monks. He wrote for his own time with immense, wide-ranging scholarship, but several important conclusions are rejected nowadays. His work, like that of his predecessors William Thorne and Thomas of Elmham (both monks of St Augustine's) have been influential in forming traditional accounts.

Pope Gregory the Great

By the standards of any age, Gregory was a great man of many achievements (**colour plate 2**). Patrician, ruler and administrator, mystic and spiritual guide, pastor and apostle, thinker and writer, he is rightly regarded as one of the makers of the Middle Ages. Born in 540, he became prefect of the city of Rome in 573. Thus he was responsible for its finances, buildings and food supplies. But only a year later, this civil servant became a monk. He founded six monasteries in Sicily on his family estates and turned his own home, on the Cælian Hill in Rome, into a monastery. There he became a monk, enjoying for four years a life of seclusion and contemplation: these years he regarded as the happiest in his whole life. A man of his experience would not be left in peace for long. In 578 Pope Benedict I ordained him deacon, with the care of organizational charity in one of the seven districts of Rome. After Benedict's death in the next year, Pope Pelagius II sent him as ambassador to the imperial court at Constantinople. This was a uniquely important post. Rome, long in decline, was still part of the empire ruled from Constantinople, relations with which had long been difficult.

Gregory's achievements here contributed to his development as theologian and ruler. In 585 however he returned thankfully to his monastery. Soon he was elected abbot. This he remained until 590, when he was chosen bishop of Rome much against his own wishes; but he accepted the charge, to the subsequent benefit of the whole Church.

His 850 surviving letters (copied into his *Register*) are both a monument to his organizational powers and a source for the study of his ideals and achievements. His care for order and good government, his versatility,

common sense and understanding of local needs stood out against a background of uncertain survival for Rome itself. There had been no Western emperor for 130 years: Ravenna, not Rome, was the centre of imperial government in Italy. Lombards from the north were a constant threat. Rome was subject to floods, food shortages and plague. Because of these disasters Gregory began his pontificate with penitential processions. Although the times appeared so bad that the end of the world seemed close, this was no excuse for inaction. On the contrary, he redoubled efforts to feed Rome with produce from Sicily, and aimed at far more than survival by starting missionary work among Lombards and Anglo-Saxons. He was also constantly interested in Europe's monasteries as important centres of prayer and learning in a disintegrating old society as well as in a barbarian new one. He often protected them from bishops' interference. His own monastery provided the liturgy in an urban church, living off its estates but deprived of access to rural pursuits. Study and teaching flourished in a regime austere enough to impair Gregory's health.

The famous story of Gregory seeing fair Anglo-Saxon boys on sale as slaves in Rome and prophesying that the race of Angles would become fellow-heirs with the angels may well be substantially true. It was recorded as tradition by Bede and narrated more fully by the monk of Whitby. But more certain evidence of his plans for England's Christianization comes from Gregory's letters. The clearest but not the earliest reference is in a letter of 599 to Syagrius, bishop of Autun: after long thought he had 'undertaken the task of preaching to the English through Augustine, then prior of my monastery and now our brother and fellow-bishop'. This supports the Whitby monk's claim that Gregory would have liked to lead the mission himself. As early as 595 he had written to Candidus, ruler of the papal estates in southern Gaul, instructing him to use surplus funds to clothe the poor and to buy from captivity English youths of 17 or 18 to be given to monasteries. A priest should be sent with them in case they were ill or in danger of death on the journey, presumably to Italy (*Letters* IX, 223; VI, 10). Some may have returned to England, either with Augustine in 597, or with the second body of clergy in 601.

The mission of Augustine

In the late sixth century, Kent and the Frankish kingdoms in Gaul had close links. Æthelberht's father had a Frankish name, Irminric, while his wife Bertha was a daughter of King Charibert of Paris (died 567) and Queen Ingoberg (died 589). In 596 Gregory wrote to the young Frankish princes Theuderic and Theudebert, shortly after the death of their father Childebert II (Charibert's nephew). Gregory told them that he had heard that the English earnestly desired the Christian faith, but that the neighbouring priests were indifferent and did nothing to help. In a similar letter to Queen Brunhild, the princes' grandmother, Gregory said that the local priests showed no pastoral concern for them (*Letters* VI, 51, 60). Were these priests Frankish or British? It is hard to be certain, but Bede repeatedly blamed the latter for the same failing. Their refusal of help could act as a spur to the Franks to provide for their failure, and make more acceptable the sending of Frankish priests on Augustine's mission.

Bede's narrative of Augustine's journey from Rome to England can be supplemented by reference to those letters not used by him and by further insight into the contemporary realities (**1**). Augustine was prior of Gregory's monastery of St Andrew in Rome in 596, but we know nothing about him before this date. He was sent on the arduous journey to England with 'several' companions. Some writers claim that Augustine took forty monks from Rome, but Bede's number of forty describes the augmented party of missionaries when they reached Kent (*Ecclesiastical History* I, 25). By then Frankish priests had joined them at Gregory's request. It may be conjectured that fifteen or twenty monks would have been a realistic number, comparable with the twelve monks and an abbot so often

sent on a new foundation at a later date. Whatever their number, the group which left Rome was purely monastic. Having overcome their initial reluctance, they travelled as far as the monastery of Lérins, off the south coast of France. Here however they sent Augustine back to Rome to explain why they now wished to turn back. They had heard that the people were barbarous, fierce and unbelievers: these Italian monks did not even know their language. They had been chosen, some think, for this task because Gregory could count on their obedience more than that of other Roman clergy. Gregory's letter to the monks strongly exhorted them to continue the work begun and to accept Augustine as their abbot, a new rank given him by Gregory. At the same time Gregory sent letters of introduction to Frankish rulers and bishops, telling them that he had instructed Augustine to collect priests to help in the mission. Gregory's several letters met the real problems. One of these was the lack of a common language: this would now be overcome. The word *interpres*, used of the Franks, meant more than 'translator'; it also meant 'expounder, explainer or negotiator'. The addition to the missionary party of men with such skills was both necessary and desirable. People of Kent and northern France might at least understand each other, but inhabitants of Rome, especially monks, could not be expected to know Old English. By providing for Frankish clerics, Gregory met one of the difficulties of the formerly hesitant monks.

From these same letters, Augustine's projected route through France can be deduced: Lérins, Marseille, Aix-en-Provence, Arles, Vienne, Autun and Tours. All these had churches of long standing. They must have travelled also through Lothar's northern Frankish kingdom of Neustria (Gregory thanked him for his help) to Boulogne or Quentavic for the Channel crossing. On their way Augustine had been consecrated bishop 'by the bishops of the Germanies'. This probably refers to the territory of Theudebert in eastern Frankia

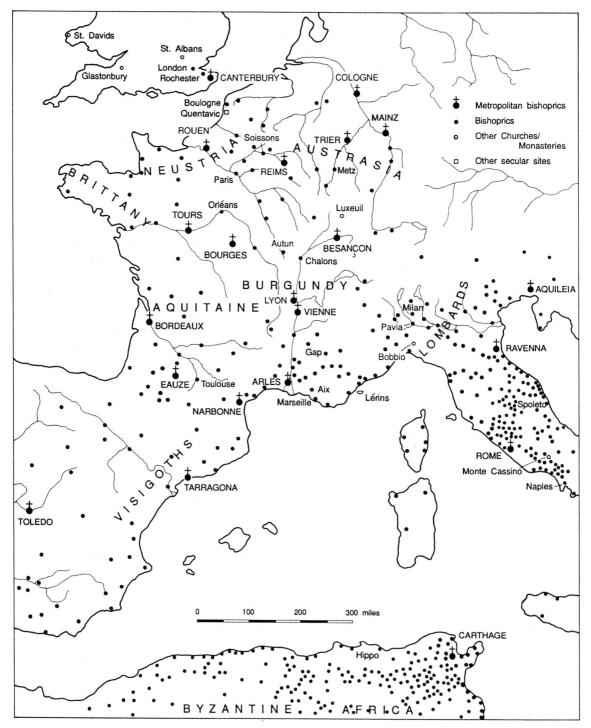

1 Map of Europe around 600, showing distribution of bishoprics and other major centres (Canterbury Archaeological Trust).

(Austrasia). This statement in Gregory's letter of 598, following his reference to him as 'fellow-bishop' in 597, makes it virtually certain that Augustine was already a bishop when he reached England (*Letters* VIII, 29, 4), and not, as Bede claimed, consecrated on a later visit to Arles (*Ecclesiastical History* I, 27). The place of his consecration is unknown, but Reims or even perhaps Trier is possible. In the above route of his passage through France, Tours is off the direct route, but either political circumstances or the immense prestige of Tours as the see of St Martin may have prompted a detour. In any case, by 597 Augustine was far better equipped for his immense task than he had been in 596: now in episcopal orders with both Italian monks and Frankish priests of proven commitment at his disposal, his party of forty was like a miniature church ready to expand.

Augustine and the conversion of Kent

Bede's memorable account of King Æthelberht's meeting with Augustine was both factual and symbolic. In it can be seen the representatives of two different societies, two different faiths, two different laws and two different ways of life. When Augustine landed in Thanet, he sent messengers to the king saying he had brought him the best of news, the 'sure and certain promise of eternal joys in heaven and an endless kingdom with the living and true God to those who received it' (*Ecclesiastical History* I, 25).

The king, warned in advance and having some knowledge of Christianity through his queen Bertha and her chaplain, Bishop Liudhard, was non-committal but not hostile. He told them to remain in Thanet, where they would be provided with all they needed. Some days later he came to see them. They met him in procession, carrying a silver cross and a painting of Christ, singing litanies and praying for the salvation both of themselves and of all the people. The king was accompanied by his principal subjects, who all heard the message of salvation, explained presumably by the Frankish priests. Æthelberht answered by promising them

food and hospitality at Canterbury, as well as allowing them to preach. He did not promise to accept their teaching nor to 'forsake those beliefs which I and the whole English race have held so long'. His caution was very understandable, his tolerance very praiseworthy. The newcomers settled in Canterbury and followed there the life of the apostles and the early Church with prayer, fasts and vigils, being 'content with what was necessary, despising all worldly goods as alien, and preaching the word of life to those whom they could'. The first church they used was that of St Martin, the church of the queen and her episcopal chaplain, situated to the east of the town. Here they first performed the liturgy, preached and baptized.

Bede's account lacks dates, notably for the king's baptism. It has often been remarked that chapter 33 of his narrative in Book I follows naturally on from chapter 26, although these are now separated by Gregory's answers to Augustine's questions. These were provided for Bede later by the priest Nothelm. It is very often asserted that Æthelberht was baptized in 597, but this is by no means certain. The principal evidence for it is a letter of Gregory to the Patriarch of Alexandria. In this he said that he had *heard* that 10,000 Anglo-Saxons had been baptized. This number cannot be pressed. Early medieval writers are notoriously 'unscientific' in estimating numbers and sometimes used biblical approximations. Even if we translate it as 'a large number' we are still faced with an unlikely time-scale. Anglo-Saxon kings, who always needed the support of their thanes, would be very unlikely to change their religion unless they could carry most of those with them. Princes in exile and kings who lost their lives by assassination or in battle are reminders of this need. Also, in several Anglo-Saxon kingdoms a preliminary acceptance of Christianity was followed by a relapse into paganism. Æthelberht and others might well have thought that traditional paganism had been very profitable. By following it, he had become the most powerful king of his time in England, he had achieved an advantageous marriage, and was poised to make his title of *bretwalda* (overlord king) more of a reality.

In describing Northumbria's conversion in about 625, Bede described the meeting of the *witan* (king's council) to decide whether or not to accept Christianity: only after this event did the baptisms take place. We hear of no such meeting in Kent, but it is reasonable to suppose that there was one, especially as Æthelberht (according to Canterbury tradition resumed by Bede) did not exert political pressure or any compulsion towards conversion. In the event, his own son Eadbald did not become a Christian during his father's lifetime. A few months seems far too short a time for paganism to be abandoned. Several place-names within a few miles of Canterbury indicate ancient centres of pagan worship, suggesting a lingering tradition. In general, it is reasonable to suppose that the old paganism was more tenacious than a cursory reading of Bede would suggest. We can only conjecture about the large numbers of conversions claimed so early: it may be that they refer to the reconciliation of some of a racially mixed Kentish population who were already Christian in sympathy.

The foundation of the churches of Canterbury

Æthelberht's baptism probably took place nearer (or in) 601, when Gregory wrote to him in June of that year a letter of congratulation and admonition. This was followed by reinforcements of personnel, books, chalices and relics from Rome, which indicate that the real turning-point had been reached. From 601 expansion could begin in earnest. First, the Cathedral was established within the Roman walled city, while the monastery was set up outside the walls. The dedications of both were Roman ones: Christ Church was the ancient dedication of St John Lateran, the cathedral church of Rome, while the two monasteries outside Rome's walls were St Peter's and St Paul's. Roman too were the dedications of the

suffragan cathedral at Rochester to St Andrew and of two lesser churches in Canterbury to St Pancras and the Four Crowned Martyrs, secondary relics of whom might well have been brought from Rome in 601 (secondary relics are pieces of cloth that had been in contact with the saint's tomb, or even dust taken from it).

Fundamental to the whole plan for Canterbury was the existence of two major churches, not one. Each would have its proper function. The monastery would be the centre of contemplative prayer and monastic life, while the Cathedral, with its mixed personnel, would be the centre of the more active apostolate. It seems clear that this arrangement was found in other towns in Western Europe: Rome, Milan, Tours and Toulouse, among others, all had from early times both a cathedral and a monastery. The liturgy (public worship) of the two churches was different: at the Cathedral, it seems, there would have been Lauds and Vespers each day (as they are usually called nowadays). They were the ancient version of a morning and evening public prayer, consisting mainly but not exclusively of the psalms. The monks, being specially committed to prayer, had Lauds and Vespers but also had vigils (the night office), with the so-called Little Hours at various times of the day. On special occasions, such as Easter Eve, the vigils would be shared by all the clergy with their bishop, as well as by many of the people. The suggestion that at Canterbury the monks came across into the Cathedral to perform the monastic liturgy there habitually seems unlikely, but on the greatest feasts like Easter or Christmas they might well have supported their bishop in this way. In his Answers to Augustine, Gregory commendably provided for Augustine to adopt Frankish or other non-Roman elements in the liturgy; this invitation to flexibility however makes reconstruction of the early liturgy doubly difficult: unfortunately there are no surviving early liturgical books from Canterbury.

The monks of the Canterbury abbey performed their traditional roles of prayer, hospitality, almsgiving and, at least within the monastic school, of teaching. In the pioneer period it seems likely that laypeople also were taught by monks. But their 'apostolic life', described by Bede, was simply traditional monastic life as St John Cassian (of Marseille, died 433) and others understood it. For them the monks represented the commitment and fervour of the first believers, but the term 'apostolic' did not have its thirteenth-century meaning as used by the orders of friars. If any monks were attached to the Cathedral clergy, they would have joined the bishop's household and not tried to live a double life.

Practical arrangements for the Canterbury churches required Gregory's guidance. All revenues of the see, as in Rome, would be divided into four parts. One would be for the bishop with his household and his guests, one for the clergy, one for the poor (including almsgiving and possibly monastic hospitality) and one for the repair and restoration of churches. Provision was also made for minor Cathedral clergy who could marry if they wished. Obviously this enactment distinguished the Cathedral sharply from the monastery.

The wider aspects of Canterbury's relations with other churches were also provided for. Neither the Frankish churches nor Canterbury would have metropolitan jurisdiction over the other, but each would have the duty of fraternal correction. With regard to future development of the Church in England, Gregory established Canterbury as a metropolitan see with eventually twelve suffragans, while further development in the North would see a metropolitan see established at York with twelve suffragans of its own. Again, neither metropolitan would dominate the other. This plan for the future proved permanent in most respects, but with the change made by Augustine for political reasons that Canterbury, and not London, would be the metropolitan see. Augustine's metropolitan status, awarded by the pope with the bestowal of the *pallium* (a woollen scarf-like vestment worn as a symbol of office), is rightly seen as the crowning glory of his episcopate and as the model for future metropolitan sees like Utrecht and Mainz.

Augustine's wider mission

At this point a résumé may be attempted. Gregory had chosen Augustine, monk and prior of his own monastery, who enjoyed his special confidence, to lead a mission to England. It seems likely that there had been some previous request for help from England itself, possibly coming through Bishop Liudhard. Gregory's expectations were not overtly imperial or political in character, but did take for granted the importance of Christian rulers, who would be expected to promote positively the spread of Christianity. Gregory's plan evolved in response to circumstances. Augustine, learned in the Scriptures, would exercise his episcopal role by preaching and presiding at the Eucharist, but would not lose his monastic roots, as his monk-companions would be established in a monastery nearby. There is no need to think that Gregory rejected his own teaching that no one 'can serve as a cleric and persist under order in the monastic rule, nor can he be bound by the restraint of a monastery who is forced to remain in the daily service of the church ... the duties of each office are so weighty that no one can rightly discharge them. It is very improper that one man should be considered fit to discharge the duties of both' (*Letters* V, 1). No doubt in the early years of the mission there was some flexibility and Augustine was in charge of both monks and clerics. By and large, however, we can suppose that the Cathedral clergy were Frankish and the monastery Italian in personnel, but that each from an early time would have Anglo-Saxon recruits, some of them former slaves.

The work of preaching to the pagans was done mainly by Cathedral clergy, but always under Augustine's direction. Two surviving sermons have been attributed to him. Both have some plausibility with regard to subject-matter, as well as liturgical style and content, but the manuscript that ascribes them to him comes from ninth-century Germany. One is a reply to complaints that the faith had been preached only very recently. To this the preacher answers that the hearers' ill will remains because they still live in sin: complaining about the doctor's late arrival is useless if the patient does not want to be healed. The other sermon concerns marriage: the Church's teaching, the prohibited degrees, the single life and sins of impurity. The preacher appeals to his hearers to do penance before communion is distributed: if they refuse penance, they will not be able to receive it. This last decision may be anachronistic and suspect, but there is no doubt that the Christian teaching on marriage would provide one major difficulty in the expansion of the Church in England.

Another reverse to Augustine's mission was his unsuccessful attempt to secure the co-operation of the British (Welsh) bishops. Bede's account of this last was, as he admits, legendary, and did not spell out all the implications. Gregory, it seems, wished Augustine to be metropolitan of the whole of southern Britain, just as the future archbishop of York would rule the North. His plan was admirable; his geography was seemingly based on documents of the Roman empire. To obtain the desirable unity, co-operation with the British was essential. Two meetings were held: one preliminary, the other decisive. Seven British bishops and many learned men are said to have been present and they refused to co-operate through attachment to their own customs and because they thought Augustine was haughty and inflexible. The issues discussed were the dating of Easter, the rite of baptism and active sharing in the apostolate to the English. Augustine offered to tolerate all other divergent customs if unity could be attained on these three. This however was refused. There is no need to suppose that all the faults were on one side, nor need we see with Bede the later deaths in battle of the monks of Bangor at the hand of a pagan Northumbrian king as fitting punishment for Celtic intransigence. But however we view the matter, it was a set-back

to the effective metropolitan rule by Augustine envisaged by Gregory (Bede, *Ecclesiastical History* II, 2).

For the rest of his episcopate Augustine concentrated on consolidation of the Church in south-east England: by establishing two suffragan sees at Rochester and London; by spreading literacy, presumably through schools at Canterbury; by encouraging the achievements of his augmented body of helpers, neither exclusively monastic nor exclusively Italian; and by following Gregory's important and far-reaching instruction to 'destroy the idols, not the temples'. Augustine's policy was to provide Christian centres, from which evangelization could take place, rather than to multiply individual, wandering preachers without a secure base.

Augustine's death and burial

The monastery of Sts Peter and Paul, subsequently renamed St Augustine's, became the burial place of the Christian pioneers of Canterbury. Augustine was buried in the chapel of St Gregory, whose active follower he had been for many years. The Gregorian connection was stressed in death, as well as in life. Augustine's epitaph reads:

> Here lies the most reverend Augustine, first archbishop of Canterbury, who was formerly sent hither by St Gregory, bishop of Rome; being supported by God in the working of miracles, he led King Æthelberht and his nation from the worship of idols to faith in Christ and ended his days of his office in peace: he died on the twenty-sixth day of May during the reign of the same king.

The year was certainly before 610 and probably 604, the same year as Gregory's death (and see p. 36). Augustine left three bishops, a number of clergy and one monastery to continue the work he had begun. His pioneering work amid immense difficulties was done; others would reap where he had sown. His veneration as a saint began, like all others, at his tomb. This would have been visited by monks and others: the earliest surviving calendars record his feast on 26 May. His example must have helped his successor Laurence in the crisis he soon faced on Æthelberht's death in 616. This threatened to end joint action in the apostolate by king and archbishop. Bertha, Æthelberht's first wife, had died and the king married again. His second wife's name and race are unknown. Eadbald, his son who succeeded him, married his stepmother in accordance with Germanic pagan custom. This caused consternation among the churchmen, familiar with St Paul's ruling on a comparable case in the church of Corinth. Fortunately for the future of the apostolate, Eadbald put her away and married Ymme (Emma), daughter of a Frankish king. Only now did he become a Christian. By this marriage, the links between Kent and Frankia were renewed and strengthened.

Augustine's monastic legacy

The best-known legacy of Augustine was his diocese with his cathedral and the metropolitan status of Canterbury. He also presumably helped Æthelberht to commit his laws to writing and to encourage literacy and stable government. Another element of his legacy was the monastic life he set up in his Canterbury monastery. Was this formally Benedictine, and did he bring the Rule of St Benedict (compiled in the first half of the sixth century) into England? Confident affirmative answers have often been made to both questions, but there is no hard evidence for either.

Gregory devoted a whole book of his *Dialogues* to the Life of Benedict, mainly a collection of miracle stories, and praised his Rule for its discretion and lucidity. It was known at Rome as one of several monastic rules then current: it is important not to equate 'monastic' and 'Benedictine' as if they were synonymous terms. To this day there are plenty of monks who do not follow Benedict's rule, especially in the East, where St Basil's rule (which Benedict praised) is still the norm. In the

2 Earliest copy of the *Rule of St Benedict*, c. 700, English (Oxford, Bodleian Library, Hatton 48, fol. 29r).

early Middle Ages various Irish rules, especially of St Columbanus, were followed. Moreover, a number of founders were eclectic in proposing rules for their own monasteries which provided the basis and explanation for their own decisions. This epoch of 'mixed rules' lasted for some centuries. England's share in the diffusion of Benedict's rule was however both early and important. The oldest manuscript of this work in existence was written in England in about 700 (**2**). Its origin is unknown, but it was at Worcester in the eleventh century.

The main agent of the diffusion of Benedict's rule in Western Europe was the English St Boniface (died 754), whose advocacy of it, backed by the success of his monastic foundations at Fulda (north-east of Frankfurt in Germany) and elsewhere, ensured it a place in Carolingian legislation from 742 onwards for all monasteries in the Frankish territories. England's importance in this process belonged to the eighth rather than the seventh century; its importance

was however based on a predominantly
Benedictine monasticism current in Northumbria
with Wilfrid and Benedict Biscop, and in Wessex
with Boniface at Nursling. Kent seems to have
little comparable evidence to offer in the form of
contemporary manuscripts or Lives, but there is
evidence from Old English manuscript glosses on
works from the school of Theodore and Hadrian
at Canterbury that at least Benedict's rule was
known there. Whether it came through Benedict
Biscop or through Hadrian or from elsewhere we
do not know. More convincing is the presence of
two manuscripts of Benedict's rule from St
Augustine's in the tenth century. This is the first
solid evidence for the presence there of Benedict's
rule as the monastery's principal guide.

The Benedictine character of St Augustine's
Abbey must have been influenced by the
presence of St Dunstan (3) as archbishop of
Canterbury from 966 until 988. He had revived
Benedictine life at Glastonbury from 940. The
movement which he initiated achieved great
importance throughout southern England. Like
other monastic revivals of the time (Cluny and
Gorze) the Rule of St Benedict was crucial,
insisting as it did on obedience, chastity, poverty
and stability. Numerous foundations were made
by Dunstan's followers Æthelwold and Oswald,
who reformed the cathedrals at Winchester and
Worcester respectively, and also many other
monasteries, in accordance with a uniform
observance set out in the *Regularis Concordia*
('The monastic agreement', which drew on the
observances of reformed continental
monasteries such as Ghent and Fleury). The
influence of these monasteries as stable centres
of dedicated Christian commitment, to say
nothing of their hospitality, almsgiving and
cultural distinction in art, architecture, music
and vernacular literature, was considerable and
lasting. These monasteries, sometimes founded
by and for long supported by kings, became
notable institutions for nearly 500 years of
English history. While often studied for
economic and social reasons, their importance
as centres of prayer and study, liturgy and

3 Self-portrait of St Dunstan kneeling before Christ, from
St Dunstan's Classbook (Oxford, Bodleian Library, Auct.
F.4.32, fol. 1).

evolving monastic ideals was unique. It seems
likely that Christ Church itself, under Dunstan's
abiding influence, adopted the rule of St
Benedict either shortly before or soon after his
death in 988. From then onwards Canterbury
had two Benedictine monasteries instead of one;
but St Augustine's was the older of the two, and
antiquity conferred prestige, if not power.

When the Norman Conquest came in 1066,
initially little changed at St Augustine's. But by
Lanfranc's arrival in 1070 as the new archbishop,
a Norman monk, Scolland of Mont-Saint-Michel
(or Scotland as he is called in the English sources),
was abbot-elect. Most other English abbeys at this
time soon also received Norman abbots. At Christ
Church Lanfranc introduced important reforms.
He not only rebuilt the Cathedral, still in ruins at
the time of his consecration, into a larger, more
clearly articulated structure, but also introduced
Norman monks from Bec to hold the most
important offices. Bec was where both Lanfranc
and his immediate successor St Anselm were
Benedictine monks. This monastery, founded by a
retired Norman knight, Herluin, became thanks
to these two scholars one of the most intellectually
advanced and distinguished in Europe. Its
monastic observance however was similar to that
of other Norman monasteries recently revived by
William of Dijon, and strongly based on Cluny
(the order of Cluny emphasized a life of liturgical
worship, offered in the context of a life of
personal poverty and chastity, with Benedict's
Rule as its principal guide; through Fleury, it was
a main influence on the *Regularis Concordia*).
The tenth-century reformers had looked to the
king for help and patronage against the intrusions
of lay owners of monasteries. In the case of St
Augustine's, there had apparently never been any
lay owners, but it was under the care and
protection of the archbishops of Canterbury. This
state of affairs, however distasteful to those
monks who sought complete autonomy and

exemption in the eleventh and twelfth centuries, had in all probability saved it from the worst 'corruption' in the ninth.

At Christ Church however all was not well. Even so devoted a partisan of Canterbury and the 'old ways' as Eadmer (an Anglo-Saxon monk who had been at Christ Church since boyhood) told how the life of pre-Conquest monks of Canterbury resembled that of 'earls', with plenty of hunting and other unmonastic pursuits. The intellectual attainments, compared to those of Bec, seemed rather limited: manuscripts betray poor Latinity with need for Old English glosses, and the range of books available could not compare, even in patristic works – such as those by Augustine of Hippo or Jerome, with the best of Norman monasteries. Lanfranc's 'policy' for the monasteries was one of tighter discipline with large new buildings and better-equipped libraries (though he was less interested, it seems, in the fine achievements of artistic scribes).

The cult of St Augustine following the Norman Conquest

Lanfranc appears to have had little interest either in some of the English saints. These seemed to him to lack firm evidence of their lives and achievements. Even Dunstan and Ælfheah (or Alphege, archbishop of Canterbury 1006–12) were initially under suspicion and their tombs were removed to the north transept. At some unknown date after Anselm's famous intervention in their favour, their tombs were restored to the Cathedral sanctuary.

Initial suspicion of English saints at Canterbury was matched elsewhere, notably at St Albans, Abingdon, Evesham and Malmesbury. But in all these places, in the late eleventh or early twelfth century, all concerned agreed on venerating the local saints: frequently they were translated to shrines in the large new churches which were more splendid than those they replaced. Writers of new Lives greatly helped in this process. Osbern and Eadmer at Christ Church were the most notable examples. Frequently Lives were used to provide lessons at

Matins and appropriate reading in the refectory. The Classical monastic Lives of Antony and Martin were well known in England as elsewhere, but at St Augustine's the Flemish hagiographer Goscelin provided new Lives of the old Canterbury saints.

This was done in the context of the 'translation' (that is, the removal of the relics from the old church into the new) of the early Canterbury saints in 1091. The important historical background to this event may be read elsewhere in this book (pp. 54–6). Here it seems sufficient to stress that this translation was a deeply unifying force in a divided community, which had recently lived through traumas of rebellion and restoration. Wido, abbot of St Augustine's, brought to a successful conclusion the architectural changes planned by his predecessor and combined them with the re-enshrinement of the bodies of St Augustine and the other early saints of Canterbury. This was an event of major significance for the monastic community, for the town and for the cult of Canterbury saints elsewhere.

Its chronicler, Goscelin of Saint-Bertin, had lived in the Wiltshire diocese for some years, at Sherborne and Wilton, under the patronage of Heremann, its bishop from 1045 to 1078. After Heremann's death Goscelin had lived in several monasteries writing the Lives of local saints in need of new documentation. Peterborough, Ely, Ramsey and Barking, as well as Wenlock and Chester, all used his services. He came to Canterbury in about 1090 and remained at St Augustine's until his death in 1107. He completed various writings on Augustine (two Lives, an account of the Translation and a book of Miracles) together with Lives of other Canterbury saints, such as Laurence, Mellitus and Justus, with Honorius, Deusdedit, Theodore and Hadrian as well as Liudhard and Mildrith. Goscelin's writings, sometimes too elaborate for modern tastes, were greatly esteemed by William of Malmesbury (died c. 1143), who rated him as the best writer on English saints since Bede and as a practitioner of fine style. Reginald of

Canterbury, who knew him personally, praised him as cheerful, kindly and honourable, one who kept clear of disputes, was the best of singers and a good teacher of grammar and rhetoric. It must be said that his Lives of Augustine have little authentic fresh material (not already in Bede), but that the Translation account (written in its present form in 1095) as well as the miracle stories do link us closely with the events of 1091 and their consequences.

The translation of Augustine's relics had begun badly. Accidents, some fatal, had taken place because, it was believed, the saints resented being disturbed. Under the presidency of Bishop Gundulf of Rochester, however, it was brought to a successful conclusion in a week. It was he who struck the first and decisive blow to open the tomb of Augustine, necessary to move the body after nearly 500 years undisturbed. What would be found? An incorrupt body like Cuthbert's? Interesting works of art of the early seventh century? Or just dust and ashes? Goscelin reported honestly. He made no claim for substantial incorruption, but did mention the sweet scents, perhaps due to ointments and spices used at the burial. The shape of the body was recognizable from the arrangement of the vestments, but a handful of dust contained nothing more substantial than a few tiny fragments of flesh. The body had decomposed, but everything in the tomb was to be moved to the place of honour in the eastern chapel of the new church. Augustine's tomb was opened on Saturday 6 September and on the next day the relics were installed in the new shrine. The choir was vested for the occasion in white and purple vestments and the sanctuary decorated with hangings and flowers as if for Easter. On the Tuesday the new tomb was sealed. On Wednesday the tombs of Mellitus and Laurence were opened, together with that of an unknown person whom they called 'Deo notus' ('known to God'). On the Thursday these bodies also were translated to new tombs. On the Friday attempts to open the other tombs failed, but Saturday saw the translation of the relics of Justus, Honorius, Deusdedit and Nothelm. This day, 13 September, was subsequently approved by Anselm as the feast of the translation of the saints of Canterbury.

Most translations of saints' relics were accompanied by 'miracles'. St Augustine's translation was no exception. In Antiquity and the early Middle Ages, before scholastic theologians worked out with precision the various types of causality and before the thinkers of the seventeenth century devised the phrase 'laws of nature', the word 'miracle' had a wider connotation. It was hardly different from *mirum*, a wonderful event which revealed the power of God, often in and through the saints. There was no question of an exception to, or suspension of, laws of nature. Goscelin classified Augustine's miracles into general and particular. In his account of the Translation he refers to cures of all kinds: of the ill and the weak, the feeble and the crippled. By mentioning that they came in the evening and departed cured in the morning, he seems to imply the ancient practice of 'incubation', or lying down to sleep, at the shrine. More important was the reconciliation, in the presence of the saint in his new shrine, of enemies long estranged. Bishop Gundulf used the occasion to preach on the Resurrection of the Dead and the perpetual reunion with the saints in heaven. He also absolved sinners and gave the blessing to all, still enjoying the authority of Lanfranc who had made Gundulf his deputy in all episcopal actions. Goscelin continued with accounts of visions or dreams, without distinguishing sufficiently whether these were experienced sleeping or awake. A well-known priest of Kent saw the heavens opened above St Augustine's church, with a ladder reaching from its roof into heaven. Angels in splendid white garments came down to the apostle of England's tomb; the whole monastery was bathed in blinding light like a huge globe of fire. A Frankish woman from East Anglia was told in sleep that she should come to Augustine's tomb, wash her side with water and then drink the water. After this she would be cured, and so it came to pass.

In his work on the miracles, Goscelin classified them further, and most of them have the purpose of showing the spread of knowledge about Augustine and his cult. Some relate the punishment of the irreverent and the sacrilegious, while those who repent of their sins are healed. A Scandinavian, we are told, stole a fine cloth from Augustine's tomb. It stuck fast to his fingers and could not be removed. Afterwards the man became a Christian. Then there are some shipwreck stories with local detail. A fleet of fifteen ships went to Normandy to pick up stone needed for Westminster Palace. Fourteen ships were lost in a severe storm: only the fifteenth survived, whose captain was a devotee of Augustine, who did not jettison his load but trusted in the saint to bring him to safety. In the time of King William an excellent Kentish man went to Constantinople to serve the emperor, presumably like other Anglo-Saxon exiles, in the Varangian guard. He won the favour of both emperor and empress, through whose generosity he built a richly furnished church in honour of St Nicholas and St Augustine. From there he went on pilgrimage to Rome and Compostela, carrying an icon of Augustine, apostle of the English. Thus Greeks of all districts including Athens praised Augustine and prayed for his intercession. Goscelin's concern to chronicle the spread of Augustine's influence and miracles led him to claim these in Northumbria, Ireland and Anjou. These stories lack historical evidence but occur in Goscelin's Lives of Augustine. More plausible is his claim that the Emperor Henry asked for relics in the late eleventh century.

The spread of Augustine's cult can also be established from the evidence of calendars and other books of church services (**4**). The earliest surviving English calendars all record his feast, but only later medieval ones record the rank or solemnity with which it was celebrated. The feast was ubiquitous in monasteries before 1100; after this date, the churches of Canterbury and those who had elected a Canterbury abbot or received relics of Augustine celebrated it at a higher rank. At Christ Church Augustine's two feasts (26 May

4 Fifteenth-century depiction of St Augustine with baptismal font, from book of *Lives of Saints* (Oxford, Bodleian Library, Tanner 17, fol. 111r).

and 13 September) enjoyed the same liturgical rank as those of All Saints or Sts Peter and Paul. At St Augustine's however the same two feasts had the very highest rank (like Christmas or St Thomas of Canterbury). In addition there was (on 27 April) a feast of all the saints whose relics were kept in the monastery. Other local saints like Hadrian, Æthelberht, Liudhard, Eanswith and her niece Mildrith also enjoyed separate feasts. In 1356 all exempt churches (that is, exempt from the jurisdiction of the local bishop) in England celebrated Augustine's feast by papal decree as one when manual work was forbidden.

Evidence for the spread of his cult outside England is found firstly in a thirteenth-century calendar of Bec: the monastery of Lanfranc and St Anselm honoured Augustine, Dunstan, Edmund and Neot. At Rome the feast was made universal by the missal of Pius V (1570); it had long been in the Roman Martyrology (the official register of Christian martyrs) and in the Sarum Missal (the medieval Salisbury missal in general use in southern England). Roman interest in him can also be seen in the early seventeenth-century rebuilding and decoration of a group of chapels adjacent to the church of San Gregorio Magno on the site of Pope Gregory's monastery of St Andrew in Rome (**5**).

The cult of saints in Christian belief

Mention of the relics of Augustine and their importance in the development of his cult requires for its full understanding at least some general knowledge of relics in the cults of saints in the Christian Church as a whole. The first error to refute is that they are a medieval accretion, best forgotten. On the contrary, there were shrines of the saints, centred on their tombs and relics, well established in the ancient Mediterranean world, well before the beginning of the Middle Ages. When Augustine came to England, he brought with him (as other

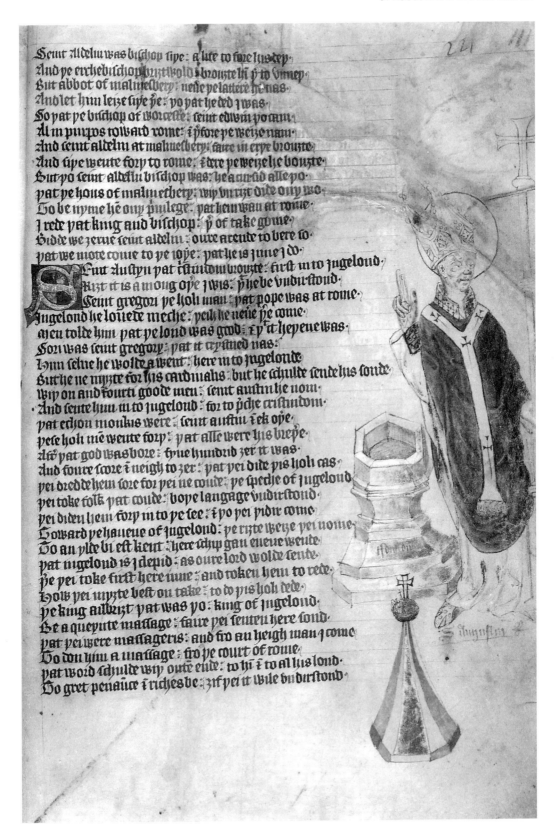

Seint Aldelm was bischop sipe · a lite to fore hisdey ·
And pe erchebischop Bryhtwold · brouzte hi p to vinnep ·
But abbot of malmesbery · nesse pe lattere he nas ·
And let him leize sipe pe · po pat he ded I was ·
So pat pe bischop of worcestre · seint edwin po cam ·
Al in purpos toward rome · I pfore pe weize nam ·
And seint aldelm at malmesbery · faire in erpe brouzte ·
And sipe wente forp to rome · I dere pe weize he bouzte ·
But po seint aldelm bischop was · hea curud alle po ·
pat pe hous of malmesbery · wip vnriзt dide ony wo ·
Ho be nyme he ony puilege · pat hem wan at rome ·
I rede pat king and bischop · p of take gome ·
Bidde we зerue seint aldelm · oure arende to bere so ·
pat we mote come to pe joye · pat he is I nne I do ·

S Eint Austyn pat cristindom brouzte · first into Ingelond ·
riзt it is amoung ope I wis · p he be vndirstond ·
Seint gregori pe holi man · pat pope was at rome ·
Ingelond he louede meche · зeuh he neue pe come ·
Men tolde him pat pe lond was good · I p it heyene was ·
Son was seint gregory · pat it crystned nas ·
Him selue he wolde awent · here into Ingelonde ·
But he ne myзte for his cardinals · but he schulde sende his sonde ·
Wip on and fourti goode men · seint austin he nom ·
And sente him into Ingelond · for to pche cristindom ·
pat echon monkis were · seint austin I ek ope ·
pese holi men wente forp · pat alle were his brepe ·
als pat god was bore · pre hundrid зer it was ·
And foure score I neigh to зer · pat pei dide pis holi cas ·
pei dredde hem sore for pei ne coude · pe speche of Ingelond ·
pei toke folk pat coude · bope langage vndirstond ·
pei diden hem forp into pe see · I po pei pider come ·
Toward pe haueue of Ingelond · pe riзte weize pei nome ·
To an ylde bi est kent · here schip gan euere wente ·
pat Ingelond is I clepid · as oure lord wolde sende ·
pe pei toke first here inne · I token hem to rede ·
How pei myзte best on take · to do pis holi dede ·
pe king ailbriзt pat was po · king of Ingelond ·
be a queynte massage · faire pei senten here sond ·
pat pei were massageris · and fro an heigh man I come ·
To don him a massage · fro pe court of rome ·
pat word schulde wip oute ende · to hi I to al his lond ·
So gret penaúce I riches be · зif pei it wile vndirstond ·

5 Rome, chapels rebuilt 1602–7 on the site of Pope Gregory's monastery of St Andrew (R. Gem).

missionaries did) the cults of saints and of their relics in the church of his origin. These had already been in existence for centuries, and in some respects go back to sub-Apostolic times.

The martyrdoms of the apostle James and the deacon Stephen are recorded in the Acts of the Apostles, but the earliest firm evidence for the cult of a martyr occurs in the contemporary account of the martyrdom of St Polycarp, bishop of Smyrna (died *c.* 166). The faithful collected his bones, 'more precious than jewels of great price', and buried them in a safe place, over which the Eucharist would be offered on the anniversary of his death. Originally local in character, the cults spread from one church to another by the exchange of calendars and martyrologies. This was accompanied by some keepsake of the dead saints such as cloths or dust from their tombs. These tombs were the places of cures, sometimes so striking and frequent that bishops moved outside the towns to the cemeteries to supervise them. Sometimes indeed the town thus gained a new centre on a different site. The shrines were regarded as places where heaven and earth met, especially in the cures accomplished by the body of the dead saint. No matter how gruesome their deaths, their joy in the new life of heaven was firmly believed, and received artistic expression in mosaics such as those of Ravenna and Rome, as well as in the poems of Venantius Fortunatus

(died *c.* 610). Sometimes their miracles concerned restitution of property or protection of their custodians: such stories are found in connection with continental and English saints. Here indeed, as very often, there was no difference between England and Europe in Anglo-Saxon times. The earliest saints chosen for dedications in England were universal saints such as the Blessed Virgin, St Michael and (soon) All Saints, as well as Roman saints like Peter and Paul, Laurence and Pancras. In Augustine's England there were no martyrs because there were no persecutors; but Anglo-Saxon missionaries like the two Hewalds suffered martyrdom, as did St Boniface. There were however several confessors of special holiness who were soon venerated as saints: Augustine, Aidan, Cuthbert, Birinus and Bede, as well as Hilda and Etheldreda (Æthelthryth) and others.

As popular demand for relics developed, so did the practice grow of separating particular bones from the saint's body. Constantinople accepted this practice long before Rome did; but in East and West there was a particularly strong demand for relics of saints who had known Christ on earth: the apostles and evangelists, St Mary Magdalene, St Lazarus and St John the Baptist. Hence the great importance for Canterbury of the gift by King Cnut and Queen Emma of an arm-bone of St Bartholomew. If we are to consider historical authenticity, the bones of the undisturbed Canterbury saints were much more likely to be authentic than a bone of an apostle, but demand for the latter seemed to confer the prestige of having a memorial of one very close to Christ himself and so 'more precious' than those of local saints.

In an unscientific age and with the clear perception of God as the source of all good, whose power was often shown in accordance with Christ's promise in and through their actions, it is not surprising that saints and relics were so highly esteemed. This was so in all walks of English (and European) society: kings, thanes, peasants and monks would all unite in venerating the relics of saints. For the monks especially they were seen as powerful protectors and intercessors; at St Augustine's Abbey they silently presided over the liturgy until the Dissolution. They also provided a unique link with heaven. This was why Gundulf preached on the Resurrection of the Dead at Augustine's translation, and why Eadmer in his treatise on relics stressed how monks would be their custodians until the Day of Judgement: as custodians not owners – they were not free to give them away. The belief in the abiding presence of saints is also seen in innumerable charters of foundation and endowment: hard-headed magnates, sometimes with blood on their hands, would give by charter to a saint, such as St Edmund, and to the abbot and monks who served him, considerable estates of land and other goods. At Canterbury however there was a distinction, according to Goscelin, between Christ Church and St Augustine's: 'there he rules, here he dwells'.

The monks' daily round of prayer, both of adoration, and of intercession for the needs of the whole Church, was performed for God, in the presence of his friends, and with the eschatological element of preparation for, and anticipation of, the joys of heaven.

The English Benedictines following the Dissolution

The Benedictine monastic life was extinguised in England by the Dissolution under Henry VIII (1535–40), but was briefly revived by Queen Mary (1554-8) at the royal abbey of Westminster. Here Benedictines, mainly elderly and bookish, lived again in the style of late medieval monasteries under the guidance of Abbot Feckenham. But in June 1559 Queen Elizabeth I brought this revival to an end. After this date young Englishmen who wished to live the monastic life joined reformed monasteries in Spain or Italy. By 1607 the sole survivor, it was believed, of pre-Reformation English monasticism was Dom Sigebert Buckley of Westminster. He (like Abbot Feckenham) had spent many years in prison for his religious beliefs, but while at liberty in Clerkenwell, old and nearly blind, received as monks of Westminster and (it was believed) of the ancient Congregation of England two priests on the English mission who were already professed members of the Cassinese Congregation of St Justina. At about this time also four autonomous priories of English Benedictines came into existence: St Gregory's at Douai (now Downside Abbey in Somerset), St Laurence's at Dieulouard (now Ampleforth Abbey in North Yorkshire) and St Edmund's in Paris (now Douai Abbey). The fourth house of St Benedict's at Saint-Malo did not survive. In 1619 a papal brief *Ex incumbenti* of Paul V united these English Cassinese monks with a larger body of English monks from the Spanish Congregation into a single body which was 'a continuation and restoration and (if necessary) a re-erection of the English Congregation'; this would enjoy all privileges, faculties etc. which the English Congregation of the Benedictine order had been granted in the past. Thus through a very tenuous historical link the juridical reality was re-established. For about 300 years however there were no abbeys or priories in England, but the monks consisted of missioners who were professed at their overseas priories, to which they returned at uncertain intervals, sometimes not until old age. Their link with St Augustine's was that they believed they were continuing the apostolate begun by him in 597.

In 1856 Benedictine monks again became near neighbours of St Augustine's, Canterbury. Father Wilfrid Alcock, a member of the Subiaco

6 Westminster Cathedral, chapel opening off baptistery, mosaic and marble decoration by Clayton and Bell, 1902–12: Pope Gregory dispatches Augustine and his missionaries to England.

Congregation, together with other English monks from Subiaco (where St Benedict had begun his monastic life), arrived to start a missionary foundation at Ramsgate Abbey in Kent. During the nineteenth century they started schools and staffed parishes in the Isle of Thanet, besides expanding (some think prematurely) into the field of foreign missions. In recent years shortage of monks has obliged some reductions in their commitments, but they are still the closest monks in geographical terms to the old Abbey at St Augustine's.

Following the restoration of the English bishoprics by Pius IX in 1850, the archbishop of Westminster, Nicholas Wiseman, adopted certain Canterbury elements on to his coat of arms as a sign that he too was following in the footsteps of St Augustine in England. By custom St Gregory's church in Rome is reserved as the titular church of the English cardinal. This link helps to explain the choice of subject of some of the mosaics in Westminster Cathedral when it was built 1895–1903 (**6**).

Whether bishops or monks or missionaries, Catholic or Anglican, many have claimed and still claim that their way of life is inspired by the example of St Gregory and of St Augustine; hence they all have an interest in the centenary of which this volume is one expression.

2

The Anglo-Saxon Abbey

Susan Kelly

King Æthelberht and the conversion

At some point in the later part of the year 597 a
momentous meeting took place on the Isle of
Thanet, the north-eastern tip of Kent, then
separated from the mainland by a broad
waterway known as the Wantsum Channel.
Some days before, a group of around forty men
from continental Europe had landed
(traditionally at Ebbsfleet, near the eastern
mouth of the Wantsum). Their leader was the
Italian Augustine, who had been sent by Pope
Gregory the Great to establish the first Christian
mission to the Anglo-Saxons of lowland Britain.
Accompanying him were several of his fellow-
monks from Rome, as well as a number of
priests from the Frankish kingdom, and no
doubt also a bevy of assistants and servants. On
landing, Augustine had sent a message to
Æthelberht, the ruler of the kingdom of Kent,
notifying him of the arrival of the mission. The
news seems to have been unexpected;
Æthelberht ordered the party to remain on the
island while he considered what to do. It must
have been an anxious time for Augustine and his
companions. Finally the king and his entourage
travelled to Thanet, to confront the newcomers.
The meeting seems to have been meticulously
arranged. It took place in the open air, because
King Æthelberht subscribed to a superstition
that magicians (and surely these foreigners were
magicians) could ply their tricks more efficiently
in an enclosed space. Augustine and his
companions were certainly not averse to putting

on a spectacular display: they arrived at the
meeting-place bearing a silver cross and an icon
of Christ, chanting litanies, praying energetically
and preaching 'the word of life' to Æthelberht
and his assembled noblemen. The king's
response was measured and dignified: he could
not abandon his traditional beliefs immediately,
but he was willing to receive the Christians
kindly and to allow them to preach without
conditions. More practically, he promised to
provide them with provisions and a dwelling-
place in the city of Canterbury, the 'metropolis'
of his kingdom. Triumphantly the members of
the mission marched in procession to
Canterbury.

By far the most interesting figure in the
encounter is Æthelberht, whose mild and
hospitable response to this foreign intrusion
seems quite remarkable. Æthelberht is the first
Anglo-Saxon king about whom we have any
substantial information, and he emerges as a
formidable ruler. His kingdom of Kent was one
of the smaller of the tribal realms which had
begun to develop in lowland Britain after
Germanic invaders had overwhelmed the
remnants of the Roman polity in the fifth and
sixth centuries; but it was already noticeably
wealthy, with riches that probably derived at
least in part from exploiting the important
trading routes that ran from the French and
Frisian ports through the Wantsum Channel and
up the Thames to London. But Æthelberht's
power spread beyond the borders of the Kentish

kingdom: he was one of a small number of early Anglo-Saxon kings who achieved an exceptional status, and who enjoyed some measure of overlordship over all the English kingdoms in the area south of the River Humber. There was good reason for Pope Gregory to focus the initial missionary effort on Æthelberht.

There were clearly also other factors involved. Archaeological finds show that the Kentish people had close cultural and commercial connections with the Christian lands of the Franks across the Channel. Some years previously Æthelberht had married a Frankish woman named Bertha, daughter of a former king of Paris and a member of the royal dynasty of the Merovingians who had ruled the Franks since the fifth century (see p. 17). This may not have been the first such inter-marriage, for Æthelberht's own father, Irminric, his predecessor as king of Kent, had a name of Frankish type. There are sources which suggest that the Merovingian kings may have claimed some kind of formal suzerainty over south-eastern England; whether this had any practical reality is unclear, but it may provide a context for the alliance between a pagan English king and a Christian Frankish princess. It was a condition of the marriage that Bertha be allowed to practise her faith without interference, and she brought Bishop Liudhard with her to Kent to act as her chaplain; it can probably be assumed that her household also contained a number of other Christian Franks. They worshipped together in what is said to have been an old Roman church dedicated to St Martin. The dedication was not necessarily one surviving from Roman times: the ancient church which Bede mentions could have been rededicated when Bertha began to use it, for Martin was a saint especially dear to the Merovingians.

Æthelberht had therefore been exposed to Christian practices for some years before the arrival of Augustine, and this familiarity helps to explain why he was so ready to welcome and support the newcomers. Moreover, Pope Gregory had exacted from the Frankish rulers a guarantee of protection and support for the mission, which probably precluded an overtly hostile reaction from the Kentish king. It may be that Æthelberht had already expressed some willingness to consider the conversion which would serve to integrate him with the post-Roman rulers in continental Europe. He certainly seems to have received baptism within a relatively short time of Augustine's arrival, and the missionaries' rapid and spectacular success was probably largely due to his sponsorship.

Royal mausoleum and monastery

The former Roman city of Canterbury in which Augustine and his companions now installed themselves would have been a ruinous and sparsely populated place. It had been deserted during the fifth century, for a period long enough for much of the Roman street pattern to disappear below a layer of rubbish and humus. Some reoccupation occurred subsequently, for excavation has revealed scattered huts built by the new Anglo-Saxon settlers, but during the sixth century Canterbury may have functioned principally as a tribal meeting-place and a market: some of this activity perhaps took place within the enormous Roman theatre, the ruins of which would have been the most prominent feature in Canterbury when Augustine arrived. By the later sixth and seventh centuries, Canterbury was beginning to develop once more into an urban centre with an important economic role. It is possible that Æthelberht played some part in the revival and restoration of what he appears to have regarded as his capital, the 'metropolis' of his kingdom. At the very least, Augustine's decision to establish his primatial seat at Canterbury, rather than in London as Pope Gregory had planned, is probably a reflection of the king's wishes. Æthelberht seems to have been a man who had thought hard about the kingship and its outward manifestations. A few years after Augustine's arrival the king issued a written lawcode, the first Anglo-Saxon ruler to do so. Significantly, the laws are in English rather than Latin, they concern mostly secular subjects and they stand in a Germanic tradition; it seems very likely that they essentially reflect an initiative of Æthelberht rather than of Augustine, even though part of their function was to assimilate the new Christian Church within the current legal framework. The issue of a lawcode, the acceptance of Christianity and (perhaps) the establishment of a 'capital' at Canterbury may all have been part of a policy by Æthelberht to redefine himself as a king on the model of his Frankish kinsmen; there is a chance that he was consciously modelling himself on the celebrated Clovis (died 511), founder of the fortunes of the Merovingians, the first Christian king of the Franks and the first to issue a written lawcode, who also established a capital (at Paris).

It is important to bear in mind these Frankish parallels when considering Æthelberht's role in the foundation of the religious house which was to become St Augustine's Abbey. Our only early source for the foundation, the *Ecclesiastical History* of the Venerable Bede (a devout advocate of monastic life), not surprisingly emphasizes the ecclesiastical and monastic aspects of the project. The initiative is ascribed to Augustine, who 'founded a monastery not far from the city, to the east'. But it seems to have been Æthelberht who was responsible for the construction. With Augustine's encouragement, the king 'built from its foundations the church of the Apostles St Peter and St Paul and endowed it with various gifts, so that the bodies of Augustine himself and all the bishops of Canterbury and the kings of Kent might be placed in it'. Evidently the establishment had a dual function, as a monastery (with an abbot) and as a burial church. Augustine himself came from a monastic background and may have felt it a priority to set up a formal monastery in the new mission station, where churchmen could concentrate on the spiritual duties of prayer and liturgical celebration; their contemplative life would complement the activities of the clergy

carrying out missionary work, who would of necessity have had much more contact with the secular world. Augustine's long-term plan may have been to imitate the arrangements in Rome, where the monks of local monasteries took over responsibility for celebrating the liturgy in the great basilicas, thus freeing the basilican clergy for their pastoral duties.

Nevertheless, there must be some doubt as to whether there would have been much enthusiasm for diverting the resources and manpower of the fledgling mission for the foundation of the new establishment, had there not been a purpose other than the promotion of monastic life. King Æthelberht is likely to have been far more interested in the new church's role as a dynastic burial-place for himself and his successors. Our (admittedly scanty) evidence suggests that pagan Anglo-Saxon kings were buried with lavish grave-goods in cemeteries, often under tumuli; the Sutton Hoo ship-burial (shortly after 625), which seems to represent the last flickering of the pagan tradition, gives us some idea of how much pomp and ceremony might attend a high-status interment. By converting to Christianity, Æthelberht had decisively cut himself off from his ancestral past: the trauma that this could involve is demonstrated by the story of a Frisian king a century later who was informed, as he approached the baptismal font, that he would go to heaven but that his ancestors were necessarily in hell, whereupon he leapt back, declining to be separated from his dead kinsfolk. The Church had to provide a newly converted king with some acceptable substitute for the pagan rituals of royal burial.

The idea of building a royal mausoleum in a Christian church, with the opportunity for display and ceremony (and the spiritual benefit of having resident clergy perpetually praying for one's soul), was already well established in the barbarian kingdoms of Europe, especially among the Franks. Clovis, the first Christian king of the Franks, founded a burial church for himself and his family outside the walls of Paris, near the shrine of the Roman martyr St Genofeva; this was the church of the Holy Apostles, later known as Sainte-Geneviève. As far as is known, all Merovingian kings after Clovis' time were buried in churches, some of them dynastic mausolea, some of them personal foundations. Under Cologne Cathedral in 1959 were discovered two possibly royal Frankish tombs, apparently dating from the second quarter of the sixth century (only a generation or two after the conversion of the Franks). One was of a young woman, richly dressed, who was interred with vessels that may have contained offerings of food and drink; the other was of a boy about six years old, buried with helmet and weapons. Clearly the transition from the pagan tradition of burial with grave-goods to the more austere Christian ritual could be a gradual one. By the time that Æthelberht and Augustine founded their new monastery outside Canterbury, the Merovingian kings across the Channel were already accustomed to being buried in lavish tombs in churches. Æthelberht would have been aware of this, if only through his Frankish consort, and is likely to have developed an early interest in making provision for his own burial and that of Queen Bertha. Augustine, for his part, probably recognized that the construction of a royal mausoleum by Æthelberht would represent an emphatic gesture of commitment to the new faith.

It was the burial function of the new church that governed the choice of its location. According to Roman law, human burial could not take place within the walls of a city or urban centre: so Roman Canterbury, like every other Roman city, was surrounded by extensive cemeteries, many of them lying along the roads which radiated out from the city gates. These rules about extramural burial were less strictly observed in the new barbarian Europe, but it would still have seemed to Augustine that the appropriate place for the new burial church was outside the city walls. The site chosen was only just outside Canterbury, with easy access to the Cathedral church inside the city; as such it was

more convenient than the area around St Martin's Church, rather further to the east (see **70**). Excavation has shown that there was a Roman inhumation cemetery within the area of the later Abbey precincts, and it is possible that there was an ancient shrine erected over one of the graves, of the type which often provided a focus for new extramural churches in early medieval Europe (St Alban's Abbey, built over the shrine of a Romano-British martyr, is an example of this kind of development).

The date of the foundation

Later St Augustine's sources fixed on 605 as the year of the Abbey's foundation, and this was enshrined in the dating clauses of three entirely spurious charters in the name of King Æthelberht, which were forged at St Augustine's in the later eleventh or twelfth century (see **9**). It is a matter of some doubt whether this traditional date has any validity. The Canterbury houses of St Augustine's and Christ Church appear to have preserved very few records of the early years of St Augustine's mission. The lack of information is already noticeable in the early eighth century. Bede, who completed his *Ecclesiastical History* in 731, was in communication with Abbot Albinus of St Augustine's (of whom more below); and yet, despite his constant preoccupation with establishing exact dates, he was unable to say exactly when Augustine died. We know that the archbishop was still alive in 604, when he consecrated bishops for the new sees of London and Rochester, and that he was dead by 610, when Pope Boniface IV wrote a letter to his successor, Laurence. Much later sources from St Augustine's Abbey claim that Augustine's death occurred in 605, supposedly in the same year as that of his patron Pope Gregory (although Gregory actually died in 604); but again this may not be based on valid information.

According to Bede, the new church of Sts Peter and Paul was not yet completed and consecrated when Augustine died, so he was buried outside and then reinterred within the church at a later date in a side chapel (or *porticus*) on the north side of the building, which was to become the official burial-place for the archbishops of Canterbury. At St Augustine's it was remembered that Queen Bertha had also died before the Abbey church was finished, so her body had later to be moved. She must have been the first member of the royal family to have been buried in the southern side chapel, which was intended as the mausoleum of the kings of Kent, and it may indeed have been the case that the main inspiration for the construction of the new burial church was the death of this Merovingian royal lady and her desire to be given a tomb worthy of her ancestors. Æthelberht himself was buried in the Abbey when he died in 616 (or between 616 and 618). For the next century and a half the Canterbury monastery was the established burial-place of the kings of Kent and their families, a truly successful dynastic mausoleum. Some members of the dynasty seem to have been interred elsewhere, in other religious houses of which they were particular patrons; but St Augustine's remained the principal dynastic burial church until the collapse of the independent Kentish kingdom in the 760s.

Benefactions to the Abbey

Not surprisingly, the Canterbury monastery was the focus of considerable generosity and patronage from the Kentish kings. One of the three forged charters in the name of King Æthelberht contains a list of treasures which are supposed to have been given by Pope Gregory to the king and then passed on by him to the Abbey: these include a silver platter, a gold sceptre or staff, a horse saddle and bridle decorated with gold and gems, a silver mirror, a silken cloak and a decorated robe. It is a curious collection. Were these the contents of Æthelberht's tomb, discovered when the Abbey's ancient royal graves were exhumed during the rebuilding of the Abbey church in the later eleventh century? (The charter was probably forged at around this time or slightly later.)

A more secure benefaction is that of Æthelberht's son, Eadbald (616–40), who built a second church, dedicated to St Mary, located a little to the east of Sts Peter and Paul but on the same axis. It was probably also in Eadbald's reign that a third church, dedicated to St Pancras, was constructed further to the east, again on the same axis. The reason for building this cluster of churches may have been to create a multifocal stage for elaborate liturgical processions and celebrations; but they would also have multiplied the opportunities for the deployment of additional royal patronage and lavish display.

The Anglo-Saxons took great pleasure in gold and sumptuous jewels, and there is some evidence that the interiors of churches might be very lavish indeed. Precious vessels and other treasures would often have been given to the Church by kings or by private individuals as pledges of piety, or they may have provided bullion which could be melted down and reworked by ecclesiastical craftsmen, or gems to be used for decorating book-covers, or ivory to be carved, or silk to be embroidered. The Sutton Hoo trove gives us some idea of how much treasure it was felt appropriate to expend in the grave of a high-status pagan; while Christian ritual frowned on the interment of such grave-goods in a tomb, there was nothing to prevent the laity from lavishing decoration on the churches where their families were buried. Unfortunately, we have no exact details about early benefactions of such treasures to the Canterbury monastery, and the objects themselves had little chance of survival, but there are notices of later gifts: in the eleventh century Queen Emma is said to have provided costly palls for the saintly tombs in the Abbey; Archbishop Eadsige (died 1050) bequeathed to the Abbey two golden and gilded vessels, 100 marks to build a tower, and a glossed psalter, which was kept chained to St Gregory's altar; and Archbishop Stigand gave a large silver crucifix.

Far more is known about the other major form of patronage to the Canterbury monastery – the gift of landed estates. The records of such grants were recorded in the form of land-charters from at least the 670s onwards (no documents of this kind survive from before that date, but it is possible that some were produced). These functioned as title-deeds, and religious houses were careful to preserve them, although the vicissitudes of war and riot, the occasional domestic conflagration or flood and the attention of generations of mice (not to mention the widespread destruction that accompanied the dissolution of the monasteries in the sixteenth century) have all ensured that only a small proportion of Anglo-Saxon land-charters has survived to the present day.

The early archive of St Augustine's is of quite respectable size, thanks to the labours of thirteenth- and fourteenth-century monks who made copies of the Abbey's muniments in registers and cartularies; the original pre-Conquest documents have all disappeared. A remarkable feature of the archive is the high proportion of title-deeds which date from the seventh, eighth and ninth centuries: it appears that the Abbey built up much of its landed endowment in this early period. Our information about the very earliest land-grants to the community is badly flawed, because the surviving charters are late forgeries: but they do show that later generations believed that King Æthelberht and his son had endowed the new church with land to the east of Canterbury (equivalent to the Abbey precincts and the Domesday manor of Longport), an estate in the area of Chislet to the north-east of the city, and another great landholding at Northbourne, some 24km (15 miles) to the east. Rather more reliance can be placed on the records of donations by King Hlothhere (673–85) and King Eadric (685–6) of land around Stodmarsh and Fordwich, in the tongue of high ground between the Great Stour and the Little Stour as they ran into the Wantsum, and there is also good reason to believe in the grant of an estate at nearby Littlebourne by King Wihtred (690/1–725).

Economic basis of the early Abbey

All these places which formed (or are said to have formed) part of the early endowment lay in the northern coastal region and river valleys of east Kent, where the earliest Anglo-Saxon settlements were established (7, see also 10 and 75). The land is fertile and easily worked, and it was to become the most prosperous and thickly settled region of Kent. But from an early stage the inhabitants of these areas came to have vested interests in other, often distant, parts of the Kentish kingdom. In the south-west of the kingdom lay the vast area of the Kentish Weald, a wooded region with clayey soils that had relatively little permanent settlement before the later Middle Ages but which was immensely important to the inhabitants of distant villages, who drove their livestock (principally swine but also cattle, horses and sheep) across the North Downs to graze in the Wealden wood-pastures over the summer. Another exceptionally important area of summer grazing was in Romney Marsh to the south, which carried large flocks of sheep, driven down from the north.

Access to the Weald and Romney Marsh was vital for the agricultural economy of settlements north of the Downs, and at an early date there seems to have evolved a system of commons whereby different villages claimed customary rights to pasture their animals in specific areas. Later many of these commons were broken up and the grazing rights passed into the possession of private landowners, such as St Augustine's. There is a glimpse of this process in one of the St Augustine's charters which describes an agreement between the community and the royal vill at Wye in 762: in return for allowing the king's agents to share the Abbey's water-mill (location unspecified), the Abbey's tenant at Chart was to be given grazing rights for his flock of swine in the Weald.

7 Map of St Augustine's Abbey estates in north-east Kent in the late Anglo-Saxon period (T. Tatton-Brown and Canterbury Archaeological Trust).

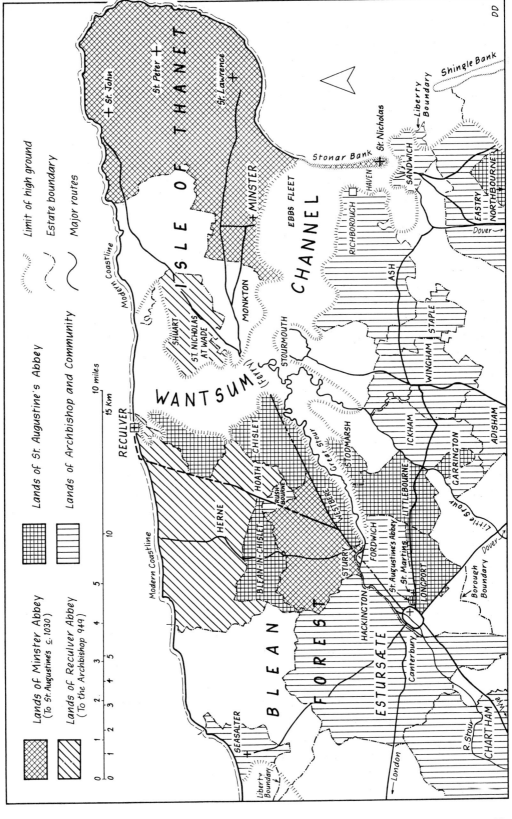

The nature of Kentish landholding meant that the acquisition of an estate could entail the simultaneous acquisition of a scatter of rights and privileges outside its boundaries: salt factories in the coastal marshes, fisheries and weirs in the rivers and coastal lagoons, permission to collect firewood in the king's forest in certain quantities and at certain times of the year, swine-pastures in the Weald and dairy farms in Romney Marsh. One charter preserved in the Abbey provides rare evidence for a mine: in 689 the community was given a piece of iron-bearing land, almost certainly in the Weald where there had been a major iron industry in Roman times. The mine may have been used to produce metal for the Abbey's own purposes, for knives and tools such as axes and saws; or it could have been exploited commercially. Religious houses seem to have been important conduits of technological information into Anglo-Saxon England. It may have been ecclesiastics who introduced from the Continent the idea of the water-mill; this may be borne out by the eagerness of the reeves of the royal vill at Wye to share a mill belonging to St Augustine's instead of building one.

Some religious communities in Kent also dabbled in trade and commerce, apparently taking advantage of their proximity to the trade routes between London and the Continent. A small corpus of eighth-century toll-privileges shows that the house of Minster-in-Thanet maintained three trading ships, and the bishop of Rochester and the abbot of Reculver had at least one each. These ships ventured to London and almost certainly to Gaul, probably acquiring luxury merchandise and perhaps also selling the produce of ecclesiastical estates. There is no documentary evidence for participation in the system by St Augustine's, but it seems unlikely that the community stood aloof. By the 760s it would appear that there was an important market-centre strung along the Great Stour around nearby Fordwich (where the Abbey had early territorial interests), channelling merchandise in and out of

Canterbury and north-eastern Kent under the supervision of the agents and toll-gatherers of the Kentish kings.

The early abbots

The wealth generated by landholdings and other sources of income was vital for the maintenance and expansion of the Canterbury monastery as an independent institution. Already during the seventh century it was beginning to develop a distinctive ethos. The first abbot was a priest and monk named Peter, one of the party that arrived on Thanet in 597, and almost certainly one of the monks from the Cælian monastery who had set out with Augustine the previous year. Peter seems to have been given a notable measure of responsibility in the early years of the Canterbury mission. Once King Æthelberht had been converted and the Christian faith had taken root in Kent, Peter was one of the emissaries sent by Augustine back to Rome with news of his successes and some practical questions about ecclesiastical organization; he probably returned to Kent in 601 or 602, accompanying a party of clergy sent by Pope Gregory as reinforcements. Little is known of the period of Peter's abbacy, but we do have a fairly secure date for his death. Bede mentions that he drowned in the Channel while on a mission to Gaul; there was some delay before his body was identified, but eventually it was given dignified burial in a church in Boulogne. Almost certainly this disaster occurred during Peter's return from attending a synod of the Frankish Church that took place in Paris in 614, for his subscription is found on the acts of this gathering, along with that of Bishop Justus of Rochester: their involvement underlines the close ecclesiastical links between Canterbury and the Frankish realm in the early years of the mission.

There is good independent evidence that the next two abbots of the Canterbury monastery, John and Ruffinianus, were both members of the party of reinforcements sent by Pope Gregory to Kent in 601/2; both of them were buried in St Mary's, the church founded within the monastery by King Eadbald, which may have become the accepted sepulchre for the early Canterbury abbots. Late medieval St Augustine's sources claim that the fourth, fifth and sixth abbots (Graciosus, Petronius and Nathanael) were also Romans who had arrived with the second group of missionaries. Nathanael is said to have died in 667, which would make it unlikely that he was part of the mission of 601/2. Perhaps further groups of Roman priests and monks travelled from Italy to help build up the Anglo-Saxon Church; but another point to bear in mind is that the later St Augustine's writers may not have had any accurate information about the origin of these abbots.

In the later Middle Ages the St Augustine's monks were immensely interested in studying the Anglo-Saxon history of their house, but it seems that the records available to them were limited and often apparently contradictory, due to earlier rewriting and interference. We rely principally on the histories written by Thomas Sprott (thirteenth century), William Thorne (fourteenth century) and Thomas of Elmham (fifteenth century), but these men were the heirs of earlier generations of Abbey historians whose work has not survived. Over many centuries the records for the early history of the monastery were studied and reinterpreted, and eventually gathered layers of contamination and fictional accretion. By the time that Thomas of Elmham was looking at the material in the early fifteenth century, he was in a position to provide a complete list of Anglo-Saxon abbots and their dates. But this list includes a large group of names from the ninth century which seem to have been taken from a separate and unconnected source, and there is reason to think that the abbatial dates were at least partly fictional. The most obvious example is provided by the case of an Abbot Sigeric, said to have been elected in 942 and to have died in 956. The source for the name was an Anglo-Saxon charter recording a grant of land to a layman, a thegn called Sigeric. A monk, probably in the

early thirteenth century, doctored the text of the charter so that Sigeric became an abbot; and sometime over the next two centuries, Abbot Sigeric was provided with exact dates. This ongoing process of imaginative reconstruction of the distant past means that we must be very wary of believing uncritically what the later St Augustine's historians say about the Anglo-Saxon period, and especially about as remote a time as the seventh century, for which there is very little corroborative evidence. And so it is possible that Graciosus, Petronius and Nathanael were not really Romans or missionaries. But if they were, then it seems likely that the Canterbury monastery would have retained a strongly Italian character during the first sixty years or so of its existence, which may perhaps have distinguished it from the other religious houses that were being founded in Kent in this period.

When Nathanael died (in 667?) the young Anglo-Saxon Church was in a sorry state. An outbreak of plague in 664 had devastated southern England, killing one of the very small number of bishops and probably many other churchmen. In the same year the decisions reached at the celebrated synod of Whitby led to an additional loss of ecclesiastical personnel, as some clergy who subscribed to Celtic traditions decided to go to Ireland rather than to remain in England and follow Roman customs. The fateful year also saw the death of Archbishop Deusdedit, leading to an extended vacancy at Canterbury. After some years a successor was chosen, and he made the traditional journey to Rome to receive the pope's blessing; but there he and almost all his entourage succumbed to another plague epidemic. Pope Vitalian decided that it was for him to appoint a new archbishop, who could revive the English Church.

Abbot Hadrian

Vitalian's first choice was the abbot of a monastery at *Hiridanum*, which was located somewhere near Naples in Campania. This was Hadrian, expert in monastic and ecclesiastical disciplines, greatly learned in both Greek and Latin and also in the Scriptures, and 'of African origin', which means that he was probably from the Byzantine exarchate of North Africa, which was in the process of being conquered by the Arabs in the mid-seventh century. Hadrian's earlier career is a mystery, but it seems to have included two visits to the Frankish lands, possibly as a papal ambassador, possibly for some other purpose. Vitalian offered him the appointment to Canterbury, but Hadrian turned it down, suggesting the choice of some other man, better fitted by erudition and age. He himself must have been a fairly young man at the time since he was to live for another forty years. The pope seems to have left the selection of a candidate to Hadrian, who finally suggested Theodore of Tarsus, a monk from Cilicia in Asia Minor, 66 years old and of immense learning. Recent study of Theodore's scholarship has made it possible to speculate with some degree of confidence about his earlier life: he probably studied for a time in Antioch, fled to Constantinople after the Arab occupation of Syria, and subsequently seems to have travelled to Rome to join a community of Cilician monks there. He was a very celebrated theologian, but he came from the Greek tradition at a time when there were issues of deep controversy between the Eastern and Western Churches. Pope Vitalian agreed to Theodore's appointment to Canterbury: but only on condition that Hadrian accompanied him to England, to supervise his activities and ensure that any Greek ideas that might be suspected of heresy were not allowed to percolate into the English Church.

Theodore and Hadrian set out together from Rome in May 668, but were detained in Gaul by the Frankish authorities. Eventually Theodore was allowed to resume his journey, arriving in Kent in 669, but Hadrian was delayed for longer, on suspicion that he was bringing a secret message from the Byzantine emperor to the kings in Britain (this may give some clue to Hadrian's earlier activities in Gaul). When he was finally released, later in 669 or in 670, he rejoined Theodore in Kent and was appointed abbot of the Canterbury monastery. Possibly this had been planned in advance, for the pope had insisted that suitable provision be made for Hadrian: so Theodore had installed as caretaker-abbot an Englishman named Benedict Biscop who had accompanied his party from Rome, and who is best known for his foundation of the great monasteries of Wearmouth and Jarrow in Northumbria (one source states that Benedict's caretaker-abbacy of the Canterbury house lasted for two years, but this seems much too long).

Hadrian was installed in the Canterbury monastery by 670 at the latest and remained abbot until his death in 709 or 710. He seems to have brought with him an entourage of followers, who also joined the community and must have deeply affected its complexion for decades. Theodore and Hadrian laboured together over the next twenty years to rebuild the ecclesiastical institutions of Anglo-Saxon England. The archbishop was the figure of authority, but he seems to have worked in partnership with the 'watchdog' Hadrian, who accompanied him on all his journeys through the English kingdoms. The relationship between the two men is almost impossible to reconstruct, given that the sources clothe it in conventional pieties; but it seems probable that Hadrian's involvement in Theodore's appointment, and the supervisory duties delegated to him by Pope Vitalian, must have added an element of equality to their technically unequal status.

It is against this background that we should consider a papal privilege in the name of Pope Agatho, which would appear to belong to the year 679 or 680. This sets out a special relationship between the Canterbury monastery and the Holy See. Only the pope was to have authority over the house, and no bishop or secular power should interfere with it. After the death of an abbot, the community was to have the right of free election of his successor; and no one was allowed to celebrate Mass in the Abbey church without the abbot's permission. Large questions hang over the authenticity of this document. It is one of a group of similar papal privileges in favour of St Augustine's, of which the rest are certainly spurious. The special rights outlined in the text, especially the prohibition of episcopal interference, were to be the principal issues of a long-standing and bitter conflict between St Augustine's and the archbishops of Canterbury from the eleventh century onwards. The other 'papal privileges' were clearly forged at the Abbey as ammunition in this controversy. But there is some reason to think that the privilege in Agatho's name does have some genuine basis (although this would not preclude the possibility that it was revised and rewritten by later generations). During the later seventh and earlier eighth centuries a number of Anglo-Saxon monasteries seem to have acquired similar papal declarations of freedom from outside interference; and the context makes it very likely that Hadrian, with his special links with Rome and the papacy, would have sought a similar guarantee of the independent status of his house.

Although Theodore and Hadrian expended much of their energy in the reorganization of the Anglo-Saxon Church, they also made Canterbury a noted centre of learning and scholarship. According to Bede, they attracted a large number of ardent students, to whom they taught Latin and Greek, the arts of scriptural exegesis and poetry, astronomy and ecclesiastical computation (that is, the complex rules behind the calculation of movable liturgical feasts). The most celebrated alumnus, the poet Aldhelm (later abbot of Malmesbury Abbey), adds to this list Roman law, astrology and musical chant. Other students included men who were to go on to distinguished careers in the Church: future bishops of Rochester, Worcester and Beverley, and Abbot Ceolfrith of Wearmouth and Jarrow.

There can be little doubt that during this time Theodore and Hadrian built up a great collection of manuscripts at Canterbury. While there is very little direct evidence about what

books were being read, some educated guesses can be made as the result of analysis of a family of glossaries preserved in much later manuscripts, which may reflect (through many removes) the study of manuscript texts at Canterbury at the turn of the seventh century. A glossary is a collection of glosses: that is, of synonyms and definitions which the reader of a manuscript has scribbled above a difficult word or phrase in the text, perhaps in response to a comment by his teacher. Such annotations were very valuable at a time when dictionaries were not available, and they were often copied when the manuscript was copied. Sometimes it was found useful to make a separate collection of the glosses to certain texts, and these were put together in a separate manuscript to create a glossary. Painstaking scholarly analysis can sometimes identify the different texts which lie behind a glossary. There are huge problems in making use of this kind of material, and the final answers are still far in the future: but it is possible to suggest that among the works studied at Canterbury were the Rule of St Benedict, works of Isidore of Seville (died c. 636), Augustine of Hippo (died 430), Gregory the Great and Orosius (died after 417), as well as grammatical tracts and canon law; less familiar names include Epiphanius of Cyprus (died 403), John Chrysostom (died 407) and Gregory of Nazianzus (died 389). The glossaries also provide us with the odd intriguing insight into the day-to-day teaching of the Canterbury school. There are a few glosses which directly link a definition with either Theodore or Hadrian; in one instance it would appear that the two teachers gave different explanations of a biblical passage.

The Canterbury school has been the focus of intensive scholarly research over the last few years. Most attention has been paid to Theodore, admittedly the greater scholar, but it may be that Hadrian's contribution had a more permanent impact. Theodore died in 690, but Hadrian survived for another nineteen or twenty years, during which time he must have been the primary teacher at Canterbury. It is likely that his forty-year abbacy had a lasting effect on the Canterbury abbey. He was succeeded by his pupil Albinus, who lived until 732. Albinus was a correspondent of Bede, and a valued source of information about the early history of the Canterbury mission. Bede mentions him several times in the preface to his *Ecclesiastical History*: Albinus was his 'principal authority and helper, a man of universal learning', who had co-ordinated the collection of historical material, in Kent and in the neighbouring kingdoms, and also in Rome.

The fall of the kingdom of Kent

The years from 670 until 732 must have seemed in retrospect a golden age for the Canterbury monastery. Some major crises were on the horizon. A good part of the monastery's prestige rested in its status as a burial church for the archbishops and for the kings of Kent. The first blow was a challenge to the monopoly of archiepiscopal burial. Space in the Abbey church of Sts Peter and Paul was growing limited: Theodore and his successor Berhtwald had had to be buried outside the side chapel designated as the archbishops' mausoleum, in the main body of the church (see p. 105). Archbishop Cuthbert (740–60) decided to solve the problem by building a new church inside the city walls, immediately adjacent to the Cathedral of Christ Church: this building was to function as a baptistery, but also as the location of new archiepiscopal tombs. He himself was buried there, and so was his successor Bregowine. Archbishop Jænberht (765–92), who had been abbot of St Augustine's, made an attempt to revive the Abbey's monopoly and insisted on being interred at the Abbey when he died, but the link was broken and thereafter all archbishops were buried at Christ Church. Later St Augustine's sources suggest that the community was hugely indignant.

Even more shattering was the fall of the Kentish royal dynasty and the disappearance of an independent Kentish kingdom, which immediately removed from the Abbey an extremely important source of patronage and prestige. Kent's power had been in decline since the time of Æthelberht, alternating between periods of stability and crisis (the region's wealth and its focal point on the trade routes made it a tempting target for the expanding kingdoms of Wessex and Mercia). The beginning of the end was marked by the death of King Æthelberht II in 762 and the disappearance of his successor Eadberht II (probably his son) within the next two years. These were probably the last kings to be buried in the Canterbury monastery, and perhaps the last representatives of the old Kentish dynasty.

By 765 the kingdom had come under the domination of the ruthless King Offa of Mercia (died 796), who ruled at first through sub-kings but later ousted the local rulers and took direct control. The situation must have been extremely difficult for a monastery which was closely linked with the defunct dynasty, and the problem is likely to have been exacerbated by the personal hostility that developed between Offa and Archbishop Jænberht, a former abbot and supporter of St Augustine's. Offa and his successors ruled Kent with a firm hand, and royal patronage of the Canterbury monastery seems to have been minimal during the period of Mercian supremacy (the only St Augustine's land-charter in Offa's name is a later forgery). Conditions improved somewhat when Kent was invaded and annexed to the West Saxon kingdom by King Ecgberht c. 825. The new West Saxon rulers were far more inclined to allow the Kentish people some measure of independent existence and to court the favour of the Kentish churches. There are several charters recording grants by Ecgberht and his successors to the abbot and to other clerics connected with the Canterbury monastery; one charter of 861 explicitly mentions that the donation was conditional upon the abbot's support for the West Saxon dynasty. But the main ecclesiastical patronage of the new rulers of Kent was focused upon the religious houses of their homeland.

The Canterbury monastery had to find a new role and new sources of support.

St Augustine's in the ninth century

Some of the solutions found to its problems are to be seen in the record of a benefaction by an aristocratic Kentish lady to the Abbey (8). It is undated, but probably belongs to the middle of the ninth century; its language is not Latin but Old English. Such vernacular documents had a relatively poor chance of survival, but this record was preserved because a copy of it was added, as an extra measure of security, into a blank space in the celebrated Gospels of St Augustine, perhaps brought by Hadrian from Italy (see further below pp. 68–9). In translation it reads:

> In the name of the Lord. Ealhburh has arranged, with the advice of her friends, that there shall be given annually to the community of St Augustine from her estate at Brabourne 40 'ambers' of malt, a full-grown bullock, 4 sheep, 240 loaves, a 'wey' of lard and cheese, 4 'fothers' of wood and 20 hens. Whoever holds the estate is to give these things for the souls of Ealdred and Ealhburh. And the community are to sing daily after their verse the psalm 'Exaudiat te Dominus' on her behalf. Whosoever shall violate this, may he be cut off from God and from all the saints and from the company of the holy in this life and eternity ... If, however, it should come to pass, as we hope it will not, that any panic shall arise through a heathen invasion or any other calamity, so that this cannot be provided that year, then twice the amount must be given in the following year. Then if it still cannot be paid, three times the amount must be given in the third year. Then if he still cannot or will not pay it, land and title-deeds are to be given to the community of St Augustine.

Ealhburh was a member of the most prominent noble family in Kent in the central decades of the ninth century: two of her brothers were successive ealdormen of Kent (officials appointed by the king with responsibility for the shire) during the period between 841 and 859. This aristocratic kindred was very active in making donations of land and rents to the Cathedral community at Canterbury, and Ealhburh's charter shows that they also supported St Augustine's. With the demise of the local dynasty, the abbot and community had to establish links of patronage with such local noble families, and fragmentary records from St Augustine's suggest that these were being built up through the ninth century. Ealhburh's charter also points to one of the Abbey's greatest assets in attracting such patronage. For the first time in the ninth century the Canterbury monastery becomes regularly associated in documentary records with the cult of St Augustine, the most celebrated ecclesiastical figure buried within its precincts. Technically the Abbey church was dedicated to Sts Peter and Paul, but from the ninth century the community was popularly known as St Augustine's (the situation was finally regularized in 978, when the Abbey church was rededicated to Sts Peter, Paul and Augustine). The possession of the relics of a famous saint was an immense asset to a religious house, a magnet for pilgrims and donations, and also a source of huge prestige. Churches promoted the cult of their relics, and encouraged veneration by liturgical celebration and by the construction of impressive shrines. By the eleventh century it seems to have been a custom for benefactors of the Abbey to place their charters ceremonially on Augustine's tomb, thus connecting themselves with the physical manifestation of the saint's presence. Another possible benefit for donors was the opportunity to be buried within the Abbey precincts, in close vicinity to the saintly sepulchres: two of the Abbey's benefactors in the ninth and tenth centuries explicitly mention their desire to find a final resting-place at St Augustine's.

Ealhburh's charter also provides an insight into the dangers that were threatening the fabric

In nomine dñi eulhburh hafaþ ʒeret mydhype
freondæ þealtamʒa þ man ælce ʒepe aʒyfe þain hypū
to sčæ aʒuftine of þū lande ætbþadanbupnan xl.
ambupa mealtes ⁊ealdhpyden ⁊iiii peþepay. ⁊xlycc blapes
⁊ane pæʒe spices ⁊ʒysef. ⁊iiii foþno puðes ⁊oc hen⁊uʒla;
Spylc man sēþland hebbe þas ðinʒe aʒyfe foþ ealdneðes
saule ⁊foþealhbupʒe; ⁊þ ahipan asinʒan ælce dæʒe æfter
hypa fefpe þæne sčalm foþ hia exaudiat ϫd ñr. Spæhpylc
man spaþyr abþece sihe ascluden fpā ʒode ⁊fpāeallum
hallʒū ⁊fpā þanhalʒun þepe onþy sūlife ⁊on ecnesse
þon synt hep ϫf þ þapa man nanūman toʒept nesse þif se
ʒesetednesse fir þon dphc nobabt þū ⁊os mund þþh
eþelped þū pyn hene diacon. beahimind. cenhelmd. hyse.
adda. cada. beapnfeph. beapn helm. ealoped. ealhbuph. ealhpapu
hop. hene. leope. þealdhelm. dudde. ofu. ofe. piʒhelm pullaf. eadpeald;
ʒifhrt þon spaʒe sæþ spape nane pypcaþ þhpylc bpoc onbecume
þuph hæþen folc ofþe hpylce oðpe eapfoþnesse þ hit man nemæʒe
þæp ʒepes ʒelæstan aʒife onoþhū ʒeape betpeo fealdum ʒif
þon ʒit nemæʒe sylle onðuddū ʒlape bēdpy fealdū ʒyf he þonʒit
nemæʒe nenelle; aʒife land ⁊bec þū hipū to sčæ aʒustine;

8 Tenth-century copy of mid-ninth-century charter, in which the lady Ealhburh makes a benefaction to St Augustine's Abbey (Cambridge, Corpus Christi College, 286, fol. 74v).

of the Anglo-Saxon Church and society in the mid-ninth century. Reference is made to the possibility of heathen invasions, which might prevent the payment of the food-rent for several years in succession. These heathen invaders were Viking pirates, who had been raiding the coasts of Kent since at least the 790s. At first these assaults seem to have been little more than a nuisance, although as early as 804 the danger was severe enough for the abbess of the monastery of Lyminge to secure a refuge for her community within the walls of Canterbury. By the middle of the ninth century the raids throughout England had become more frequent and more devastating, and were ultimately to culminate in an invasion that led to the Scandinavian conquest of the kingdoms of Northumbria and East Anglia and a large part of Mercia. Thanks to the energetic response of the West Saxon rulers, among them Alfred the Great (died 899), England south of the Thames resisted occupation, but these were terrible times. In 850 or 851 a Viking army is known to have stormed and sacked the city of Canterbury, and this was probably only one out of a number of occasions when the Scandinavian hosts threatened the city.

St Augustine's was in a very vulnerable position outside the walls; almost certainly the community would have taken refuge in the city at times of crisis, leaving the Abbey buildings to be sacked by the raiders. Anglo-Saxon churches, filled with gold and treasures, largely undefended, were an inevitable target for the pagan Vikings. In the kingdoms which they conquered very few churches continued to function, and even in Kent many outlying monasteries seem to have disappeared in the course of the ninth century. Apart from physical attacks on their buildings, the churches could suffer incapacitating losses of income

when their fields were burned and their livestock driven off; Ealhburh's charter suggests that a raid could result in three years' loss of profit from an estate. In addition, the regular collections of bullion needed to pay Viking tribute and to buy off their armies were a constant drain on resources. It was probably against this background that St Augustine's lost a large estate in Thanet which was restored to it in 925.

The late Anglo-Saxon revival

St Augustine's was one of only a very few early Anglo-Saxon monasteries that was still in existence in the tenth century. There is no evidence that the continuity of religious life was interrupted, although the Abbey's later medieval historians seem not to have had a proper list of abbots for the crucial period in the second half of the ninth century. Some notices of benefactions by local laymen may be proof that the community was still functioning (although it is not clear that they truly belong to the period). For the most part, the history of the Abbey is desperately obscure until well into the tenth century. It was during this period that the West Saxon kings conquered the Scandinavian-held areas to create a unified English kingdom. There was also a movement for the regeneration of the battered Anglo-Saxon Church through the promotion of the virtues of Benedictine monasticism, which burst into flower after the accession of the sympathetic King Edgar in 959.

Through Edgar's intercession, one of the leaders of the Benedictine movement was immediately appointed as archbishop of Canterbury. Dunstan had been the abbot of Glastonbury Abbey, where he had nurtured a community of learned and enthusiastic monks. It is a great disappointment that little information is available about the impact of his activities in Canterbury. There is a hint that he held St Augustine's in particular favour, but it is only a hint: in a Life written soon after his death, it is mentioned that he was accustomed to go to the Abbey church at night to pray and that he there experienced a vision. At St Augustine's it was remembered that he rededicated the Abbey church in 978, which may reflect a programme of rebuilding and refurbishment. It is possible that Dunstan sponsored the reform of St Augustine's along stricter lines during his period of office, but direct evidence is lacking. It was probably the archbishop who arranged for the appointment of a Glastonbury monk named Sigeric as the new abbot in c. 980; some five years later the latter resigned to become bishop of Ramsbury and subsequently archbishop of Canterbury. By the end of the tenth century the abbey seems to have become a recognizable centre of the scholarly activity that had been a hallmark of the Benedictine movement. A number of surviving manuscripts has been ascribed to the scriptorium, although it is not always possible to distinguish these from the products of the Christ Church scribes (see below p. 80).

From the 990s the English had to endure a resurgence of Viking raids, which the current King Æthelred found it impossible to counter effectively. The strategy of trying to buy off the Vikings with huge sums of money proved ill conceived, and eventually an all-out invasion led to the installation of the Scandinavian king Cnut as king of England in 1017. Kent had suffered badly during the second round of Viking wars, the worst episode being the sack of Canterbury in 1011 during which the raiders captured Archbishop Ælfheah and Abbot Ælfmær of St Augustine's, as well as other ecclesiastics who had taken refuge in the city. Ælfmær was allowed to escape (perhaps after payment of a ransom), but the archbishop was killed. According to one source the Vikings burnt and plundered Christ Church; it is unlikely that St Augustine's escaped unscathed.

King Cnut proved a (perhaps unlikely) benefactor of the Abbey, allowing it to re-establish its fortunes with what appears to have been a closely planned project. The richly endowed early monastery known as Minster-in-

Thanet (whose community may in the ninth century have migrated to St Mildred's Church in Canterbury) seems to have been dissolved at some point in the early eleventh century. Abbot Ælfstan of St Augustine's managed to obtain some former Minster lands in exchange for other property, and then sought permission from Cnut to translate from Thanet to St Augustine's the body of St Mildrith (later known as Mildred), a renowned seventh-century saint who had been abbess of Minster. The acquisition of Mildrith's relics was a valuable coup, adding greatly to the Abbey's prestige as a pilgrim-centre. Perhaps equally important was the consequence that Ælfstan could now present the Abbey as St Mildrith's 'heir' and as such entitled to other estates which had once belonged to her monastery. It may also have been in the capacity of Mildrith's 'heir' that Ælfstan made a bid in the reign of Cnut's son Harold Harefoot to control the tolls of the Wantsum port of Sandwich. Baulked in this initiative, he tried unsuccessfully to channel ships away from Sandwich towards an anchorage on Thanet, as is discussed in more detail below (pp. 62–5). Ælfstan seems to have been a man of great practical ability, and there is reason to think that his efforts made a considerable contribution to the endowment and income of St Augustine's.

The Abbey seems to have ended the Anglo-Saxon period on a high note, with recognition that it should enjoy an elevated status as the most ancient monastery in England (but it must be conceded that the evidence for what actually happened is blurred and uncertain because of later propaganda and mythologizing). According to a late eleventh-century source, Bishop Heremann of Ramsbury made a speech at a synod in Rome about the glories of the Anglo-Saxon Church, in which he claimed that by ancient custom the archbishop of Canterbury and the abbot of St Augustine's should be seated in prestigious positions when they attended assemblies in Rome. Pope Leo IX (1049–54) ordered research into the records, which

apparently corroborated the claim. (Was this a decree dating from the time of Theodore and Hadrian?) In 1049 Abbot Wulfric II travelled as the king's emissary to a papal synod held in Reims, where he was received with great honour (at least, according to the much later St Augustine's sources). Finally, when his successor Æthelsige went to Rome in 1063, the pope is said to have awarded him the immensely significant honour of the right to wear a bishop's mitre and sandals; in effect this would have been recognition that St Augustine's was the leading monastery of England. If this did actually happen, then it was a short-lived triumph, for the right is said to have lapsed when Æthelsige fell foul of the new Norman king William between 1066 and 1070.

Whatever the truth of the matter, St Augustine's in the years leading up to the Conquest seems to have been riding on a wave of enthusiasm and confidence. Major building works were initiated by Abbot Wulfric. There is some evidence of notable patronage, including a project by the king's goldsmith, Abbot Spearhafoc of Abingdon, to construct large-scale statues in precious metal to stand over the tombs of the Frankish bishop Liudhard (by now sanctified) and of Queen Bertha. King Edward the Confessor made over to the Abbey his rights over two-thirds of the borough of Fordwich, perhaps in compensation for its disappointment over Sandwich. The course seemed set fair, but the Norman Conquest ushered in a period of conflict and great challenges.

3
The Anglo-Norman Abbey

Ann Williams

The Norman invasion of 1066 was felt most sharply in south-eastern England, which bore the brunt of the actual fighting. In Kent itself, Canterbury, which surrendered as soon as the issue was decided, was spared any damage, but both Romney and Dover were sacked and burnt by the Conqueror's army, and Dover suffered further disruption the following summer, when Eustace of Boulogne tried (unsuccessfully) to seize its newly established castle. Kent had been part of the earldom of Wessex, held in turn by Godwine (died 1053) and his son, King Harold II. In 1066 or 1067 King William divided the earldom, bestowing the eastern part on his half-brother Odo, bishop of Bayeux. Odo also received most of the lay estates in Kent (as opposed to those of the Church) and used them to enrich his own followers. Those pre-Conquest Kentish magnates who did not fall at Hastings were soon dispossessed and exiled or reduced in wealth and social standing as tenants of the incoming Normans and Frenchmen.

The property of the Church did not suffer the same vicissitudes as that of the lay magnates, but St Augustine's could not remain untouched by these events. To judge from the *Anglo-Saxon Chronicle*, the 'E' version of which was kept at St Augustine's in the mid-eleventh century, the house had been on good terms with the family of King Harold II, and might for that reason be disapproved of by the Conqueror. Moreover its current abbot, Æthelsige (1061–c. 1070), perhaps owed his appointment to Archbishop

Stigand, who was also bishop of Winchester, where Æthelsige had been a monk. Certainly St Augustine's was one of the few houses to remember Stigand kindly. The archbishop's deposition at Easter (4 April) 1070 seems to have brought down Æthelsige as well; he fled to temporary exile in Denmark, and though he was later reinstated, it was as abbot of Ramsey (1080–7), not of St Augustine's.

The Norman Conquest and settlement required both secular and ecclesiastical adjustments from the ancient religious houses. On the ecclesiastical side, they had to adapt to the foreign heads appointed to English bishoprics and abbeys, some of whom were committed to implementing the changes in ecclesiastical organization and discipline emanating from the reformed papacy. The pre-Conquest Church had not been closed to these influences, but the influx of foreigners after 1066 brought a new urgency to the question of reform. On the secular side, they had to meet the quotas of military service imposed by King William, and defend their wealth in land and treasure from the rapacity of the continental settlers.

The abbacy of Scolland (1070–87)

In some ways St Augustine's was well placed to weather these changes. Though less wealthy than Christ Church, it was unquestionably the dominant house within Canterbury, favoured by the later pre-Conquest archbishops over the community of their own church. The fall of

Archbishop Stigand and the flight of Abbot Æthelsige must have been alarming, but Æthelsige's successor, Scolland, though a Norman, was likely to be sympathetic to the traditions of his new house. He came from Mont-Saint-Michel, a house with some English connections. While still an exile in Normandy, Edward the Confessor had endowed Mont-Saint-Michel with land in Cornwall and (perhaps) rights in the port of Romney, Kent, though whether the grant ever took full effect is doubtful. Mont-Saint-Michel was a notable centre of manuscript production (Scolland himself was an accomplished scribe), and the style of decoration developed there in the mid-eleventh century shows an acquaintance with English, as well as continental models. It is noteworthy that Orderic Vitalis (died *c.* 1142), who was critical of many of the Conqueror's appointments, approved of Scolland as 'a renowned abbot famed for his learning and virtue', promoted 'to restore the customs of Canterbury'. In 1070, it seems that the monks of St Augustine's could contemplate their future with some confidence, but the appointment of Lanfranc, consecrated as archbishop of Canterbury on 29 August 1070, produced a change of perspective.

Archbishop Lanfranc (1070–89) and ecclesiastical reform

Lanfranc was an Italian from Pavia, trained in the law schools of north Italy before removing first to Bec, of which he became prior, and thence (as abbot) to the ducal monastery of St Stephen at Caen. The Norman Church had been more deeply influenced than that of England by the ideas of the reformed papacy, the main thrust of which was to free the Church from secular control by kings and nobles. Though as a reformer Lanfranc must be counted among the conservatives (he supported the king against the more extreme ambitions of the reformed papacy) he was committed to instilling a firmer discipline into the English Church, and introducing better standards of scholarship into

its members. Under his direction, Christ Church, something of a backwater before the Conquest, developed its traditions of learning; it soon became a centre for work on the *Anglo-Saxon Chronicle*, once kept at St Augustine's. By *c.* 1077, Lanfranc had rebuilt the Cathedral church, destroyed by fire on 6 December 1067. He composed a new rule for the community, the *Monastic Constitutions*, subsequently exported to other English houses under his direct influence. Monks were imported from his old home at Bec, including Henry, who became prior of Christ Church, Gundulf, formerly prior of St Stephen's at Caen and soon to become bishop of Rochester, and Ernulf, Gundulf's successor but one at Rochester, who was put in charge of Christ Church's school.

Lanfranc saw the archbishopric of Canterbury as the primatial see not merely of England but of all Britain. This vision initiated a long dispute between the archbishops of Canterbury and York. Before Lanfranc's arrival in England, Thomas of Bayeux had been appointed to York, but when, as archbishop-elect, he came to Lanfranc for consecration, Lanfranc refused to perform the ceremony until Thomas made a written profession of obedience to himself as primate and swore an oath of allegiance. Thomas refused, until he could hear evidence supporting these demands. In the autumn of 1071, the archbishops travelled together to Rome, where the dispute was laid before Alexander II, who prudently referred it back to England for judgement. At a council held in the king's presence at Easter 1072, Thomas was persuaded to make a limited profession to Lanfranc personally. The text of the agreement was then sent to Rome for ratification, and Lanfranc requested (but did not receive) a papal confirmation of his primacy. Canterbury's claims were in fact stubbornly, and in the end successfully, resisted by the archbishops of York.

Lanfranc's vision of Canterbury's primacy rested upon an idiosyncratic reading of Bede's account of the early archbishops, especially

St Augustine himself. That the monastery founded by St Augustine played an important part in the promotion of Lanfranc's case is suggested by the role of Abbot Scolland in Lanfranc's contention with Thomas. At the time of Lanfranc's arrival, Scolland was only abbot-elect of St Augustine's, and it was not until a few days after the Easter council of 1072 that Lanfranc finally consecrated him. Though the most recently blessed of the English abbots, he nevertheless witnesses the text of the 1072 agreement at their head, appearing in the same position in the decrees of the 1075 council; his attestations to the royal charters of William the Conqueror are given similar prominence. No pre-Conquest abbot of St Augustine's had been accorded this position, nor was it maintained beyond the abbacy of Scolland's immediate successor. Scolland's promotion is probably connected with his support for Lanfranc's primatial ambitions. Indeed he seems to have been a member of the delegation which took the decisions of the 1072 council to Rome; it was on this occasion that he received permission from Alexander II to translate the body of St Augustine into the new church he was planning to build at his abbey.

The Christ Church historian Gervase of Canterbury, writing in the 1180s, saw Scolland's abbacy as a time of harmony between St Augustine's and the archbishopric; Lanfranc, he says, 'loved [Scolland] as a son and protected him from all harm'. The later historians of St Augustine's put a different gloss on the matter. Thomas Sprott praised Scolland's vigilance in the matter of recovering the Abbey's lands, but not his subservience to Lanfranc, who took advantage of him to restrict the Abbey's privileges. These strictures are repeated by William Thorne, who goes so far as to compare the archbishop to 'a snake hiding in the grass'.

These criticisms reflect the changing relationship between the two Canterbury communities. Though prepared to use the traditions of St Augustine's to further his own ambitions, Lanfranc showed no undue favour to the community. Moreover his reforming policies inevitably affected the traditional rights of St Augustine's. One of the aims of the eleventh-century reformers was to assert the control of bishops over their sees and subordinate all other communities (including Benedictine monasteries) to the diocesan bishop. The office of archdeacon, the bishop's executive officer, appears in Lanfranc's time, as do the beginnings of that separation of lay and ecclesiastical jurisdiction which eventually led to the establishment of a hierarchy of church courts, for the hearing of cases concerning churchmen and church matters. St Augustine's, however, had always claimed freedom from archiepiscopal jurisdiction, a stance never challenged before the Conquest, when the Abbey, founded by Gregory the Great's missionary archbishop, was revered as the mother-church of the English. This was a situation which neither Lanfranc nor his successors were willing to tolerate, and resulted in a series of bitter disputes which lasted throughout the twelfth and into the thirteenth century.

Though outright conflict broke out only after Scolland's death, ill-feeling between the two Canterbury churches was clearly building during the years of his abbacy. It was probably in the 1070s (or perhaps a little earlier) that the monks of St Augustine's embarked on a series of forged charters in the names of Æthelberht of Kent and St Augustine himself, supported by equally spurious papal privileges; the purpose was to provide documentation for the Abbey's earliest history and its privileged position as St Augustine's own foundation (9). They were the written equivalent of the splendid new church, built to display the shrines of the early archbishops, which Abbot Scolland was building throughout the 1070s. The forgeries

9 Twelfth-century copy of a spurious charter of King Æthelberht to St Augustine's Abbey, the text forged in the late eleventh century: Æthelberht is shown enthroned on top of the initial letter (London, British Library, Cotton Vespasian B.XX, fol. 277r).

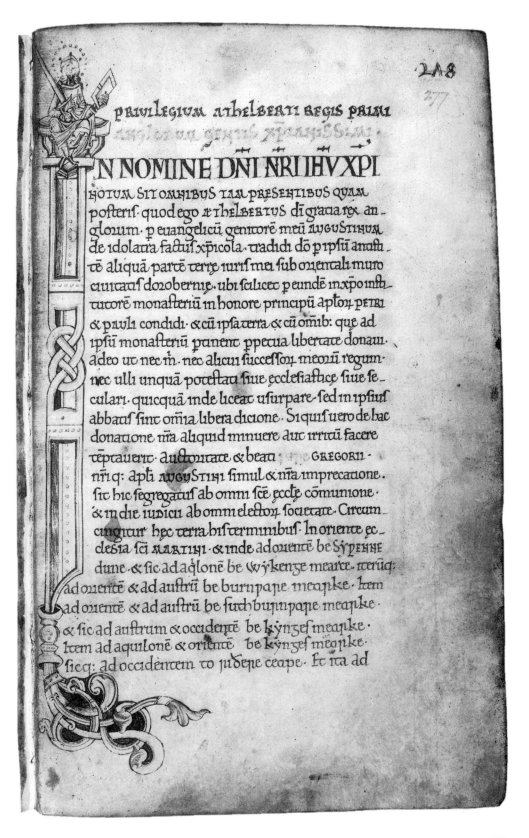

248
277

PRIVILEGIVM ATHELBERTI REGIS PRIMI
anglorum gentis xp̄ianissimi·

IN NOMINE DNI NRI IHV XPI

NOTVM SIT OMNIBVS TAM PRESENTIBVS QVAM
posteris· quod ego æTHELBERTVS d̄i gratia rex an
glorum· p euangelicū genitorē meū AVGVSTINVM
de idolatria factus xp̄icola· tradidi d̄o p ipsū anti sti
tē aliquā parte terrę iuris mei sub orientali muro
ciuitatis dorobernie· ubi scilicet p eundē in xp̄o insti
tutorē monasteriū in honore principū apto+ PETRI
& pavli condidi· & cū ipsa terra & cū omib: que ad
ipsū monasteriū ptinent ppetua libertate donaui·
a deo ut nec m̄· nec alicui successo+ meorū regum·
nec ulli unquā potestati siue ecclesiastice siue se
culari· quicquā inde liceat usurpare· sed in ipsius
abbatis sint omia libera dicione· Si quis uero de hac
donatione n̄ra aliquid minuere aut irritū facere
tēptauerit· auctoritate & beati papę GREGORII
n̄riq: apl̄i AVGVSTINI simul & n̄ra imprecatione·
sit hic segregatus ab omni sc̄e ęccl̄e cōmunione·
& in die iudicii ab omni electo+ societate· Circum
cingitur hęc terra his terminibus· In oriente ęc
clesia sc̄i MARTINI· & inde ad orientē be SYPENNE
dune· & sic ad aq̄lonē be WYKENGE meaire· rerūq:
ad orientē & ad austrū be burnpape meapke· Item
ad orientē & ad austrū be surchburnpape meapke·
& sic ad austrum & occidentē be kynges meapke·
Item ad aquilonē & orientē be kynges meapke·
sicq: ad occidentem to iudeie ceape· Et ita ad

53

were perhaps not all made at the same time, nor by the same agents; one of the forgers involved, possibly at a later stage, was Guerno, a monk of Saint-Médard, Soissons, who confessed his fault (for which he was paid) on his death-bed, sometime between 1119 and 1131. Guerno's charters were exposed and destroyed, but others long survived in the Abbey's armoury. The privilege in the name of St Augustine himself, with its leaden *bulla* (papal seal), was used in a dispute between Abbot Roger of St Augustine's and Archbishop Richard in 1181, when doubts were expressed about its authenticity.

The abbacy of Wido (1087–*c*. 1093)

The tension between archbishop and Abbey erupted into open rebellion after the death of Scolland on 3 September 1087. The violence which accompanied the imposition of his successor, Wido (Guy), which Gervase of Canterbury saw as 'the root of the troubles', is described in the *Acta Lanfranci*, written at Christ Church in the late eleventh or early twelfth century. Lanfranc consecrated Wido (who may have been one of his monks at Christ Church) and presented him to the community of St Augustine's with the command that they should recognize him as abbot: 'unanimously and with fervour the monks replied that they would neither obey nor receive him'. Lanfranc turned out his most vociferous opponents and installed Wido by force. Ælfwine the prior and some others were removed to Christ Church, and Lanfranc ordered the arrest of 'those who were more vehement and had been the ringleaders'. The dissident monks had taken refuge at their church of St Mildred's by the castle. They were given until the ninth hour to return, or be treated as renegades. As dinner-time approached, the more faint-hearted (and hungry) decided to submit; the remainder were 'scattered among the monasteries of England', and a small band, led by one Alfred, who tried to flee were captured and imprisoned in the castle. Eventually Lanfranc allowed all those who had been punished to return and be

reconciled with their abbot. Only one, Columbanus, who had threatened to kill Wido, was publicly flogged at the door of the Abbey and driven from the city.

Lanfranc himself died on 28 May 1089. Soon afterwards the monks, aided by some of the citizens of Canterbury, attacked Wido's house with intent to kill him. His household defended their position, and in the ensuing struggle several people on both sides were wounded and even killed. Wido himself managed to escape and took refuge at Christ Church, now without an archbishop, for William II kept the see vacant for nearly five years after Lanfranc's death. It was Gundulf, bishop of Rochester, who intervened to restore order. The ringleaders of the monks were punished and again scattered to other houses; they were replaced by twenty-four Christ Church monks, headed by Antony, sub-prior of Christ Church, who became prior of St Augustine's. The Canterbury citizens who had participated in the attack on Wido's house were arrested, and those who could not prove their innocence were blinded.

The intransigence of the monks turned on their assertion that the abbot-elect of St Augustine's had the right to be consecrated in his own abbey church. Lanfranc was clearly expecting trouble when he invested Wido, for he was accompanied by Odo of Bayeux, representing (as earl of Kent) the secular authority in the shire. Nor was Gundulf's solution to the problem any more successful, in the long run, than that of Lanfranc. After the death of Wido there was a similar, though non-violent, dispute over the consecration of his eventual successor, Hugh I de Flori (Fleury?). It was only after long argument, and the intervention of King Henry I, that Hugh agreed to let Archbishop Anselm consecrate him, on 27 February 1108, and then not at Christ Church but in the church of the bishop of Rochester's manor at Lambeth. The Christ Church historian Eadmer, a devoted admirer of Anselm, remarked sourly that 'those who were present at the ceremony declared that to have been able to be consecrated at Canterbury would have been much more honourable, and that it was a greater distinction for an abbot to ask the Father of the nation for his blessing in the metropolitan see of Canterbury than in the chapel of the bishop of Rochester'. The conflict over consecration of the abbot-elect was prolonged into the twelfth century, with much forging of charters and appealing to Rome on both sides. Abbot Roger (1175–1213) even secured a papal blessing from Alexander III, who also conferred on him the right to wear the mitre and sandals, implying exemption from episcopal control.

The expulsion of the rebellious monks seems to have had little impact on the preservation of St Augustine's traditions. There is no way of knowing how many monks were removed in 1089, nor what proportion of the total community they represented, nor whether (as with the earlier expulsions) they were eventually allowed to return. Nor is it known how many of the twenty-four monks imposed by Gundulf remained at St Augustine's, nor for how long, though Prior Antony was back at Christ Church, as sub-prior, by 1108. At least some members of the original community survived into the 1090s, and at least some of the newcomers embraced the traditions of the house with enthusiasm.

As for Abbot Wido, he retained his abbacy, but his actions suggest a wish to placate his community. His chance came as work progressed on the new church begun by Abbot Scolland. Much of the pre-Conquest building had already been demolished and most of the relics from it had been temporarily rehoused; Odo of Bayeux had advised on the removal of St Hadrian's sarcophagus without damage to the bones therein. All that remained was to demolish the porticus of St Gregory on the north side of the nave, which contained the most ancient and revered relics: those of St Augustine himself and his immediate successors. These Scolland had hesitated, even with papal authorization, to disturb. It was left to Wido to stage-manage the

process, as a dramatic restatement of the Abbey's ancient traditions, and its status as the treasure-house of early English Christianity. The translations were achieved with extravagant splendour in 1091. Clearly Wido had a point to make, both to contemporaries and for the future. To ensure the commemoration of the event, he had invited the Flemish monk and hagiographer Goscelin of Saint-Bertin to join the community. Goscelin, a notable musician, perhaps composed some of the liturgical music for the translation, and was commissioned by Wido to write an account of it.

Literature and music at St Augustine's: Goscelin of Saint-Bertin

Goscelin had come to England at the invitation of Heremann, bishop of Ramsbury and Sherborne, perhaps as early as 1058 and certainly before the Conquest. After 1078, he fell out with Heremann's Norman successor, Osmund de Sées: a victim (as he says) of 'viperine envy and step-fatherly barbarity', he wandered from monastery to monastery for the next ten or so years, writing commissioned lives of the pre-Conquest saints (see p. 26). He was at Ramsey during the abbacy of Herbert Losinga (1087–91), successor to Æthelsige (the once abbot of St Augustine's). During his stay there, he worked for Abbot Wido on the life of St Mildrith of Minster-in-Thanet, an abbey founded in expiation for the murders of Mildrith's maternal uncles, Æthelberht and Æthelred, whose relics had been enshrined at Ramsey since the late tenth century; an account of their death had been written by the Ramsey monk Byrhtferth.

Goscelin's move to St Augustine's was his last, and he remained there until his death, in the second decade of the twelfth century. One of his fellow-monks was the distinguished poet Reginald of Canterbury, who, though a Frenchman from Faye-la-Vineuse, was as much an Anglophile as Goscelin himself, and, like him, wrote in praise of the saints of Canterbury. He has some glowing words on Goscelin's musical talent: 'your singing revives spirits that are growing cold; you gladden all hearts with songs when you sound loud and clear, and soothe rough natures with lyre and voice'. A generation later, William of Malmesbury considered Goscelin second only to the Christ Church monk Osbern in musical skill, and the best hagiographer since Bede. He especially praises Goscelin's *Translatio sancti Augustini*: 'he gave such a polished account of the events ... that for contemporaries he seems to have pointed with a finger and for future generations to have brought it before their eyes'.

Goscelin completed the *Translatio* between 1098 and 1100, after Wido's death, and followed it up with Lives of St Augustine and of the other early archbishops and abbots. His works continue the themes which had preoccupied the community since the days of Lanfranc. His Life of Augustine emphasizes the archbishop's authority over York and the north, sometimes to the extent of misrepresenting his source (Bede's *Ecclesiastical History*), and could thus be read as support for Canterbury's primatial claims. He is, however, equally insistent on the traditional rights of St Augustine's. In none of his works does he refer to the events of 1087–9, but in the *Translatio* he affirms the right of the abbot-elect to be blessed in his own church, and makes extravagant claims about the honours conferred on Wido's predecessors. It is he who claims that his old master, Bishop Heremann, so convinced Pope Leo IX of the special status of St Augustine's that, at the Council of Reims in 1049, Abbot Wulfric was seated next in honour to the abbot of Monte Cassino himself; and that Wulfric's successor Æthelsige was accorded the right to wear mitre and sandals by Pope Alexander II (see p. 49). Neither assertion is entirely credible. The *acta* of the Council of Reims do not give Wulfric any special prominence, and the Reims historian, Anselm, places him only fifteenth in order of the abbots present. As for Æthelsige, the later historians of St Augustine's rather give the game away, for they cannot conceal the fact

that neither Æthelsige nor his successors until Abbot Roger (for whom see above) actually exercised the alleged privilege granted by Pope Alexander. These claims, like the forged charters discussed above, were weapons in St Augustine's armoury against archiepiscopal demands, and it is significant that the forgeries are included in the same manuscript (British Library, Cotton Vespasian B xx) that contains Goscelin's Lives of the early saints.

Goscelin and his friend Reginald of Canterbury were perhaps the most distinguished writers at St Augustine's in the late eleventh century. Reginald was an accomplished Latin poet, who wrote a series of verses in praise of the Canterbury saints, including Augustine and his successors. His main work was a six-book epic on the life of the fourth-century desert saint Malchus, copies of which he sent to various friends and acquaintances in England and north France. One was addressed to Gilbert Crispin, abbot of Westminster and a former monk of Christ Church, for whom Reginald says the poem was composed. Others were sent to Ernulf, by now prior of Christ Church, and to the hagiographer and musician Osbern of Canterbury. Clearly the rivalry between the two houses over land and liberties did not preclude ties of friendship between the inmates of the two communities.

The estates of St Augustine's

In terms of its landed wealth, St Augustine's was one of the richest English abbeys, exceeded only by Glastonbury, Christ Church Canterbury, Ely, Bury St Edmund's and Westminster. Its estates were concentrated in eastern Kent (**10**), and included the manors of Lenham, Littlebourne, Longport and Northbourne, as well as the more recently acquired properties of Minster-in-Thanet and the borough of Fordwich, a centre of both local and foreign trade. The estates were in part exploited directly for the needs of the community, either through reeves (manorial bailiffs) or through 'farmers', who paid a fixed annual sum, which they recouped from the

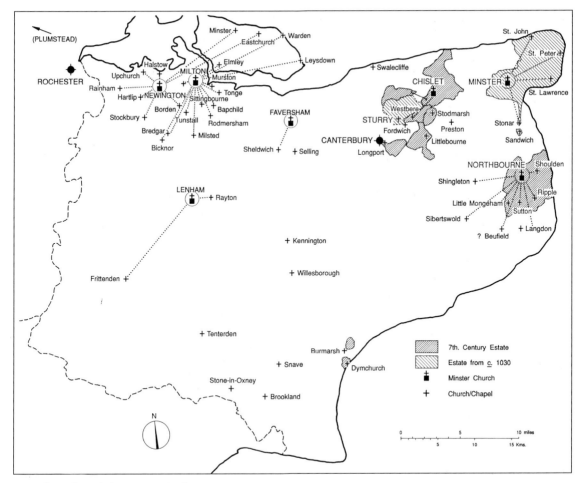

10 Map of St Augustine's Abbey estates in east Kent in the early Norman period (T. Tatton-Brown and Canterbury Archaeological Trust).

actual profits of the estate. Both systems were subject to abuse, and complaints about rapacious and extortionate manorial officials are common throughout the eleventh and twelfth centuries. Other estates, or parts of estates, were let to tenants, or held by freeholders, whose rents and services included the discharge of the Abbey's obligation to provide military service to the king.

Before 1066, each landholder's liability to military service was proportionate to the tax assessment of his estates, but the Conqueror introduced a system whereby a set quota of knights was assigned to each landowner, which might be discharged either in men-at-arms or in money. These quotas were unrelated to the size or value of the holdings; that of St Augustine's was fifteen knights, a modest figure considering the Abbey's wealth. On the Domesday figures,

its estates were worth £471.15s in 1066, and (though fluctuating in the intervening period) at £569.6s in 1086; these figures include Deal, held by the abbot as a canon of Dover. Moreover Domesday shows that in 1086 several manors were let for rents greater than the given values, and the same is probably true for the pre-Conquest period.

In addition to this, the Abbey had extensive property within Canterbury: seventy burgesses were attached to the Abbey's manor of Longport, to the east of the city, and the rents of fourteen more had been given in exchange for land used in the construction of the royal castle, as had the churches of St Andrew and St Mary de Castro. This urban property must have added considerably to the Abbey's income, but Domesday Book does not provide any details. The Abbey was also entitled to the tolls paid by foreign merchants operating on its property in Canterbury, though in the latter years of King Edward's reign these had been appropriated by the king's officer in Canterbury, Brunmann the portreeve, and had to be recovered. Before the Conquest St Augustine's had possessed the rights over its lands which Domesday calls 'sake and soke' (roughly speaking, 'jurisdiction'); this entailed the right to take from those dwelling on the land concerned the judicial fines for all but the most serious offences, but also covered various rents, renders and services which Domesday sums up as *consuetudines* ('customary dues'). The abbot was also entitled to the heriots of all free men dwelling on his church's estates (heriot was the render of weapons, armour and money paid to the lord on the death of his retainers); and to the king's (as opposed to the bishop's) share of the fines for adultery. All these privileges were confirmed by the Conqueror.

The estates of the Abbey survived the Norman settlement virtually unscathed. Only one dispute is recorded in Domesday, over land at Badlesmere held in 1086 by Ansfrid Maleclerk of Odo, bishop of Bayeux and earl of Kent, but claimed by St Augustine's on the authority of a writ of Edward the Confessor. The local hundred court (the hundreds were administrative subdivisions of the shire) supported the Abbey, and the shire court testified that before 1066, the abbot had 'sake and soke' over Badlesmere, then held by Godric Wisce. Godric's son, however, who was apparently still holding Badlesmere as Ansfrid's sub-tenant in 1086, claimed that his father had freedom to commend himself (that is, choose himself a lord) wherever he would (which the monks denied). It seems that either Godric or his son had taken Ansfrid as his lord, whereupon Ansfrid appropriated their land at Badlesmere as well. The dispute illustrates the distinction between rights over land ('sake and soke') and rights over men (commendation) and legally Ansfrid had no case, for personal commendation had no bearing upon title to land; nevertheless (as often happened) the judgement of the shire and hundred had not been enforced. The fact that Ansfrid himself was in the following of Odo of Bayeux, who, as earl of Kent, presided over the shire court, may have something to do with this. At all events Ansfrid continued to hold Badlesmere as Odo's tenant, nor is there any evidence that St Augustine's ever regained it.

To defend its possessions, the Church needed powerful friends, and successive abbots cultivated the local magnates, especially those who held public office in the shire. Abbot Æthelsige allowed Haimo, sheriff of Kent, to take over the royal rights in Fordwich granted to St Augustine's by King Edward. Such generosity could be dangerous. Æthelsige's successor, Scolland, obtained a royal writ restoring Fordwich, but Haimo's son, Haimo II, only relinquished his claims in 1111, in return for a lease on various other lands belonging to St Augustine's (the charters recording these transactions are dated on the same day).

Other local magnates were remembered as spoilers of St Augustine's land. A memorandum recording the Abbey's losses in the immediate post-Conquest period accuses Hugh de Montfort, commander of Dover Castle, of removing lands at Swanton, Eastbridge and Horton, and Richard of Tonbridge (Richard fitzGilbert de Brionne, ancestor of the Clares) of taking away the manor of Barming; the lands concerned appear under their names in 1086, without mention of the Abbey's claims. Most of the losses recorded, however, were of small parcels of land, some of which had been restored by 1086. Selling, taken by Odo of Bayeux, had reverted to the abbot, and Odo had also restored lands at Shingleton and Betteshanger, abstracted by two of his men, Rannulf de Colombières and Osbern fitzLedhard respectively.

Odo of Bayeux, as earl of Kent and half-brother of the king, was a patron well worth cultivating. There was some dispute over the Abbey's meadowland at Canterbury and Odo took part of its land at Littlebourne into his park, but he gave other lands in compensation, at Leeds and Garrington, the latter once held by Esbearn bigga, son of Æthelric bigga, a benefactor of St Augustine's before 1066. On the whole Odo figures as a protector of St Augustine's, and was remembered by the community as a friend and benefactor. It was perhaps through his good offices that Abbot Scolland recovered his rights in Fordwich, for in addition to the king's share of the town's revenues, Odo gave his own third part, held as earl of Kent. It was probably Odo too who granted to the church the rights which they claimed in Sandwich (see below). By the time of the Domesday survey, however, the bishop's political activities had led to his arrest and imprisonment and only on his death-bed in September 1087 would William I consent to free his half-brother.

Odo also restored half of the manor of Plumstead, which (according to the charter of restitution issued by the king) had been taken from the Abbey by Earl Godwine and given to his son Tostig. The charter, recorded by Thomas of Elmham, is not above suspicion, especially since the details do not accord with those of Domesday. This does indeed record two manors at Plumstead, one in the abbot's possession and the other also held by him but as Odo's tenant. The latter is presumably what Odo restored, but Domesday gives the pre-Conquest holder as Beorhtsige Cild, who also held land in Surrey and perhaps elsewhere. It is possible that at some later date the unfamiliar name Beorhtsige was read as the name of Godwine's son Tostig. If the land was at any time held by Godwine, it is unlikely to have been by seizure, for he and his family seem to have been on good terms with the Abbey. (The 'E' version of the *Anglo-Saxon Chronicle*, which was being compiled at St Augustine's in the mid-eleventh century, is noticeably partial towards Godwine and his sons.) If Godwine did hold this part of Plumstead, it was probably because one of the abbots had granted it to him.

St Augustine's also benefited from the king's largesse. William I gave the churches and tithes of the royal manors of Milton Regis and Faversham. The church of Milton was particularly valuable, since it was one of the old minsters which had been the basis of ecclesiastical organization since the conversion (see below). King William also restored the church of Newington, whose parish seems to have been carved out of that of Milton. Indeed the manors were still interconnected in 1086, when Newington was held by Albert the Lotharingian, a royal chaplain, in succession to Queen Edith (died 1075).

The tenants of St Augustine's

The Abbey's good relations with Odo of Bayeux explains why, though many of the Abbey's tenants were also Odo's men, all seem to be holding with the Church's assent. Two of them, Ansfrid Maleclerk and Wadard Miles, received lands belonging to the manor of Northbourne from Abbot Scolland. He was presumably providing for St Augustine's military quota of fifteen knights, for in the Abbey's *Noticia terrarum* (see p. 172), the Northbourne tenancies are headed 'lands of the knights' (*terre militum*), and several were held for military service in the twelfth century and later. A list of land owing knight-service compiled in the time of Abbot Hugh II (1126–51) includes Sholden, which can be identified as the land at Northbourne held in 1086 by Gilbert Maminot (bishop of Lisieux). Lands at Ashenfield, Garrington and Repton, held in 1086 by Ansketel de Rots, Ralph de Saint-Wandrille and Ansered, appear in the same list, which also records land at Thanet, owing three knights' service, and at Chislet, owing one; in 1086, three *milites* held three ploughlands at Minster, and four French *milites* had land worth £12 a year at Chislet.

Few of the lay tenants of the Abbey are more than names and some not even that; two of its knights were Abbot Scolland's nephews, but all we know of them is that they were killed in a brawl by some knights of the archbishop. Odo or Odelin, who held one of the Northbourne tenancies in 1086, seems to have married an Englishwoman. As Odo Miles, he left his tenement, which lay at Sutton, to the Abbey, and after his death his widow *Luvia* (in Old English Leofgifu) relinquished it to Abbot Hugh I de Flori (*c.* 1108–26), in return for a payment of £5 and land at *Heyham* (unidentified) for her lifetime. The agreement was made with the leave of Matthew the monk (presumably of St Augustine's), who may have been their son. Sutton reappears in later lists of the Abbey's knight-service, but whether the tenants were descended from Odo and Leofgifu is unknown.

Wadard and Vitalis, both followers of Odo of Bayeux, are rather better recorded. Both appear on the Bayeux Tapestry, whose designer may have been connected with St Augustine's. Wadard is depicted in the section showing Duke William's encampment at Hastings after his landing at Pevensey, and Vitalis is the scout reporting to the duke on the approach of King Harold's army (**11**). Wadard Miles was given lands at Ripple and Langdon, belonging to Northbourne, by Abbot Scolland, and also held of the Abbey at Mongeham. He was a tenant of Odo not only in Kent but also in Surrey, Dorset, Warwickshire, Oxfordshire and Lincolnshire, and his lands later formed the barony of Arsic. He was dead by 1110, when Abbot Hugh de Flori proved his title to these lands against Mannaser Arsic.

Vitalis was the founder of the prosperous Kentish family of Shoford. He held land of the archbishop as well as of St Augustine's and the bishop of Bayeux, and had property in Canterbury, where he founded the church of St

11 Vitalis, a Norman tenant and benefactor of St Augustine's Abbey, as depicted on the Bayeux Tapestry where he reports to Duke William the sighting of King Harold's army (City of Bayeux).

Edmund Ridingate; the dedication to an English saint is worth noticing as evidence of Vitalis' assimilation to his new homeland. The king employed him in requisitioning ships to transport Caen stone for the building of the royal palace of Westminster and when Scolland began his rebuilding of the abbatial church, Vitalis acted in the same capacity, receiving confraternity with the community in return. Vitalis died soon after the great survey of 1086, and his lands passed to his son Haimo fitzVitalis, founder of St Mary's Bredin, Canterbury. Another son was a monk of Rochester, and his daughter Matilda married William Calvellus, portreeve of Canterbury about 1100, and founder of the Cauvel family. Before 1086, this William had founded a small Benedictine nunnery dedicated to St Sepulchre on land in Canterbury belonging to St Augustine's, whose nuns appear as the Abbey's tenants in Domesday Book.

A tenant of St Augustine's not recorded in Domesday is Hugh fitzFulbert, to whom Scolland granted land at Sibertswold for his lifetime; Hugh was dead by 1086, when the land appears in the abbot's possession. William Thorne says that Hugh made 'a lavish donation of all his property' for the right to be buried in the monks' cemetery, but this is an exaggeration, for Hugh's successor, Fulbert of Chilham, continued to hold his estates and transmitted them to his heirs. Doubtless Hugh had made some more modest donation, as did Herbert fitzIvo, who gave the tithes of his estates at Harrietsham, Ospringe, Temple Ewell and West Cliffe for membership of the Abbey's confraternity. By such means did the Abbey integrate the newly established continental families into a local social network of mutual support.

Ecclesiastical property

As well as its material possessions, St Augustine's had rights over a large group of Kentish churches. The *Liber Albus* or *White Book* (see p. 172) gives a list of these, mostly on estates belonging to or claimed by the Abbey. In some instances it also records the payments which these churches made annually at Easter for chrism (the consecrated oil used in baptism). Though updated in the mid-twelfth century, the list (like similar compilations from Christ Church and Rochester) reflects the organization of the English Church on the eve of the Conquest. At that time four grades of church were recognized. First were the 'head-minsters', the cathedral churches and those of the great Benedictine abbeys, like St Augustine's itself. Next came the 'old minsters' or 'mother-churches', some of which dated back to the earliest days of English Christianity; they were staffed by groups of priests with pastoral responsibility for large areas (their *parochiae* or parishes). Last came the two grades of lesser churches: 'estate-churches' which had burial rights and therefore graveyards, and 'field-churches' which had no such rights, but merely served the basic needs of isolated communities.

The estate-churches and field-churches were established largely by lay landowners for their own manors. From the tenth century kings had legislated on the relationship between such churches and the old minsters, which retained much of the renders (like tithe) owed by the laity to the Church. Throughout the tenth, eleventh and twelfth centuries, however, the balance between minsters and estate-churches was shifting, as the huge *parochiae* of the former broke up into the smaller and (to us) more familiar parishes of the estate-churches, each served by a single priest.

In the eleventh century, many estate- and field-churches continued to pay dues to the minster or mother-church within whose parish they lay, and when that church itself passed into the possession of a 'head-minster' its dependencies followed it. Such groups can be seen in the list of St Augustine's churches. Northbourne, for instance, was the mother-church of Beusfield, East Langdon, Little Mongeham, Shingleton, Sholden, Sibertswold, Sutton and the chapel of Ripple. Northbourne had belonged to St Augustine's before 1066, and Minster-in-Thanet, acquired in 1030 (see below), brought another group of

61

dependent churches with it. Others were acquired after 1066: Abbot Scolland recovered Newington and its dependent churches, which had been lost before the Conquest, and King William added the mother-church of Milton Regis with all its dependencies. Rights in Newington were also claimed by the archbishop and the list in the *White Book* reveals that its church, with those of Lenham, Fordwich and Faversham, was paying dues to Christ Church, not to St Augustine's, adding plaintively 'how this happens unless by our negligence is unknown'.

Though the income from the dependent churches was not great, they represented an important source of patronage, for the abbot had the right to present to (that is, appoint the priests of) such churches. The abbot also had jurisdiction over his churches, and Lanfranc's insistence on his diocesan authority, which required the attendance of the priests of St Augustine's churches at his court rather than that of the abbot, was bitterly resented. The development of episcopal administration in the twelfth century produced long-drawn-out lawsuits between successive abbots and archbishops over rights of presentation and jurisdiction, which rumbled on until 1237.

Also resented was the obligation for St Augustine's itself to pay chrism dues to Christ Church, recorded not in the *White Book* list, but in the *Domesday Monachorum* of Christ Church itself. The Abbey paid 50s.7d cash, 30 loaves, 2 sheep, 2 amphorae of mead and one of ale (these payments in kind, rather than cash, indicate that the render was of some antiquity). The odd 7d were paid over in a formal ceremony: 'the sacristan of St Augustine is to place seven pence on the altar of Christ or shall give them into the hand of the sacristan of Christ Church'. In 1143, Abbot Hugh II of Trottiscliffe succeeded in persuading Archbishop Theobald to abolish the payment in return for a grant of property worth £4 (80s) a year. According to Thorne, the monks felt that the archbishop had done too well out of the deal, but the dispute was not so much about money as status.

Minster-in-Thanet and the Sandwich dispute

The Abbey's manor at Minster deserves special treatment (**12**, and see **7**). At some time before 1030 (as discussed above, p. 48), Abbot Ælfstan of St Augustine's was able to buy half the landed endowment of the former abbey of Minster; the vendor is unnamed, but Ælfstan allegedly gave him Folkestone in exchange, which is later found in the possession of Earl Godwine. Godwine certainly assisted Ælfstan in a subsequent dispute over the Minster estate, the remainder of which was acquired when the relics of St Mildrith were translated to St Augustine's. This was bitterly resented by the inhabitants of Thanet. Ælfstan had to open the tomb in secret, and when the saint's removal was discovered, his party was pursued to the ferry at Sarre by an angry crowd, led by Leofstan, who was perhaps a kinsman of the abbess Leofrun, captured by the Vikings in 1011 (she was possibly the last abbess of Minster). In the 1040s, the Abbey's title to the Minster estate was challenged by Leofwine the priest, a canon of Dover, and perhaps also related to Abbess Leofrun. The eventual compromise, which involved payment of a life pension to Leofwine, was brokered by Earl Godwine (who may have been patron of the Dover community).

To bolster their possession of Mildrith's relics and land against similar suits, the monks wrote or commissioned at least two versions of her legend, and concocted a writ in the name of Cnut conveying her relics and her property to the Abbey. The Life of Mildrith commissioned by Abbot Wido from Goscelin of Saint-Bertin was presumably intended to replace these early attempts at her hagiography. He was soon required to defend the Abbey's rights against a new challenge. The clerks of Lanfranc's new

12 Early fifteenth-century map of Isle of Thanet from Thomas of Elmham's history of St Augustine's: the map shows the churches on Thanet and the boundary of the estate of Minster established in the seventh century (Cambridge, Trinity Hall, I, fol. 28v).

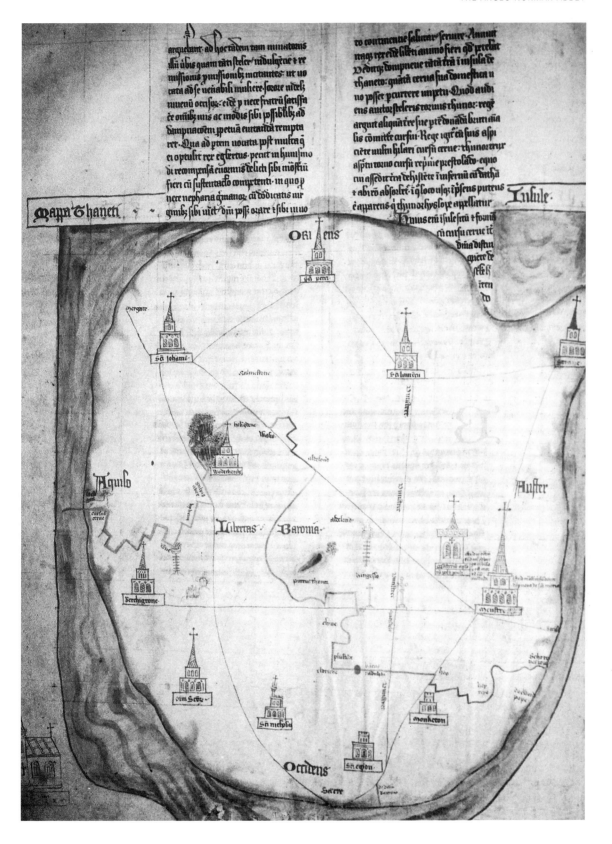

church of St Gregory in Canterbury (founded *c.* 1085) began to claim, apparently from the late 1080s, that Mildrith's relics had been transferred to Lyminge, whither the Minster community had fled in the ninth century for fear of the Vikings, and that Mildrith was one of the saints translated from Lyminge by Lanfranc for the endowment of their own house. Written texts were produced in support of these claims, apparently the work of the German hagiographer Bertram. In his rebuttal, the *Libellus contra inanes sancte virginis Mildrethae usurpatores* ('a little book against the madmen who would appropriate the blessed virgin Mildrith'), Goscelin easily picked holes in these accounts, but St Gregory's was still claiming to possess Mildrith's relics as late as the fifteenth century.

In the critical climate produced by the new learning of the reform movement, many houses were concerned to prove that their relics were genuine and rebut claims that they were in fact in another place. In the 1120s Eadmer dispatched a furious letter to the monks of Glastonbury, who claimed, against Christ Church, to have the relics of St Dunstan, fulminating against the use of foreign hagiographers who wrote lies for money. The cults of saints played a key role in contemporary spirituality, and could moreover provide a lucrative source of pious offerings from pilgrims. The saints of a community were also its undying landlords, whose presence in their shrines guaranteed possession of the properties associated with them. In his dispute with Leofwine of Dover, Abbot Ælfstan had already argued that the translation of St Mildrith's relics to St Augustine's conferred possession of her lands in Thanet.

The estate of Minster-in-Thanet was and is situated on very rich (modern Grade I) agricultural land, but its value lay in its position as well as its intrinsic worth. In the eleventh century, Thanet was still an island, separated from the mainland by the Wantsum Channel. Sandwich, at its southern end, was not only an important trading and fishing port, but was also, as the possessor of what Nicholas Brooks has described as 'the largest sheltered anchorage

for naval fleets in eastern England', a centre of strategic importance in the warfare of the eleventh century. The royal fleet, stationed at London, was accustomed to deploy at Sandwich at the beginning of the campaigning season; hence the king's right to a bodyguard provided by the magnates of east Kent at either Sandwich or Canterbury.

Rights in the port of Sandwich were granted by Cnut to Christ Church, to which the western half of Thanet (the manor of Monkton) already belonged. St Augustine's acquisition of the Minster estate in eastern Thanet was a potential embarrassment, for it included property within Sandwich itself, known as 'Mildrith's acre'. This potentiality was realized when Cnut's son and successor, Harold I, appropriated Sandwich for himself, and gave the third penny of its tolls to St Augustine's (see also p. 48). The third penny was the earl's, as opposed to the king's, share of the revenues, and since at this time the archbishop was acting as earl in Kent, the move was clearly directed against him personally. But the memorandum from Christ Church which records the event (which accuses Abbot Ælfstan of bribing the king) shows that opposition to the king's grant was orchestrated by the community, whereas the archbishop was willing to compromise.

In the event, Harold I's grant was revoked, and Ælfstan was refused permission to construct a wharf on the Stonar Bank, opposite 'Mildrith's acre', in Sandwich. This is further described at the time of Domesday as an *ager* ('acre'), upon which was a church (presumably St Peter's, which later belonged to St Augustine's) and 30 messuages (the messuage is a unit of urban property consisting both of the land and any buildings erected on it). It is significant that this property is described only in the St Augustine's account of Sandwich (in the *White Book*); it is omitted both from the Christ Church description in the *Domesday Monachorum* and from the Domesday account of the town, based on material supplied by Christ Church.

St Augustine's not only maintained its toehold in Sandwich, but also built up a rival anchorage on Thanet itself, at Stonar. Stonar's importance is shown by the fact that it was claimed by the Londoners as belonging to their city, but in 1090 William II confirmed St Augustine's possession. Twenty years later the Abbey was involved in another dispute, this time with Christ Church. At some time between 1116 and 1118, the king being in Normandy, his son William ætheling (meaning 'son or grandson of a ruling king') ordered the sheriff of Kent to assemble the 'honest men' of Sandwich to declare the truth concerning the ship belonging to the abbot of St Augustine's: 'and if that ship went on sea on the day when the king last crossed the sea, then I order that it shall keep going on sea till the king comes back to England'. A slightly later writ in the name of the ætheling's mother, Queen Matilda, commands Ansfrid, steward of the archbishop of Canterbury, to restore to the abbot his ship and all his goods, and orders that the men who took his property shall stand trial before the king when he requires it of them.

The ramifications of this are revealed in a suit before the shire court of Kent in 1127. Archbishop William complained that the abbot's men had been enticing foreign trading-vessels to tie up at Stonar, where some 'little houses' had been built for their reception, and were taking from these merchants the tolls which should have been paid to his own men at Sandwich. Moreover the abbot's men were operating a rival ferry between Thanet and Sandwich, for the convenience of the Abbey's tenants on the island; this is presumably the ship seized by the archbishop's men in the earlier dispute, which the queen and William ætheling ordered to be restored. This time, however, the jurors of Sandwich and Dover found for Christ Church, and the judgement eventually formed part of the later custom of Sandwich.

Historical writing at St Augustine's

Before 1066, the monks of St Augustine's had felt little need to set down their traditions in writing; even the 'E' version of the *Anglo-Saxon Chronicle*, compiled at St Augustine's in the mid-eleventh century, includes nothing specifically on the Abbey, though some entries show a strong local bias. After the Conquest, however, the need to defend lands and privileges led many religious houses to overhaul their archives, copy their title-deeds into cartularies, and preserve a written account of their traditions. Christ Church was one of the earliest to do so, though its eleventh-century cartulary, perhaps written *c.* 1073–83, has to be reconstructed from extracts copied or abstracted in later compilations.

Something similar seems to have happened at St Augustine's. Its four surviving cartularies were written in the thirteenth and fourteenth centuries, but contain much earlier material. Particularly interesting are the eleventh- and twelfth-century charters and other documents in the *White Book* of St Augustine's, and in a second cartulary now in the British Library (BL Cotton Julius D ii). Though their contents are not identical, these manuscripts share enough material to suggest that they were compiled from a common source, possibly the lost *Textus sancti Adriani*, used by Sprott, his continuator Thorne, and Thomas of Elmham. Some idea of its contents has been reconstructed by Susan Kelly. It was perhaps a Gospel Book (this is one of the regular meanings of *textus*) associated in some way with the seventh-century abbot Hadrian, with added quires (gatherings of leaves) on which material concerning the Abbey's lands could be entered. The *Noticia terrarum*, one of the three Domesday-related descriptions of the Abbey's lands in the *White Book* (see p. 172), is actually said to have been copied from this manuscript, which also contained an early papal privilege and two charters relating to the early endowment of Minster-in-Thanet. There was also some historical material, perhaps a set of annals (that is, organized year by year), for Sprott and Thorne cite the *Textus* as their authority for the death of St Augustine in 605. Material was being added in the late twelfth century, for Thorne copied from it a charter issued by Roger as abbot-elect, between 1175 and 1179.

The early charters, combined with the works of Goscelin and of more wide-ranging historians, were the sources for later histories of the Abbey by Thomas Sprott, William Thorne and Thomas of Elmham. Indeed Elmham considered charter evidence superior to any other, especially when the originals survived to be consulted. The St Augustine's historians have not been treated kindly by modern commentators, who have criticized them as 'narrow, parochial and dull' (Eric John) and as 'the most consistently inaccurate [historians] in the country' (Martin Brett). A more favourable assessment by Richard Emms sees Sprott and Thorne as uncritical but honest purveyors of the Abbey's traditions, and Elmham as something more: 'a pioneer antiquary, a forerunner of those in Tudor and Stuart times fascinated by the medieval past'.

It could also be argued that the narrow horizons of Sprott and Thorne reflect the shrinking role of St Augustine's in national politics. Its pre-Conquest abbots had been high in the king's counsel, acting as his ambassadors and perhaps performing other administrative functions. A much discussed passage in the chronicle–cartulary of Ely Abbey, written in the twelfth century, claims that from the time of Æthelred II until the Conquest, the duties of chancellor had been performed in rotation by the abbots of Ely, St Augustine's and Glastonbury. No such tradition is recorded at St Augustine's or at Glastonbury, and the statement cannot be accepted as it stands, but there would be nothing remarkable in the abbots of such houses being employed in the royal administration. By the twelfth century, however, the position was changing. Monasteries were no longer the sole repositories of literacy, learning and scholarship, but were being supplanted by the cathedral schools and the emerging universities and these provided the pool of educated men from which twelfth-century rulers recruited their administrators. Henceforth it was not monks but the secular clergy who would prosper in the service of the king.

Yet even if its place in national history was diminished, St Augustine's in the later Middle Ages was not wholly preoccupied with its own internal affairs. The Abbey was still one of the richest landlords in Kent, and the fact that it held no land of any consequence elsewhere perhaps encouraged identification with Kentish interests. One of the most celebrated stories purveyed by Sprott and Thorne describes how, after the death of Harold II at Hastings, Archbishop Stigand and Abbot Æthelsige rallied the Kentish nobles 'to oppose Duke William and fight with him for their ancestral rights'. Led by the archbishop and the abbot, they laid their ambush at Swanscombe Down, and when the duke walked into the trap, challenged him either to stand and fight, or to confirm their ancient freedom. William, 'seeing himself in a tight spot', chose the second option:

> and thus the ancient liberty of the English and their ancestral laws and customs, which before the arrival of Duke William were in force equally throughout the whole of England, have remained inviolable up to the present time in the county of Kent only, and that too through the agency of Archbishop Stigand and Abbot Æthelsige.

Of course this story is completely unhistorical; Stigand was probably not even in Kent in the autumn of 1066 (he is said to have submitted to the duke at Wallingford). The interest of the tale, first found in Sprott, lies elsewhere. It must be connected with the fact that, from the 1270s at least, the royal justices operating in Kent were being petitioned to accept the distinctive customs of the county. By 1293 these efforts seem to have been successful, and thereafter the customs of Kent were recorded in writing and circulated in the fourteenth and fifteenth centuries. The historians of St Augustine's provided a legendary context for these customs, synchronized with the Norman Conquest, the ultimate term for all valid tenures. Though its national influence had declined, the Abbey still had a significant role to play in the local Kentish community.

4
The arts and learning

Sandy Heslop and John Mitchell

The Roman mission

Images and visual aids to conversion seem to have been used by Augustine's mission to the court of Æthelberht of Kent from the beginning. Bede recounts how the missionaries were first received by the king in the open air on the island of Thanet, because of his misgivings about their magic powers. But

> they came furnished with divine, not with magic virtue, bearing a silver cross for their banner, and the image of our Lord and Saviour, painted on a board; and singing the litany, they offered up their prayers to the Lord for the eternal salvation both of themselves and of those to whom they were come. (*Ecclesiastical History* I, 25)

It is probable that the use of visual symbols and images of this kind formed part of a particularly Roman strategy designed to facilitate the conversion of the heathen. Pope Gregory I, who had sent Augustine to Kent, was a leading exponent of the idea that images can serve as books for the unlettered. In a letter to Bishop Serenus of Marseille, in which he expressed this concept, Gregory remarks that visual images are particularly effective in communicating ideas to pagans. Although he does not explicitly recommend missionaries to use images in this way, the idea is implicit in his writings. The theme is picked up by Bede in a number of contexts, but most tellingly in reference to the painted pictures which Benedict Biscop brought back with him from Rome, in 679, to set up in the church of St Peter at his newly founded monastery at Wearmouth in Northumbria.

Augustine's silver cross is one of the first recorded instances in English sources of this symbol, which was to have a particular resonance for Insular art in the islands of Britain and Ireland from the sixth to the ninth century. The carved stone high crosses, the cross-carpet pages which are one of the characteristic features of the grander Insular Gospel Books, and the great Anglo-Saxon meditational poem, the *Dream of the Rood*, are three exceptional manifestations of the particular love which Anglo-Saxons and Celts showed for the cross in the early medieval period.

These relics of the Roman mission no longer survive, but Henry VIII's antiquary, John Leland, who chronicled the dispersion of the possessions of the English monasteries in the 1530s, saw at St Augustine's Abbey what was said to be the cross which St Augustine had brought to England, bearing an inscription, 'crux Augustini', and he mentions the existence of another cross 'made of porphyry, ornamented with a few strips of silver, and some people affirm that this was also a cross of St Augustine'. The image of Christ, painted on wood, was very likely a Roman panel-painting, like the miraculous icon of Christ still preserved in the chapel of the Sancta Sanctorum at the Lateran Palace in Rome, or the image of Mary, known as the *Salus Populi Romani* ('salvation of the Roman people'), at Santa Maria Maggiore in Rome. An idea of a contemporary image of Christ may be gained from the mosaics of *c.* 579–90 in the basilica of San Lorenzo fuori le Mura in Rome (**colour plate 14**).

The Insular predilection for the symbol of the cross is readily apparent in the immediate aftermath of the arrival of the Gregorian mission, in the personal jewellery favoured by the Kentish elite. The gold disc brooches set with garnet and cut glass, which are such a characteristic feature of grave-goods in Kentish cemeteries in this period, almost invariably have a cross as the dominant element in the design of their display faces. A similar cruciform configuration is to be found on a splendid circular gold pendant set with garnets, from a burial at Old Westgate Farm, a site just outside the walls of Canterbury, to the west (**colour plate 15**). The fashion for disc brooches with cruciform design of this kind had been introduced from the kingdom of the Merovingian Franks, probably in the second half of the sixth century. Kent was drawn into the Frankish sphere of influence during the period, and the material culture of south-eastern England shows some marked similarities with Frankish craft production in the latter half of the sixth century. The introduction of this type may have been instrumental in establishing the popularity of the cross as a symbol in Anglo-Saxon England.

The clearest expression of this Frankish connection was the marriage alliance between King Æthelberht and the Merovingian princess Bertha. The strong Frankish presence, which the missionaries must have encountered when they came to Canterbury, is illustrated most dramatically in a small group of items, consisting of five coins and a medalet mounted as pendants, a disc brooch of Merovingian type and a Roman pendant cornelian intaglio, known as the 'St Martin's Hoard' (**colour plate 16**). The coins include: a Merovingian gold *solidus* (the standard late Roman and Byzantine denomination); four gold *tremisses* (one-third of a *solidus*), two of which are Merovingian, one possibly West

German and one Italian Byzantine; and a gold medalet bearing the name of Bishop Liudhard. It has usually been supposed that these were found in the vicinity of the church of St Martin, in Canterbury, which had served as a chapel for Queen Bertha and Liudhard, and was subsequently used by Augustine's missionaries. However, it has been pointed out that Roach Smith in his initial publication of the material, in 1845, says that the hoard was found in 'the grounds of the monastery of St Augustine', and that the various items were probably found in a number of female graves, rather than in a single deposit. If this is correct, these coins and ornaments would bear eloquent visual witness to the courtly connections of the occupants of some of the high-status graves in the vicinity of St Augustine's Abbey church, and to their taste for continental Frankish fashions.

Augustine and the first Roman missionaries must have brought with them the essential paraphernalia needed for establishing a church in England and for celebrating the liturgy. Certainly Bede says that four years later, in 601, Pope Gregory dispatched from Rome liturgical vessels, altar cloths, vestments, books, and relics of the apostles and martyrs (*Ecclesiastical History* I, 29). None of the furniture or fittings of the original monastic church dedicated to Sts Peter and Paul has survived. However, there is one early book which is known to have been in the possession of the monastery later in the Middle Ages and which may have come from Rome within Augustine's lifetime. This is the so-called Gospels of St Augustine, a lavishly decorated Gospel Book (Cambridge, Corpus Christi College 286). The manuscript is written in two columns to the page, in a typically Roman uncial script, which appears to date from the second half of the sixth century. Tradition associates the book with Augustine. To judge from some corrections to the text in a somewhat ungainly Insular hand, it must have been in England by *c.* 700 and sometime in the eighth century another English hand added uncial legends to the little scenes illustrated in the book. Internal evidence shows that it was certainly at St Augustine's in the eleventh century. It is possible that it was one of the two Gospel Books which Thomas of Elmham, writing in the second decade of the fifteenth century, identified with the books which were known to have been sent by Pope Gregory to Augustine.

The manuscript was originally embellished with portraits of the four Evangelists, and with at least two storied pages, each of which consisted of twelve small scenes framed with a rectangular grid (**13** and **colour plate** 3). In addition, it probably opened with a set of canon tables (see p. 72) set within brightly coloured arcades. This book is the sole surviving example of the imported de luxe Late Antique manuscripts of Mediterranean origin whose example determined the course of book production and decoration in the British Isles, and it also seems to have played a direct role in the creation of a house style of decoration for Gospel Books at St Augustine's. There is no evidence however that the portrait type of St Luke, the one surviving Evangelist in the book, who is shown in the typical attitude and dress of a late Roman teacher, was ever picked up by book painters at Canterbury in the early Middle Ages. Likewise the idiosyncratic design of the page, with tiny scenes from Scripture filling the spaces between the twin columns which stand either side of the Evangelist, is never found again. The idea of displaying a long sequence of episodes from the life of Christ in a regular chequer-board framework on one page had no immediate descendants, and was not revived until the mid-twelfth century, when four pages of little scenes arranged in a similar manner were appended to the Eadwine Psalter at Canterbury Cathedral. However, the symbol of the bull-calf, in the lunette above St Luke, is the same in attitude and design as the symbol at the beginning of St Luke's Gospel in the great early ninth-century Bible from Canterbury (British Library, Royal 1.E.VI, fol. 43r) discussed below.

It is very probable that the set of symbols in the Gospels of St Augustine was adopted in the Stockholm Gospels, also probably a Canterbury book (see below), of the third quarter of the eighth century, and that they were expanded into full-length creatures in the Book of Cerne, a ninth-century prayerbook with strong Mercian associations, made at a time when Canterbury was still culturally in the Mercian sphere of influence. The inventive strategies undertaken by early Anglo-Saxon artists when borrowing ideas from imported exemplars is nowhere more clearly evident than in the surviving progeny of the Gospels of St Augustine.

Two de luxe manuscripts of the eighth and ninth centuries

There are only two lavishly decorated books of the mid-Anglo-Saxon period which can be associated, with some degree of confidence, with St Augustine's. Both have been identified with books that in the later Middle Ages were believed to have been brought to Canterbury by Augustine himself, although in fact both post-date the arrival of the Roman missionaries by more than a century. These were described in some detail by Thomas of Elmham, in his early fifteenth-century history of the community. The first is the so-called Vespasian Psalter (British Library, Cotton Vespasian A.i) and the second is a fragmentary copy of the Gospels which formed part of a large Bible, probably in two volumes (British Library, Royal 1.E.VI).

The Vespasian Psalter is a de luxe manuscript, written in an expert uncial script on finely prepared white vellum (calf skin), and embellished with an exceptionally rich scheme of painted imagery and ornament. It now has one full-page picture and originally had at least one other (**colour plate** 4). All the psalms open with elaborate first letters, often extraordinarily ingenious and inventive, and each verse is headed by a coloured capital letter, alternately red and blue, set within a running ladder of red dots. The book is unusual, among early Insular manuscripts, for the extent to which gold is used in its illumination. Thomas of Elmham describes the book as having, in his day, an elaborate cover with a flat silver image of Christ with the four Evangelists.

13 Gospels of St Augustine, scenes from the life of Christ; Italian, second half sixth century (Cambridge, Corpus Christi College, 286, fol. 125r).

Whether this psalter was designed originally for use in the monastery or whether it was made for a private individual and only later came into the possession of the community, is hard to say. The psalms were the principal text used in monastic devotions and were chanted right through by the brothers each week. A book of this sort would have been very appropriate as an expression of monastic devotion and as a source of reference in the Abbey church. On the other hand, the psalter was the principal vehicle of private prayer and was the book with which most people learnt to read Latin in the Middle Ages. The quality of the materials used in the production of the manuscript, the brilliant colours of the illumination and the quite lavish use of gold and silver would be what one might expect of a book designed for the private use of an aristocratic member of the ecclesiastical or monastic hierarchy or of an elite secular patron in the eighth century.

The way the text is laid out lends some support to a monastic destination: this manuscript is the earliest surviving example of a psalter text divided into the liturgical sections that were sung by monastic communities at Matins and Vespers throughout the week. However, the sections in the Vespasian Psalter do not always coincide with those which were to become the later monastic norm. This may be an early experimental variant on the normal Roman usage. The divisions are marked by major initial letters, each followed by an elaborate line of display capitals set against a band of ornament. Two of the initial letters are historiated: the D at the head of Psalm 26 encloses little figures of David and of Saul's son, Jonathan, holding spears, and the D of Psalm 52 has David the shepherd killing the lion that threatened his sheep and goats. Thomas of Elmham described a scene of Saul anointing David at the front of the book. This episode may have embellished a third historiated initial: the B at the head of the first psalm. The page which carried the first psalm and the first three verses of Psalm 2 is lost, but one side would have provided just sufficient space for an initial historiated letter followed by the nine missing verses. The figural initials in the Vespasian Psalter are remarkable for being the earliest known letters containing narrative imagery. The book probably opened with a full-page picture, which is now set before Psalm 26.

This is a striking image of David composing the psalms, surrounded by scribes, musicians and dancers, within a brilliantly ornamented arched setting (see **colour plate 4**). A coloured offprint on folio 142 (the transferred impression of a lost page) shows that a highly coloured carpet page, dominated by a so-called patriarchal cross with two horizontal bars of unequal length, stood at the end of the text of the psalms and before the other canticles (the songs of praise from the Old and New Testaments which were habitually appended to the psalms in early medieval psalters).

Like many of the great early Insular illuminated books, the Vespasian Psalter is a synthesis between imported Late Antique models and an exuberant indigenous tradition. The uncial script of the text is directly derived from late Roman practice. The cross-carpet page, on the other hand, is a thoroughly Insular phenomenon, which is first met with in late seventh- and early eighth-century Irish and Northumbrian manuscripts like the Gospel Books from Durrow and Lindisfarne. The large image of David as author of the psalms is also a conflation of the two traditions. The idea for the composition of the psalmist seated at the focus of a ring of subordinate figures was doubtless inspired by an image of David from an imported Late Antique psalter. This must have been a variant of a widespread compositional type in which a group of authors are shown seated around their spiritual and intellectual leader – for instance, Socrates and the seven sages in numerous Roman floor mosaics, or the wise centaur Chiron and Dioscourides seated together with authorities in the various branches of medical science, in the frontispieces of the sixth-century copy of Dioscourides' *De materia medica* in Vienna (Vienna, Nationalbibliothek, Cod. Vind. Med. gr. 1).

The pictorial idiom of the central group is an effective simplification of Late Antique figure style with simple but dramatic two-tone colour modelling used to create palpably three-dimensional, if somewhat pneumatic, figures.

Drapery is articulated with strong black outlines, with interior coloured contouring and banding, and brilliant schematic highlights, to define somewhat ambiguously rounded surfaces. The arched frame, on the other hand, is filled with angular configurations of polychrome ribbon interlace in the columns, a swirling running sequence of curling, interlocking trumpet patterns and whorls in the arch, and a strip of key-pattern forming the base. All these are staple components of the vocabulary of Hiberno-Saxon artistic practice in the period. However, here too foreign elements are introduced: the three many-petalled gold rosettes in the arch, and the eagles and paired quadrupeds in the capitals and bases of the columns. These creatures may well ultimately derive from some imported eastern figured textile. Similarly the symmetrically composed almost zoomorphic plants flanking the arch are peculiar hybrids, Anglo-Saxon transfigurations of motifs of Mediterranean origin.

The Vespasian Psalter is usually assigned to the second or third quarter of the eighth century. In pictorial idiom and figure style it is related to a slightly later manuscript, a Gospel Book, the so-called Codex Aureus in Stockholm, also written in formal uncial script and also sumptuously illuminated. The Codex Aureus was presented to the cathedral of Canterbury, in the late ninth century, by the Ealdorman Ælfred and his wife Werburg, who had redeemed it from a heathen, presumably Danish, army. Whether this codex and the Vespasian Psalter were actually produced at a Canterbury scriptorium in the eighth century is at present impossible to determine for certain. Additions made to the Psalter by the Christ Church scribe Eadui Basan, suggest that it was in the city in the first years of the eleventh century, and by Thomas of Elmham's time it was considered to be one of the founder's books. It is perfectly possible that the Vespasian Psalter was produced expressly for St Augustine's, but there is no way of proving this.

The Anglo-Saxon gloss to the Psalter contains many Mercian elements and it has been argued that this book together with the Stockholm

Gospels, the fragmentary copy of the Gospels (Royal 1.E.VI) and a small group of other related southern English illuminated manuscripts were produced in scriptoria operating in the Mercian heartlands. This view is now generally discredited, but the possibility of a Mercian interest in the genesis of some of these books cannot be discounted since south-eastern England was under Mercian hegemony in the second half of the eighth century and the early ninth.

The second de luxe book of this period that can be associated with St Augustine's is a fragment of a giant Bible, British Library, Royal 1.E.VI, containing most of the four Gospels and part of the Acts of the Apostles. It is usually identified as the remains of the *Biblia Gregoriana*, divided into two volumes, which Thomas of Elmham describes in his account of the books associated with the Roman mission. There are problems of identity, but even if the two were not one and the same, the book Thomas refers to must have been very similar to Royal 1.E.VI, with, at the front of the book, pages of vellum stained purple and rose, which, when held up, transmitted coloured light in a striking manner. Whether the Royal Bible originated in the scriptorium at St Augustine's is also uncertain, in the present state of our knowledge. However, the presence of a shelf-mark (indicating the book's location within the library) and an ex libris (recording the library's ownership of the book) show that it was in the library of the monastery, more or less in its present fragmentary state, by the fourteenth century.

Royal 1.E.VI, written in Insular majuscule on huge sheets of vellum, two columns to the page, with an extensive scheme of painted and ornamented pages, lavishly embellished with gold and silver, must have been one of the most magnificent books of its time. Of its ornamental pages there survive five with arcaded frames containing the canon tables, the lists which demonstrate in tabular form the concordance and discordance of the narratives in the four canonical Gospels (**14**), three more of splendidly ornate display capitals, each of which describes a lost

full-page picture, and one of the four initial pages that opened each of the Gospels (**colour plate 5**).

Instead of the usual twelve or sixteen pages of canon tables, the Royal Bible fragment has only

14 Royal Gospels, canon tables; Canterbury (St Augustine's?), first half ninth century (London, British Library, Royal I.E.VI, fol. 4r).

five. This is typical of large single-volume bibles like the Codex Amiatinus, written at Jarrow *c.* 700, of the bibles associated with Theodulph of Orléans and of the great Tours bibles of the first half of the ninth century. The arcades with their exiguous columns, step capitals and bases recall the canon arcades in the Codex Amiatinus, which are known to have been copied directly from a sixth-century south Italian model. However, here the architectural elements are filled with panels of ornament, drawn from the typical Insular repertoire. Crouching in the capitals and enmeshed in the panels of ribbon interlace are little animals, so-called Anglian Beasts. These are typical of the repertoire of artists working in central and southern England in the later eighth century and ninth.

Originally five full-page pictures were inserted at various points in the text. These were accompanied by purple-dyed pages carrying appropriate descriptive texts in ornate gold and silver display capitals. All the pictures have been removed but three of the accompanying descriptive legends survive. At the very front of the book, acting as a frontispiece, was a composition with the Lamb of God surrounded by the symbols of the four Evangelists – an image proclaiming the harmony of the four authors of the Gospels in Christ. The subject was commonly used at the beginning of Gospel Books in the early medieval period, particularly in Carolingian scriptoria. Similarly, before St Mark's Gospel there was a full-page image of John the Baptist baptizing Christ in the River Jordan, with the Holy Spirit descending from the opening heavens; and before St Luke an image of the archangel Gabriel announcing the birth of John to his father, Zacharias, in the Temple. The descriptive pages relating to the pictures accompanying the Gospels of Matthew and John have not survived. It is impossible to say with certainty what their subjects would have been, but the episode associated with Matthew was probably the Nativity, and that accompanying John could have been a miracle scene like the conversion of water into wine at Cana or a more

theophanic event like the Ascension. There does not seem to have been any one canonical way of illustrating the Gospels in Ireland and mid-Anglo-Saxon England, but the remains of somewhat similar schemes are preserved in a number of Insular books: the Durham Gospel fragment, the St Gall Gospels, the Book of Kells and the Turin Gospels.

Following these frontispieces, each Gospel in Royal 1.E.VI was introduced by a grand purple-dyed initial page and an accompanying side on which the first verses of each book were written out in ornate display script. Of these eight pages only one is preserved: the initial page to Luke (see **colour plate 5**). This is a remarkable composition which combines initial, Evangelist portrait and Evangelist symbol on one page. Against a deep purple ground, the first letter a large Q, together with the following letters of the first two words, *quoniam quidem*, are written out within an arched frame. In the lunette of the arch is a remarkably naturalistic representation of the symbol of St Luke, the bull-calf, grasping a book and set amidst the parting clouds of an epiphanic vision. Above in a medallion set at the apex of the arch is a frontal half-length bearded man, also holding a book, possibly the Evangelist, but more likely Christ. A fundamental conceit is realized here with extraordinary clarity and compression – the Word of God, embodied in the gold and silver initial words, in the process of being transmitted from its author, Christ, through the mediation of the Evangelist, who is shown in his transfigured symbolic aspect.

In this book, as much as in any other English book of the period, the impact of both Late Antique exemplars and of contemporary continental practice is apparent. The composite initial page reveals an awareness of disparate traditions of imagery and an ability to draw on them and synthesize them into a new idiom in a remarkably inventive way. The configuration of the arch, with the medallion-image at its apex, and the pose of the bull-calf are both derived, directly or indirectly, from Late Antique models; the arch from a lost Gospel Book, the symbolic beast from the Gospels of St Augustine in Cambridge. However, the idea of magnifying an initial letter by placing it under an arch was something new in book design. It was probably an invention of the artist-scribes who produced the magnificent Gospel Books of the so-called Court School of Charlemagne, in the years around 800. It would seem that the designer of Royal 1.E.VI was aware of the latest developments in the scriptoria working for the Carolingian court. The great purple-stained pages and the lavish use of gold and silver accord with this ethos. Characteristic features of the most sumptuous manuscripts produced in the Late Antique world – gold, silver and costly purple dye – had been deployed by Anglo-Saxon scribes in the later seventh and eighth centuries in their most prestigious productions, and more recently they had been used to comparable effect in books made for the circle of Charlemagne.

In its original state, the Royal Bible must have been an extraordinary book, and, if the Gospel section is anything to go by, it would have contained an exceptionally elaborate and extensive complement of narrative imagery and ornament spanning the books of both the Old and the New Testament. If it really was produced in the scriptorium at St Augustine's, for use in the Abbey church, it would suggest that the monastery was second to none in the material resources and scribal expertise at its disposal in the early ninth century, and that the community was implementing an ambitious strategy of visual display.

Metalworking at the Anglo-Saxon Abbey

Excavations in recent years at Christ Church College, in the area of the old outer court of the monastery, immediately to the north of the church, have brought to light evidence for a succession of phases of metalworking, mostly in iron, which probably relate to craft activity within the monastery. There is evidence for ironworking from the seventh to ninth century, in the vicinity of the late medieval bakehouse and brewhouse, debris from the casting of large

15 Copper-alloy pin with horse-head terminal; from the outer court of St Augustine's Abbey; eighth century? (Canterbury Archaeological Trust).

bronze objects from the eleventh to the twelfth century has been found under the cellarer's range, and a large industrial furnace of the same period was also discovered in the same area. The precise nature of the industrial operations associated with these remains has yet to be established. Numerous items that might be expected in the context of a monastic establishment have been found in this area. These include combs of antler and bone, copper pins, strap-ends, a needle, a buckle, two ceramic spindle-whorls, a number of knives and a broken stylus. Among the most elaborately decorated pieces are a copper-alloy pin with two horse-heads set back-to-back forming its upper terminal, probably of eighth-century date (**15**), and an eighth- to ninth-century Anglo-Saxon strap-end with a dove engraved into its silvered upper surface (**16**).

It is not yet possible to get a comprehensive picture of craft production and the visual culture of the monastery in the Anglo-Saxon period, but various stray finds throw some light on the material wealth enjoyed by the community during this period.

Among the most spectacular items are two small cloisonné enamels. One of these is a tiny square mount, 11 by 11mm (less than half an inch), in gold cloisonné, with a delicate device in blue, turquoise, yellow and white enamel (**colour plate 17**). The colour of the glass and the design of the stud suggest a date in the ninth century. The second enamel found at St Augustine's is a small flat gilded copper disc, 27mm (*c.* 1in) in diameter, carrying an elaborate quatrefoil design

17 Fragments of gilded lead with repoussé decoration; from St Augustine's Abbey; ninth century? (English Heritage, AML 765884).

of interlacing ribbons with little palmettes between the four lobes (**colour plate 18**). Most of the colours are opaque, but the green is translucent. This is probably eleventh-century work. The precise use to which ornaments of this kind were put is impossible to ascertain, but the disc could have embellished the richly decorated cover of a book or a metal vessel, and the little square mount must have been set on some similar piece of de luxe metalwork.

Two fragments of gilded lead strip may derive from an elaborate piece of ecclesiastical metalwork, perhaps an antependium (altar-frontal), a shrine or a reliquary of some sort (**17**). One of these seems to be part of an arcade decorated with symmetrical running plant scrolls in repoussé, framed by bands of raised pellets; the other is a curving band, ornamented with imitation gem-settings. The form of the scroll and the alternate rectangular and oval gem-settings may suggest a date in the mid-Anglo-Saxon period, perhaps the ninth century, rather than the post-Conquest date previously ascribed.

A number of elegantly formed copper styluses are typical of high-status monastic sites and bear witness to the activity of writing ephemeral notes and texts on waxed tablets, practised by a literate community (**18**). The pointed ends of

16 Strap-end with dove engraved on silvered display surface; from the outer court of St Augustine's Abbey; eighth or ninth century (Canterbury Archaeological Trust).

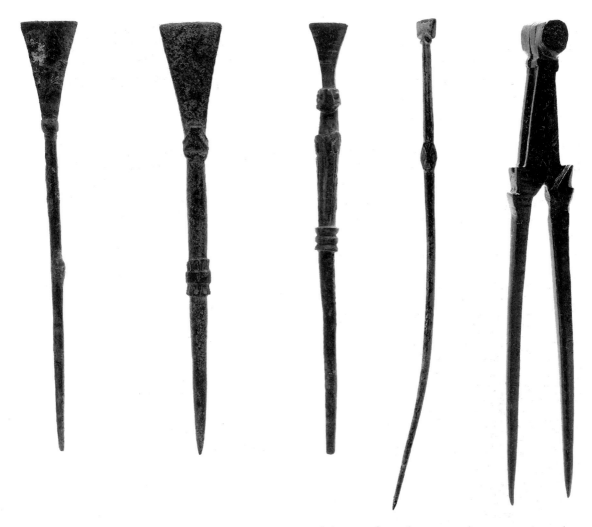

18 Four styluses and a pair of compasses, copper alloy; from St Augustine's Abbey; dates uncertain (English Heritage, AML 78203057–60 and 7716146).

these could also have served in the scriptorium for ruling pages of vellum for writing. A small pair of copper-alloy compasses from the site may also have been used in the scriptorium. The date of these items is uncertain, but some of them may be from the Anglo-Saxon period.

Late Anglo-Saxon books and the monastic library

In chapter 48 of his Rule for monks, St Benedict specifies several periods for 'sacred reading'. These vary between summer and winter, but during the former, when the light was better, a minimum of two hours per day was envisaged. Since the Rule also forbade personal possessions, it followed logically that the books had to be communally owned, and this was the justification for a monastic library. The nature of the books provided doubtless varied from place to place, depending on the availability of texts, the enthusiasms of those making the collection and the view of what was appropriate. A wide range of material could be regarded as suitable for study, since it was argued that God revealed himself through the workings of nature and human history as well as through holy scripture.

The evidence for early libraries comes in a number of forms: surviving manuscripts, lists of books, and less reliably through the quotations used by medieval writers which reveal which sources had been accessible to them. For some early monasteries, for example Jarrow in Northumbria where the historian Bede was a monk, we have evidence of various kinds. For other houses, and sadly St Augustine's is one of them, we have nothing substantial to help us form a picture of the material available. The lavishly illuminated psalters, bibles or Gospel Books, such as those that do indeed survive from St Augustine's, would either have been used in the liturgical context of church services, or have been treated as precious objects associated with the treasury: they are not library books for contemplative reading. While it is likely that the latter would have included commentaries on various books of the Bible, perhaps some Lives of saints, and devotional compositions, this can only be surmise in the case of St Augustine's and is anyway no help in establishing the particular character of the collection, which might give us an insight into what was distinctive about the culture of the Abbey.

However, among the books known to have been in the library in the later Middle Ages there are a few of early date. A case in point is a copy of Jerome's *De viris illustribus* (On famous men, British Library, Cotton Caligula A.xv) dating from the late eighth century. It is not clear when it was acquired or where it was produced, though north-eastern France has been suggested. It is perhaps less probable that a book of this age would have been bought or donated after the Norman Conquest (when it is far more likely that a modern copy would have been commissioned), so this is one of a number of indications that part at least of the Anglo-Saxon library might have remained in the Abbey's possession.

Substantial support for this argument begins to accumulate from the middle of the tenth century. This is the period when it first becomes possible to suggest, on the basis of the style of the writing, that there was a local scriptorium producing books for the monastery. For example, among the works of one scribe are Amalarius of Metz's *Offices of the Church*

(**colour plate 8**), St Benedict's *Rule* (Cambridge, Trinity College 0.2.30) and the *Satires* of Juvenal and Persius (ibid. 0.4.10). Unfortunately only this last, and least appropriate, can be identified with any certainty as having been in the St Augustine's library. It therefore remains possible that the other books were being produced for distribution to other owners. As this scribe also contributed to the splendidly illuminated continental copy of Cicero's Latin translation of Aratus' poetic work on astronomy, *Phaenomena* (**19**), which was also at St Augustine's, we may envisage that he worked within the confines of the Abbey rather than merely in the vicinity.

Another manuscript which has been attributed to St Augustine's on the basis of the style of its script is a copy of Isidore of Seville's *De natura rerum* (On the nature of things, British Library, Cotton Domitian i). On one of its pages is a list of the books that once belonged to a man called Athelstan. It includes, yet again, Persius' *Satires* but is largely constituted by books on grammar and literary style, for example the two grammatical works by Donatus written in the fourth century, two texts on metre, one on parsing, and apparently an early colloquy or imagined dialogue between a teacher and his pupils. Such a collection makes best sense as the private library of a schoolmaster and raises the possibility that Athelstan taught at St Augustine's itself. There are however a number of other equally plausible explanations, such as that Athelstan retired to the Abbey and gave his books to its library, or indeed that the Isidore found its way there independently, perhaps at some much later date. None the less, it is worth considering the idea that St Augustine's played an educational role during the tenth century. It might help explain the three surviving copies of Boethius' *Consolation of Philosophy* (**20, 21**), a text composed *c.* 524–6 and widely used later as a schoolbook, and considered so significant at the period as to be one of the handful of Latin texts translated into Anglo-Saxon (Old English) by King Alfred in the 890s as part of his educational reforms. One of the Latin copies from St Augustine's contains a beautiful drawing of Philosophy, shown as a standing woman, as she is described by Boethius in his opening vision of her appearance to him in his prison cell while awaiting execution.

19 The constellation Perseus from Cicero, *Aratus' Phaenomena*; St Augustine's Abbey, last third of tenth century (London, British Library, Harley 647, fol. 4r).

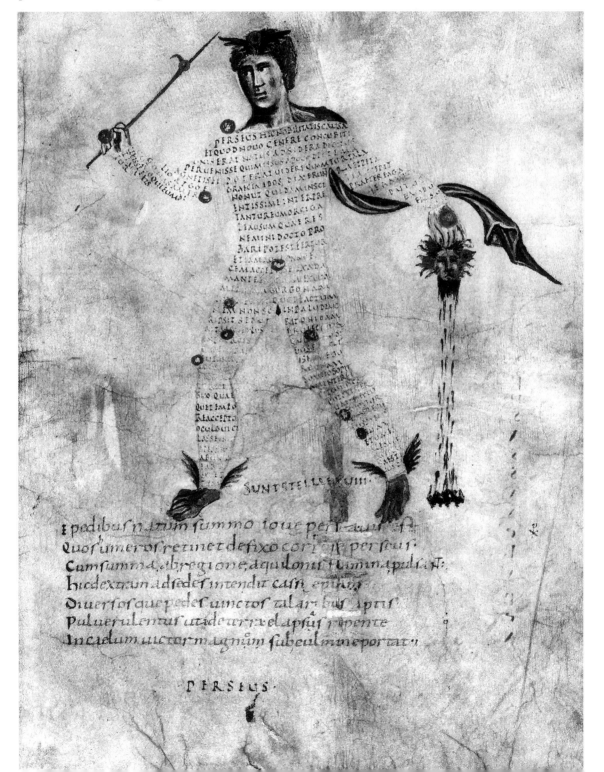

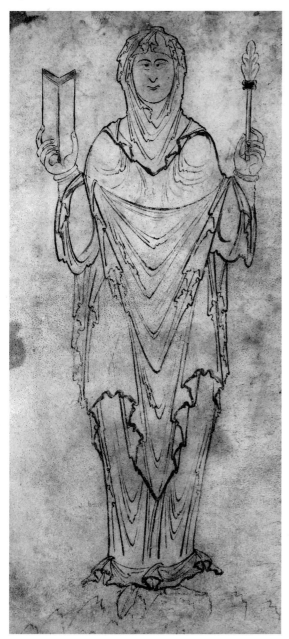

20 Personification of Philosophy from Boethius, *Consolation of Philosophy*, St Augustine's Abbey, late tenth century (Cambridge, Trinity College, O.3.7, fol. 1r).

There remains a general problem about the extent to which the making of books was concentrated in religious communities, and, even if it was, whether members of the community were themselves the scribes and artists. This is a particular issue in cities like Canterbury, or Winchester, where there were two large churches. Did they duplicate or share the provision of a scriptorium and perhaps even of a library? The evidence is equivocal.

One can sometimes tell from the contents whether the book would have been more likely to come from or be used in a monastery (as St Augustine's certainly was from the time of Archbishop Dunstan) or a house of secular clerics, as Canterbury Cathedral may have remained into the early eleventh century. For example, the so-called Bosworth Psalter of the late tenth century (**colour plate 6**), written to be used in the context of the daily monastic services, or the contemporary *Rule of St Benedict* (British Library, Harley 5431) are far more likely to have been commissioned for the monastery of St Augustine's than for the secular Cathedral, and the exemplars from which they were copied are also more likely to have been found there. But once again it must be stressed that such texts would have been used in church for the liturgy, and did not strictly form part of the library which provided books for personal meditative reading by the monks elsewhere in the monastery – as enjoined by St Benedict's Rule (chapter 48).

Although there are uncertainties, in the late Anglo-Saxon period a distinctive culture at the Abbey does begin to come into focus. For example, in the later Middle Ages, the Abbey owned early manuscripts of texts such as Juvencus' Latin poetic rendering of the Gospels, composed in the fourth century, and the metrical rendering of the first seven books of the Old Testament, wrongly attributed to Aldhelm, both probably already in the library in the tenth century. It is perhaps against this background interest in versions of biblical texts that we should see the acquisition of perhaps the most ambitiously illuminated manuscript surviving from late Anglo-Saxon England, a version in English of the books of the Pentateuch and Joshua (**colour plate 7**).

Known as Ælfric's Pentateuch, after the translator of a large part of its text, this book was probably produced in Canterbury in the

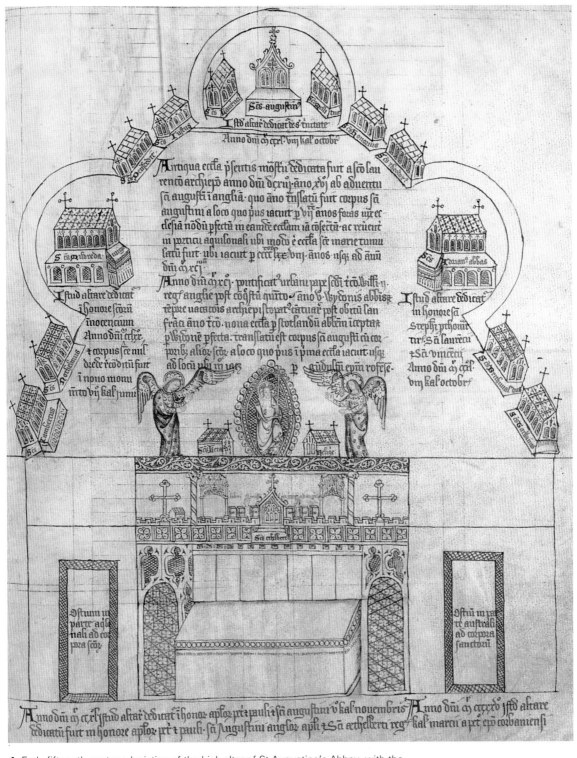

1 Early fifteenth-century depiction of the high altar of St Augustine's Abbey, with the shrines of Augustine and other saints in the chapels and ambulatory beyond; from Thomas of Elmham's history of the Abbey (Cambridge, Trinity Hall I, fol. 77r)

2 Pope Gregory the Great (right), with Augustine of Hippo (centre) and Jerome (left); one of the earliest representations of Gregory. Painting added between seventh and ninth centuries to ivory diptych of Boethius (Brescia, Civico Museo Cristiano, Avori, Inv. no. 5).

3 Gospels of St Augustine, portrait of the evangelist Luke; Italian, second half of sixth century, later at St Augustine's Abbey (Cambridge, Corpus Christi College 286, fol. 129v).

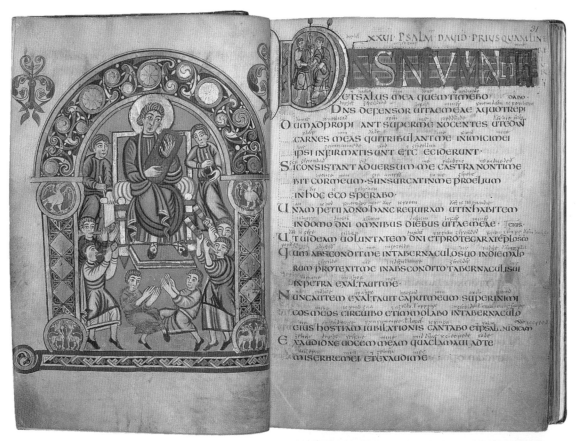

4 Vespasian Psalter, full-page illumination of King David harping and facing page with opening text of Psalm 26, with David and Jonathan in initial D; text in uncial script; Canterbury, St Augustine's Abbey? second quarter of eighth century (London, British Library, Cotton Vespasian A.i, fols. 30v–31r).

5 Royal Gospels, opening text of St Luke's Gospel, with evangelist symbol and bust of Christ in arch above; on purple-stained vellum; Canterbury, St Augustine's Abbey? first half ninth century (London, British Library, Royal 1.E.VI, fol. 43r).

6 Bosworth Psalter, opening text of Psalm 1, in a
book designed for Benedictine monastic usage;
Canterbury, St Augustine's Abbey? late tenth
century (London, British Library, Additional 37517,
fol. 4r).

7 Ælfric's Pentateuch, an Old English translation of the first six
books of the Bible; depiction of Noah's ark; Canterbury, mid-
eleventh century (London, British Library, Cotton Claudius B.IV,
fol. 15v).

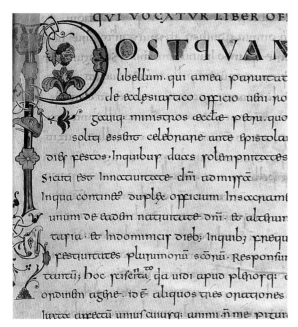

8 Amalarius, *Offices of the Church*, initial letter P; Canterbury, St Augustine's Abbey? mid-tenth century (Cambridge, Trinity College B 11.2, fol. 4r).

9 Martyrology, initial for the month of March; Canterbury, St Augustine's Abbey, *c.* 1100 (London, British Library, Cotton Vitellius C.XII, fol. 121r).

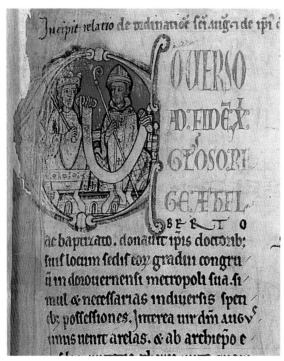

10 Lives of Saints, initial with St Augustine and King Æthelberht; Canterbury, St Augustine's Abbey? *c.* 1100 (Oxford, Bodleian Library, Fell II, fol. 45r).

11 Lives of Saints (from the companion volume to plate 10), initial with the martyrdom of St Cesarius; Canterbury, St Augustine's Abbey? *c.* 1100 (London, British Library, Arundel 91, fol. 188r).

12 St Augustine's Abbey, foot of north wall of original church of Sts Peter and Paul looking west, with tombs of Archbishops Laurence, Mellitus and Justus (English Heritage).

13 St Augustine's Abbey, church of St Pancras; in foreground upstanding wall of mid-eighth-century west porch (English Heritage).

14 Rome, mosaic of Christ enthroned between St Peter and St Paul, chancel arch of basilica of S. Lorenzo fuori le Mura; *c.* 579–90.

15 Canterbury, Old Westgate Farm, gold and garnet pendant with cruciform design, from a burial; diam. 40mm (*c.* 1½in), Anglo-Saxon, early seventh century (Canterbury, City Museums, inv. no. CANCM:CB/R2 78 456).

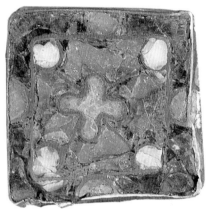

17 St Augustine's Abbey, gold and cloisonné enamel mount; width 11mm (*c.* ½in); ninth century (English Heritage, AML 777597).

16 Canterbury, the 'St Martin's Hoard', comprising: five sixth-century gold coins and a medalet; a seventh-century gold, garnet and glass disc-brooch; and a gold and cornelian pendant. The medalet with the name of Bishop Liudhard is upper right (Liverpool Museum inv. no. M7013–M7020).

18 St Augustine's Abbey, copper-alloy and cloisonné enamel circular mount; tenth or eleventh century (English Heritage, AML 78203053).

19 St Augustine's Abbey site, map of the New Lodgings and gardens *c.* 1640; not thought to be an accurate survey (Canterbury, Dean and Chapter Archives, map 123).

20 Watercolour, view of former guest hall and chapel with Ethelbert tower, *c.* 1793, by J.M.W. Turner (Northampton, Mass., Smith College Museum of Art, inv. no. 1926: 2–1).

middle of the eleventh century. One reason for suggesting this is that many details in the pictures bear close comparison with the Bayeux Tapestry, itself now generally agreed to have been made in Kent for Bishop Odo of Bayeux

(see **11**). There has been considerable debate about the extent to which the manuscript might itself be derived from an earlier (now lost) pictorial exemplar. However, even if there was the stimulus of some lavishly illustrated earlier source to explain the scale or the layout of the visual narratives, the representations of many of the artefacts, such as the crown and sceptre worn by the pharaoh, are taken from

21 Opening page of Boethius, *Consolation of Philosophy*; St Augustine's Abbey, late tenth century (Oxford, Bodleian Library, Auct. F.1.15, fol. 5r).

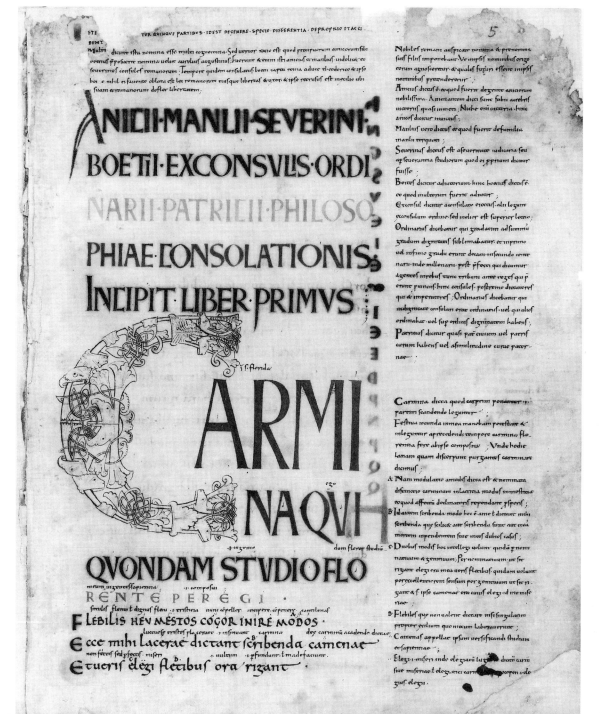

contemporary Anglo-Saxon culture. The time taken to devise such a complex cycle in addition to the time taken actually to execute it is further evidence that substantial resources were devoted to it. However, despite the evidence of local production and a level of patronage appropriate to a major institution, there remains a general problem about the purposes for which such a book could have been wanted in a monastery. It is really too lavish for the library and in the wrong language for the liturgy.

Art, liturgy and historical scholarship after the Norman Conquest

As in so many other respects, the Norman Conquest marked something of a watershed in the artistic patronage at St Augustine's. This is particularly obvious in book production in a number of different respects. For example, changes in the liturgy introduced as part of Archbishop Lanfranc's reforms of the English Church necessitated the creation of new sets of books for Mass, and for the daily office and chapter meetings. Several of these books survive, dating from around the year 1100, and show a consistency of script and decoration which suggests well-co-ordinated local production.

Foremost in importance among them is a missal, now in Corpus Christi College, Cambridge (MS 270). Its text is of considerable significance since it shows a number of distinct correspondences with the missal of the Norman abbey of Bec where Lanfranc had been a monk, and then prior, for over twenty years. By far the most likely explanation for these correspondences is that the Cathedral of Canterbury, where Lanfranc was in charge from 1070, adopted a large number of Masses from Bec and that these were, in turn, accepted or imposed at St Augustine's. In both the Canterbury houses a few major English commemorations were retained from the pre-Conquest period, for example St Alban and St Etheldreda; as well, of course, as the saints associated with the two monasteries themselves – each of which paid particular attention to

those buried in its church. So, in the St Augustine's Missal we have Masses for each of the first seven archbishops.

A similar pattern is evident in other books. The St Augustine's Psalter, now in Rouen (Bibliothèque municipale, A.44), has a litany of saints which shows the same hybrid quality, with a small selection of English material added into a list ultimately derived from Bec.

But the pattern was not always that of adapting a Norman core. The text of the Martyrology, now in the British Library, derives from a version current in England from at least 1000 (represented by Cambridge, Corpus Christi College 57). Interestingly, it is also very close to the Martyrology used at the Cathedral, and it raises the question whether this homogeneity is the result of a Norman attempt to unify practice between the two houses on the basis of a pre-Conquest text, or whether the same text was already in use in both monasteries before the Conquest.

The Martyrology, compiled by the ninth-century French monk Usuard, was read at the daily meetings of monks in the chapter house. The St Augustine's copy contains several beautifully drawn initials in coloured inks (**colour plate 9**). Originally there were twelve, one for each month of the year, and their subject-matter shows an inventive combination of material such as signs of the zodiac and characteristic agricultural activities for the months in question. These are generally shown within a structure composed of the letters KL (for the word *Kalendae*) and complex scrollwork. While the mixed content of these initials, letters, figures and foliage is quite a recent development on both sides of the Channel, the vitality and delicacy of the drawings recalls the style of the Anglo-Saxon art of Canterbury in the early eleventh century. Thus we see an artistic equivalent to the liturgical compromises discussed above. In the case of these initials, a revival of interest in the local pre-Conquest graphic tradition was being used to realize a modern compositional genre.

Some of the same points can be made about the Lives of Saints in the British and Bodleian Libraries (**colour plates 10, 11**). In many cases here, though, the foliate element is suppressed in favour of purely narrative or iconic imagery set within the structure of the initial letter. Although small in scale, the ambition of these compositions is very striking, compressing into inches a sequence of scenes that, in other contexts, might occupy several pages.

It is frequently argued that in the style of both script and art this group of manuscripts is distinctively of St Augustine's rather than Christ Church. This is taken as evidence that there were separate scriptoria in the two monasteries. There may well be some truth in this. For example the scribe of the Missal is only found working in books which seem to have been made for the Abbey. However, the 'impressionistic' drawing style is also found in books which come from the Cathedral's library (such as the two-volume Josephus now in Cambridge – St John's College A.8 and University Library Dd.1.4). Furthermore, the surviving books from the Cathedral at this date are indeed almost entirely from the library, not liturgical texts, and these might be expected to differ from books used in church services. Evidence from other monasteries at this period, for example Abingdon, makes clear that these two categories of books could be produced by quite different teams of scribes: liturgica by monks and library books by lay professionals. It may be then that some of the apparent distinction between the two monasteries in script is caused by the fact that preponderantly different types of material have survived from each of them.

Liturgical reform was only one aspect of the change at St Augustine's. The Norman abbots, and the continental recruits who came in their wake, had different expectations about what a well-stocked library should contain. The first post-Conquest abbot, Scolland, came from the Norman abbey of Mont-Saint-Michel, and that seems to have been the source of some books which entered the St Augustine's library, such as

Paul the Deacon's *History of the Lombards*, Ado of Vienne's *Chronicle of the Franks* and a series of genealogies, including those of the Franks and the Normans themselves (British Library, Royal 13.A.XXII and XXIII). As these seem to date from about 1070, it is quite likely that they were especially written for the English library. They indicate an interest in history, which is also demonstrated by the contemporary copy of the *Encomium of Queen Emma* (**22**). Emma, a daughter of a duke of Normandy, had married successively two kings of England, Æthelred II and Cnut, and been the mother of two more, Harthacnut and Edward the Confessor, and was subsequently remembered as a patron of St Augustine's to which she gave precious silk textiles to cover the bodies of the saints.

It was at this period, with the advent of the hagiographer Goscelin of Saint-Bertin, that St Augustine's Abbey first began to define its own historical traditions in writing. It is to Goscelin that we owe our knowledge of much that occurred in the Abbey's artistic patronage in the years around the Conquest. For example he tells us that Abbot Ælfstan (died 1046) invited a fellow Benedictine, Abbot Spearhafoc of Abingdon who was a famous painter and metalworker, to St Augustine's where he made effigies of great size and beauty of Queen Bertha and Bishop Liudhard, both of whom were buried in the Abbey. This seems to have formed part of an enhancement of the cult of Liudhard which survived the Conquest. There is a Mass for him in the St Augustine's Missal of *c.* 1100.

But by far the greatest single enterprise of which Goscelin informs us was the translation of the relics of the Canterbury saints which took place in 1091: the rehousing of the remains of the early archbishops in the new, Norman presbytery giving them renewed prominence and visibility. As shown in the early fifteenth-century drawing in Thomas of Elmham's history (**colour plate 1**), the shrines of Augustine himself, of Mildrith and Hadrian have altars attached, but the dating and sequence of the elaboration of the shrines in material and liturgical terms is not

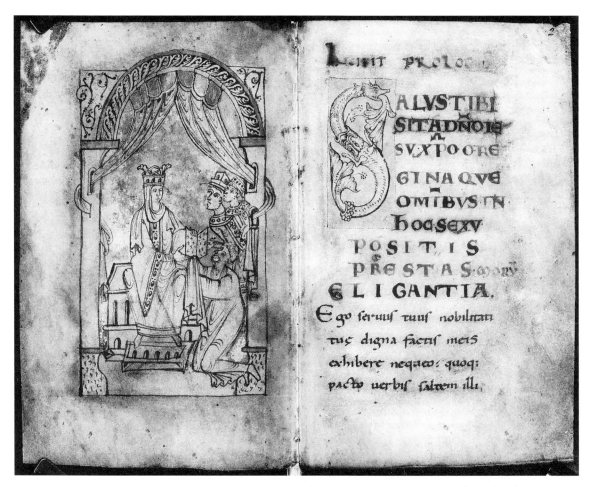

22 Opening pages of the *Encomium of Queen Emma*; the queen receives the book from its author, watched by her two sons Edward and Harthacnut; Normandy? third quarter eleventh century; from the library of St Augustine's (London, British Library, Additional 33241, fols. 1v–2r).

clear. Thorne, a historian of the Abbey writing in the late fourteenth century, records activity associated with the shrines in 1221, significantly the year following Thomas Becket's translation at the neighbouring Cathedral, and 1300. However, the layout described in Goscelin's account from around 1100 is essentially the same as that in Elmham's drawing and is likely to have been retained throughout the intervening centuries. Quite possibly there was from about the time of the translations also an image of Christ enthroned between angels, on a beam behind the high altar. Goscelin tells us

that sculpted images of angels with Christ in majesty, which had been above Augustine's tomb in the Anglo-Saxon church, miraculously survived all the upheavals and it is possible that they were reused in the new building. Even if they were replaced by contemporary works reflecting the same subject-matter, it seems that the stress on continuity was uppermost in the community's thoughts.

During the abbacy of Hugh de Flori, who had completed the church, the stone choir screen or *pulpitum* was erected to separate the monks from the laity in the nave. Hugh also imported a great bronze candlestick for the choir, almost certainly a seven-branched candlestick since its nickname, Jesse, apparently alluded to the seven gifts of the Holy Spirit associated with the 'Tree of Jesse' (Isaiah 11:1–2) and would also have echoed the symbolism of Augustine and his six companions in the apse of the church as seven candelabra, as Goscelin had described them. Hugh also commissioned a silver frontal for the high altar and a set of vestments worked with gold and gems which was apparently still in use when the chronicler Thorne was writing in the fourteenth century.

In the light of the almost total disappearance of the liturgical ornaments of the Abbey (23), such information seems invaluable. And yet it has to be treated with some circumspection. Unlike Goscelin's eyewitness accounts which, with the exception of obvious hyperbole for effect, must be taken at face value, later authors were prone to invent, or at least reconstruct from often inadequate data, the information they recounted. Thorne, for example, was fiercely loyal to his abbey and at pains to represent it as at least the equal of the neighbouring Cathedral. The new east end of the Cathedral, begun in the mid-1090s, was itself almost certainly a response to the glory of St Augustine's after the translations of 1091 and was famous for its coloured glass, its painting and marble. One can easily see how rivalry between the two houses might encourage their adherents to attempt to outdo each other both in the embellishment of the buildings and in the embellishment of the texts which purported to describe them. That said, the early twelfth century was undoubtedly the period when the material magnificence of the great churches of high medieval England found its first, mature expression, and St Augustine's is very likely to have been in the vanguard of this development. For not only was the church itself one of the earliest to be begun, but the translations of its many saints established new standards of ceremonial and display for others to measure themselves against.

The library in the fifteenth century

Any assessment of the intellectual culture of a medieval abbey needs to take full account of the contents of its library but, as we have already seen, there are difficulties in establishing this for the early centuries at St Augustine's since the

major surviving catalogue of the collection dates from as late as the 1490s. By way of compensation it is a very methodical and informative work. It has been estimated that the library at this stage contained some 1900 volumes, but many of these contained several shorter works. Of these rather less than half were what would now be considered religious works: books of the Bible, commentaries, sermons or devotional texts. The majority were roughly categorized into subsections of, for example, natural history, history, philosophy and the liberal arts, medicine, poetry, alchemy and law. There was also a small section for books in English and French.

Both the numbers of books in each rough category and the juxtapositions are revealing. There are, for example, over a hundred volumes on medicine and about one hundred and fifty on law. Interestingly the latter are treated in the catalogue as a distinct group, whereas the medical texts are listed, and were apparently shelved, in a

23 Copper alloy with mercury gilding; fragment with incised and punched decoration, perhaps from a shrine; length 32mm (1¼ in); twelfth century (English Heritage AML 743658).

VITRUUII · DE ARCHITECTURA LIBER · I ·

CUM DIUINA TUA MENS ET NUMEN IMPERATOR CESAR IMPERIO POTIRETUR
orbis terrarū inuictaq; uirtute cunctif hostib: stratif · triumpho uictoriaq; tua ciuef
gloriarent · & gentef omf subacte tuū spectarent nutū · populufq; romanuf & senatuf
liberatuf timore · & ampliffimif tuif cogitationib: confiliifq; gubernarent · Non audeba
tantif occupationib: de architectura scripta · & magnif cogitationib: explicata edere
metuenf · Necnon apto tēpore impellanf subirem tui animi offensionem ·:·

Cum uero attendere te non solū deuita cōmuni omium cura · publiceq; rei constitutione
habere · Sed etiam deoportunitate publicorū aedificiorū · ut ciuitaf pte nonsolum
prouincif eet aucta · uerū etiam ut maiestaf impii publicoy aedificiorū aegregiaf
haberet auctoritatef; · Non putaui ptermittendū quin primo quoq; tēpore de
reb: ea tibi edere · ideo qd primū parenti tuo de eo fuerā notuf · & eiuf uirtutif studiofuf

Cū autē concilium caeleftium insedib: immortalitatif eū dedicaffe & · & impiū parentif imp
potestatē transtulisset · idem studiū meū ineiuf memoria pmanenf · me contulit
fauore · Itaq; cum · M · aurelio · & · p · minidio · & · cn · cornelio · ad apparatione baliftarū
& scorpionū · reliquorūq; tormētorū refectione fui presto · & cū eif cōmoda accepi
que tum primo mihi tribuisti · recognitione pforonif cōmendatione seruasti;

Cum ergo eo beneficio essem obligatuf · ut ad exitū uitę non haberē inopie timore ·
haec tibi scribere coepi · qd animaduerti multa te aedificauiffe · & nunc ędificare

Reliquo quoq; tēpore · & publicorū & priuatorū aedificiorū pamplitudine rerū gestarū
ut posterif memorię traderent cura habiturū conscripfi prescriptionef terminataf ·
Vt eaf attendenf · & ante facta & futurę qualia fiant opa pte posses ſota habere ·

Namq; hif uoluminib: · Aperui omf discipline rationes ·:·

DE ARCHITECTIS · INSTITUENDIS ·:·

24 Preface and table of contents from Vitruvius, *On Architecture*; English? early eleventh century?; from the library of St Augustine's (London, British Library, Cotton Cleopatra D.I, fol. 2v).

sequence after astronomy and computistics, an order suggested, no doubt, by the importance of horoscopic calculation in the treatment of illness. Similarly the books on grammar, almost a hundred of them, were succeeded by the books of Classical poetry (fifty or so) which exemplified the heights of Latin style.

It is at once clear that, unless it functioned in part as a lending library outside the Abbey, there can have been little need for the multiple provision of copies of many of the texts that explains the sheer number of volumes. The fact is that what we are looking at is an accumulation, in some sense accidental, of gifts and donations as well as at the result of a deliberate 'purchasing policy'. In many cases the names of donors are specified. Several of these were abbots, who may indeed have been paying to have books made which the librarian felt were needed, but some are ordinary monks. Their collections seem often to represent personal taste. Thomas Arnold, for example, gave history books, including one on the Trojan Wars, a series of anonymous romances in French (such as *Lancelot* and *The Quest of the Grail*) and the French biographical *History of William the Marshal*, a famous paragon of twelfth-century knightly virtue; but there was only one book of devotions, again in French, among his gift of fourteen volumes. One cannot help but wonder how a man apparently obsessed at least in his imagination with deeds of valour adapted to the cloister!

While the catalogue gives us an overview of the library, the surviving books bring us face to face with the realities of wealth, taste and curiosity of successive generations. Any selection from the three hundred or so that have been identified is going to be partial, and the three which are illustrated here are not a representative sample (for example no biblical

commentary or law book is included). None the less they are revealing.

The Abbey possessed three copies of Vitruvius' treatise on architecture. Written in imperial Rome, it represents both practical advice to architects and a claim to enhance their status. One of these is now in the British Library (**24**) and appears to have been written in the early eleventh century, probably in England (though a claim for France in the late ninth or tenth century has also been made). Perhaps from the beginning, it was bound up with a copy of another Classical technical treatise, *De re militari* (On military matters) of Vegetius, again of uncertain origin. They were probably together at St Augustine's by the late eleventh century, when several initials that had not been supplied by the original scriptoria were added in what looks like a Canterbury hand. The prospect of two texts on architecture and defence being acquired at this period is, of course, very suggestive. Two major churches and a castle were begun very soon after the Conquest, and it raises the prospect that these Classical books were intended to inform patrons, master mason and engineers.

A quite different text, but with ancient antecedents and some practical function, was the *Herbal* of Apuleius. The copy, now in Oxford, was probably made in Canterbury around 1100 (**25**). Dealing with the medicinal properties of plants, it is early evidence of an interest in health in all its aspects which is so apparent in the late fifteenth-century library catalogue. The attractive paintings of different species are mostly distant derivatives of the illustration of Late Antique exemplars. In many cases the representations have been so distorted by repeated copying as to be barely recognizable, or even downright misleading. Such books stand then as monuments to the desire to perpetuate the heritage of Classical learning and art as much as to provide a straightforward, usable handbook. To that extent it is a later manifestation of some of the same impulses that led to the creation of the ninth-century *Aratus* manuscript in Carolingian

dar. mirifice fucer ardura stomachi sedar. nom herbe cerfolium.
Nascit locis cultis ut hortis. ad dolore stomachi. 1.
herbe cerefoln urides cimas tres colligis. & puleiu
ilignous. y mell coctr unu comisces. & papauer uiride.
l nducis i stomachu. libaberis. Nom herbe sisim
oxynta agit brui. ad uesice dolor & stranguir.
.1. herbe sisimbru aceo suco ∋ .11.
aduesice dolore & stranguria
dab cu aqua calida. n febrierant
cu uino dab. libabetur. n om herbe oleastru.
A geis dr sinernion. Aluy poselin.
Alu selmagon. Itali uoc olisatra.
egypti dicu dexerchon. ad uesice
dolore .1. he oleastru trita cu passo. & potui
data. stranguria emendat. nom herbe
lilium. A geis dr corinion.
ad morsu serpentis .1.
he lilu foliu conteres.
& expssu sucu potui dato.
& ipsu eet tu morsui ipo
nis. sanabit. ad luxu
.11. her lilu folia tunsa
& iposita. efficacit sanas. & si tumor fuerit.
tumore sedato.
nom herbe cymalua. ad ueteraneor
dolor .1. her tramallu radice t fruuteu eius. &
uiny cyatus .11. ei suco coctr .11. mixtis. dab ieiuno bibe.
sanabit. ad uerrucas tollendas. her tramali
sucu cu uino mixtu sup eo pnis. deuin oeis fontis obliga.
ad fistulas sanandas. 111. her tramali lac mixtu cu tbo
ris suco situruis iposueris. sanabit. ad lepsu. 1111. her tu
mallifflore cu resina decoq. & lepsu lineis. & u sinio crescere.

25 (*Opposite*) Various herbs, from Apuleius, *Herbal*; Canterbury, *c.* 1100; from the library of St Augustine's (Oxford, Bodleian Library, Ashmole 1431, fol. 27r).

26 (*Below*) Scenes of Irish life, from Gerald of Wales, *Topography of Ireland; c.* 1200 (London, British Library, 13.B.VIII, fols. 28v–29r).

France which had apparently been in the Abbey's library since the tenth century.

But not all learning and exploration of the world was derivative. In many respects the central Middle Ages were a time of direct curiosity translated into empirical enquiry. Indeed books such as the *Herbal* often included supplementary material based on recent observation. A far greater and concerted monument to this fresh and confident approach to the world is represented by the *Topography of Ireland* by the cleric Gerald of Wales (died 1223). One of the three surviving illustrated copies comes from the St Augustine's library (**26**). Here, with licence which depends on a certain amount of prejudice also evident in the text, are illustrations of the natural history and wonders of Ireland and the customs of the people.

While we cannot now look at books such as the *Vitruvius*, the *Herbal* or the *Topography* from the perspective of a medieval monk of St Augustine's, we can infer from them a good

deal about the priorities and intellectual mettle of the community. Tradition was obviously very important (how many people these days would read a textbook over a thousand years old as a source of practical information?). So too was a far more wide-ranging enquiry than we might at first associate with the contemplative life and the praise of God. Among monastic communities as a whole there was considerable variation of opinion about what constituted appropriate reading matter. The Cistercians, for example, preferred spiritual reading and biblical exegesis almost to the exclusion of all else; Classical poetry or natural history is a rarity in their libraries. St Augustine's, by contrast, seems to have been at the liberal extreme. Albeit the collection was built up by donation as much as by purchase, it reflects the tastes of the community and its friends. If not a centre of great intellectual activity, the Abbey was apparently sympathetic to virtually the full range of thought and speculation conceivable within the medieval world view.

5
The Anglo-Saxon and Norman churches

Richard Gem

Augustine and the foundation of the Abbey

The construction of the first church of St Augustine's Abbey in the years between 597 and 619, together with the Cathedral in Canterbury, constitute the beginning of Christian architecture in southern England, and also the point at which it connects with the traditions of the Continent. However, it would be a mistake to imagine that the arrival of Augustine's mission simply transplanted to the soil of Kent the type of Christian architecture that was to be seen in his home city of Rome. Canterbury began as a mission station, and it was only slowly over the centuries that it was to develop an artistic culture to match its ecclesiastical status as a metropolitan see.

The Rome of Augustine and Gregory was heir to the magnificent Christian churches that had been created in the fourth and fifth centuries under the Roman emperors and popes, and what new projects were still undertaken owed much to the tradition of these earlier buildings. Representative of the late sixth century is the church erected over the tomb of the martyr St Laurence by Pope Pelagius II (579–90). The church (**27** and see **colour plate 14**) is modest in scale and has a nave surrounded by aisles and galleries on three sides, and originally with an apse at the west end. The walls were built of brick, but this was clothed on the interior with marble and with exquisite mosaics. Examination of the marble columns and the architraves above them, however, shows

that most of them were not manufactured specifically for the building; rather they are spoils taken from earlier structures, dating from periods when such lavish materials were more easily available.

Unfortunately we know little about the buildings of the actual monastery of St Andrew on the Cælian Hill, founded by Gregory and where Augustine was a monk: but it is reasonable to suppose that it was different in character from the church of St Laurence, or from any of the major city churches of earlier date. Gregory came from an aristocratic family and had inherited a mansion on the Cælian Hill, which in 574–5 he converted into a monastery and there adopted a strict ascetic lifestyle. The site stood immediately across the road, the *Clivus Scauri*, from the long-established city church of Sts John and Paul, where an earlier member of the family, Gordian, had been a priest. Gordian's son Agapitus became pope in 535 and, encouraged by the senator Cassiodorus, established a library in the mansion, which was intended to become a Christian university, but the project failed and the library came to be incorporated into Gregory's monastery. Of the other monastery buildings we have little clear evidence, but from later descriptions they appear to have comprised an informal grouping of buildings, including three churches or chapels, a dining hall, the monks' cellar and a courtyard with a fountain (compare **5**). Yet even these minimal details are

27 Rome, basilica of S. Lorenzo fuori le Mura, church built by Pope Pelagius II, 579–90, with a later shrine over the tomb of St Laurence (Courtauld Institute, Conway Library).

important in trying to understand the new monastery which Augustine founded when he left Rome for Canterbury, for they must have constituted a pattern in his mind.

Augustine and his fellow-missionaries would not have set out from Rome in 596 with a set of architect's drawings or with a team of construction workers; though, no doubt, they did carry with them books and items needed for the liturgy. When it came to building, Augustine would have to make the best of the local circumstances he found at his destination. The native Anglo-Saxon tradition was one of building in timber, since masonry construction had fallen largely into disuse in Britain in the post-Roman period. If, therefore, Augustine wished to build in masonry, he would have to import the necessary craftsmen from the nearest available source, which would be from among the Franks. Although we have no direct documentary evidence from Augustine's time, a century later the bringing in of masons and

glaziers to northern England is indeed recorded. A further strand in the background to the early churches of Canterbury, therefore, is provided by late sixth-century building traditions in France.

Augustine had arrived by sea in the south of France and had travelled up the Rhône valley (see **1**). Here many churches survived from the late Roman period, but new buildings were continuing to be erected. At Vienne the surviving basilica of the Apostles (Saint-Pierre) dates in part from the latter half of the fifth century and is the best-preserved such building in France. It was a cemetery church, standing outside the city wall, and received the burials of a number of the early bishops of Vienne. The church had a wide nave with no aisles, and the walls were decorated with blank arcading and paired columns. At the east end was an apse between square side chambers, and beyond these a small atrium. At Lyon the basilica of St Justus served as a cemetery church outside the upper city, and again was used for the burials of a number of the early bishops. The building, as revealed by archaeological excavation (**28**), was reconstructed on a substantial scale in the sixth century, following the type of the somewhat

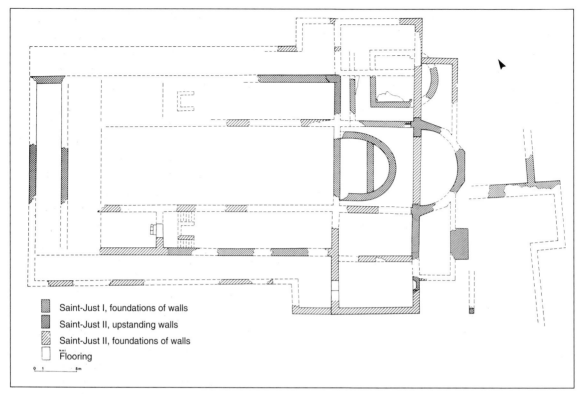

Saint-Just I, foundations of walls
Saint-Just II, upstanding walls
Saint-Just II, foundations of walls
Flooring

0 1   5 m

28 Lyon, basilica of St Justus; plan of excavated
structures: Phase I, late fourth or early fifth century;
Phase II, sixth century (after H. Delhumeau and N. Duval).

29 Autun, church of St Martin;
plan of building of *c.* 600 as recorded in
a plan of 1685 (redrawn R. Gem).

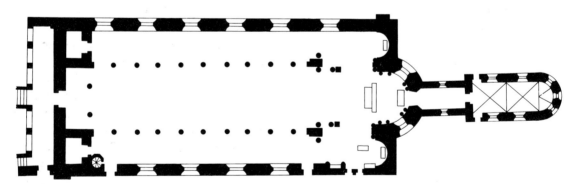

earlier church of St Laurence also in Lyon. It
had an aisled nave with flanking outer
porticoes; to the east of the nave was a transept,
on to which opened an apse. Beside the apse
were rectangular side chambers, and a series of
crypts underlay the building at various points.

Further north on Augustine's route lay the city
of Autun, where the basilica and monastery of St
Martin was built in the 590s by Bishop Syagrius
and by Queen Brunhild, both of whom were

among those persons to whom Pope Gregory had
addressed letters relating to Augustine's mission.
The church survived until the eighteenth century
and is known from descriptions and a plan (**29**).
The latter shows a building with nave and aisles,
terminating at the east in three apses; however,
the colonnades of the nave stopped some distance
west of the apse to make space for a separate
choir bay. The choir was possibly surmounted by
an elaborate superstructure, such as those

described elsewhere in France by Gregory of Tours and Venantius Fortunatus (contemporaries of Augustine). Beyond the apse was a separate funerary chapel, perhaps intended for Brunhild. At the west end of the nave was a narthex between two low towers. The building was of unmortared ashlar masonry, held by cramps, while the columns were of marble and the decoration included mosaic work. One gains the impression that Frankish monarchs at the end of the sixth century were still able to command the construction of buildings in the late Roman style.

In the Frankish kingdoms of Austrasia and Neustria, further north, less survives and there has been little relevant archaeological research to throw light on sixth-century architecture (notable exceptions are Rouen, where recent work has shown that the late fourth-century cathedral continued in use through this period; and Trier, where the monumental fourth-century cathedral was rebuilt c. 525–66). This lack of evidence is very unfortunate in relation to understanding early Kent, since it is precisely from these north-eastern Frankish regions that construction workers are most likely to have been brought by Augustine or King Æthelberht to Canterbury. Documentary sources at least throw some light on Paris, where in the 530s King Childebert I founded the church of the Holy Cross and St Vincent (later Saint-Germain) outside the city. There he and members of his family continued to be buried, including Lothar II, cousin of Queen Bertha, who was king of Neustria in the time of Augustine. The church had a monastic community, founded by Bishop Germanus of Paris, who was himself buried there. A later description indicates that the church was cruciform in plan and had marble columns, a gilded vault or ceiling, golden murals (probably wall mosaics) and a mosaic floor; externally it had a roof of gilded bronze tiles. Clearly here, as at Autun, the late Roman tradition continued, but it would be helpful to know more about the detailed arrangements of a wider range of buildings of the mid- and late sixth century in the region between Paris and the Channel.

Turning now to Kent itself, it is necessary to begin outside the city walls of Canterbury, with the church of St Martin, which Bede says had been built in the Roman period and had been restored for Christian worship by Bertha and her chaplain Bishop Liudhard when she had married Æthelberht. It was here also that Augustine and his companions first began to celebrate the liturgy. Research in recent times has suggested that the site in the late sixth century may have been that of a royal residence of Æthelberht and Bertha, lying on the hill east of Canterbury and in the fork between two roadways, one leading to Richborough and Sandwich, and the other to a *wic* or trading settlement on the River Stour at Fordwich (see **7** and **70**). The present church is of several periods of construction (**30**). The first building comprised the western half of the present chancel, together with an extension of the same width beneath the present nave. The chancel section is constructed of Roman bricks (some of which are clearly reused), bonded together with a hard mortar coloured pink by the addition of crushed brick (**31**). In the south wall is a doorway with a stone lintel, and this originally led to a small side chamber. It could be that this building was a simple church from the outset, or alternatively that it was an earlier building of unknown function later reused as a church.

In the second phase of St Martin's the early narrow nave was replaced by the present structure (**32**). The technique of building was quite different from the first phase, but resembles another form of Roman construction: the walls were of blocks of stone, with bricks used only for occasional courses between the stone; the mortar is again of the pink type. The stone is a limestone imported from a region north and north-east of Paris, but we cannot say for certain whether this importation took place in the Roman period or later. There are shallow buttresses at the corners of the nave and in the middle of the side walls. The only other original features are two windows, now blocked, in the west wall. Dating either the nave or the chancel of St Martin's is problematic. The roughly romanizing character of the nave

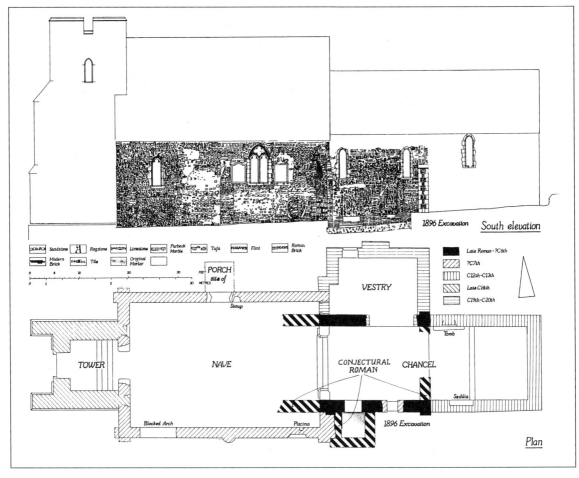

30 Canterbury, church of St Martin; plan and south elevation; for discussion of the date see the text (Canterbury Archaeological Trust).

masonry suggests a date not later than the seventh century according to one archaeologist: however, it is so different from the constructions at St Augustine's Abbey that it is difficult to accept it as precisely contemporary, or by the same builders as these. On the other hand, the brick walls of the first phase are much more similar to the dated works at the Abbey, and have perhaps a better claim to be associated with Bertha's church.

While they were worshipping at St Martin's, the missionaries received from the king a dwelling within the city walls of Canterbury for their use. Archaeological work within Canterbury over the last two decades has shown the Roman city in decline, and perhaps abandonment for a

31 Canterbury, church of St Martin; early south wall of chancel, constructed in Roman brick, and later nave beyond (National Monuments Record).

32 Canterbury, church of St Martin; reconstruction perspective of the Anglo-Saxon church following the building of the Phase II nave (J.A. Bowen).

generation, preceding the first Anglo-Saxon occupation in the middle of the fifth century. A large number of small huts, with a sunken ground-level within, were built among the ruins of the Roman town, and this type of structure continued from the fifth into the seventh century (**33**). No evidence has so far been discovered of larger hall-type buildings, constructed with earth-fast timber posts framing the walls. Such are what might be expected for higher-status dwellings, and perhaps these were located elsewhere within the walled area, as well as outside it.

According to Bede, King Æthelberht following his baptism finally granted to Augustine a site within the city walls of Canterbury for the establishment of his episcopal seat. Augustine then proceeded to repair a church which he had been informed was built by Christians in the Roman period, and this he dedicated to Christ the Saviour. Recent excavations beneath the nave of Canterbury Cathedral, however, have shown that the earliest church was on a quite different alignment from that of the streets and buildings

of the Roman city. At the least, this throws significant doubt on whether Augustine's cathedral was indeed the restoration of a church which had formed an integral part of the Roman city in the period when this was still flourishing as an urban entity (though it does not preclude a construction in the period of urban decline). Adjacent to the Cathedral Augustine now established his official residence.

For the best understanding of the architecture of this crucial period in English history we must turn, however, not to the Cathedral but to St Augustine's Abbey, which lay between the Cathedral and St Martin's, outside the city walls and along the north side of the road which ran to Richborough and Sandwich (see **70**). The Abbey church of Sts Peter and Paul, constructed in the years between 597 and 619, is known through excavations conducted in the early years of the twentieth century, but never properly published, and through further small-scale work in the 1950s (**34**). One part of the building, however, remains open to inspection by visitors (**colour plate 12**). Another important source for reconstructing the arrangements within the church is the remarkable account of the demolition of the building made in the late eleventh century by the writer Goscelin.

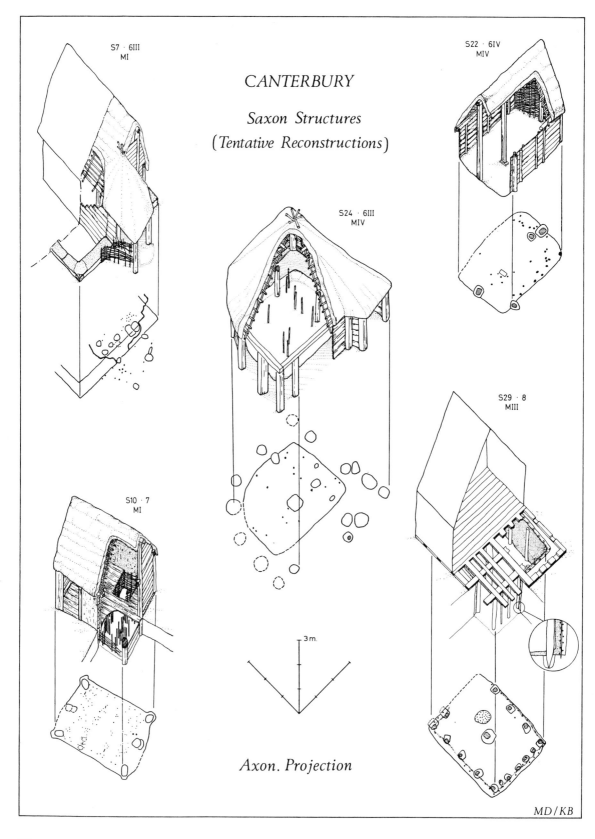

S7 · 6III
MI

S22 · 6IV
MIV

CANTERBURY

Saxon Structures
(Tentative Reconstructions)

S24 · 6III
MIV

S10 · 7
MI

S29 · 8
MIII

3m.

Axon. Projection

MD/KB

33 Canterbury, reconstructions of timber buildings from the town of the fifth- to seventh-century period (Canterbury Archaeological Trust).

The surviving lower courses of the walls of the church are constructed of reused Roman bricks, laid with a pebbly mortar; they are covered on both faces with a thin plaster rendering. The floors were of mortar with crushed brick. The building had a nave, 11.7m long and 8.1m wide (c. 38 by 26½ ft), and this was surrounded on its north, south and west sides by subsidiary chambers known as *porticus*, 3.6m (12ft) wide; the north and south porticus were subdivided into two by thin walls (**35**). The walls of the nave were solid and

access to the porticus was gained by simple doorways. At the west end a wide opening in the outer wall of the porticus must have formed a main entrance to the church. The east end was rebuilt in the later Anglo-Saxon period and its original form can be reconstructed only tentatively. It is clear from the evidence that the line of north and south porticus continued further east, and it is only beyond the point at which these terminated that the main apse can have sprung. Between the nave and apse there would have been a cross-wall with arches

34 St Augustine's Abbey, composite plan of excavated Anglo-Saxon structures of all periods (R. Gem and English Heritage).

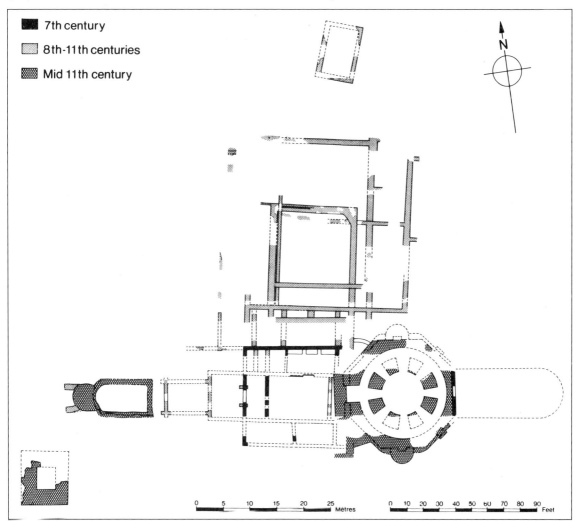

7th century

8th-11th centuries

Mid 11th century

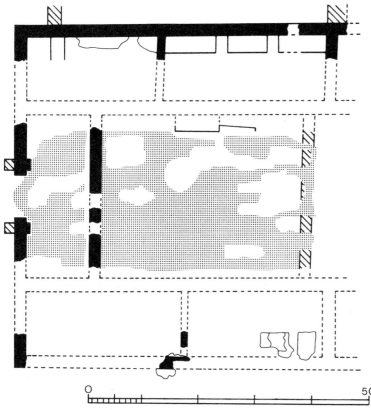

35 St Augustine's Abbey, undated excavation plan by W.S. showing walls, floors and tombs in nave area of Sts Peter and Paul; redrawn by R. Gem. Black shows primary walls and cross-hatching secondary; the floor, shown stippled, is of more than one phase.

36 *(Below)* St Augustine's Abbey, reconstructed plan of the early seventh-century church of Sts Peter and Paul (R. Gem). Hatched right to left, excavated walls; left to right conjectural. Altars: 1, Sts Peter and Paul; 2, St Gregory; 3, St Martin. Tombs of Archbishops: a, Augustine; b, Laurence; c, Mellitus; d, Justus; e, Honorius; f, Deusdedit; g, uncertain; h, Theodore. Other tombs: p, Bishop Liudhard; q, Queen Bertha; r, King Æthelberht.

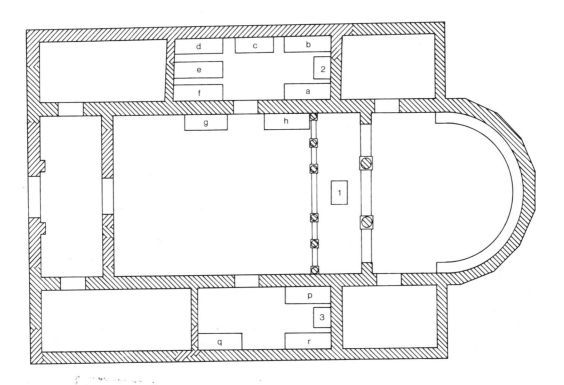

37 St Augustine's Abbey, reconstruction of the church of Sts Peter and Paul in the seventh century (J.A. Bowen after R. Gem).

through it; but the exact position of this must remain hypothetical (**36**, **37**).

The new church was, of course, intended as a functional structure, but very little precise evidence has survived to show how it was used, and we can build up only a hypothetical picture. The most important feature in the building would be the altar used for the celebration of Mass, and this probably stood in the east end of the nave under a canopy. Behind the altar would have been an arcade separating off the apse, where seats would have been provided for the clergy,

probably on a semicircular bench along the wall. Accessible from either the apse or from the nave would have been the two easternmost porticus, which would have served for the storage of vestments and books, and for the preparation of the bread and wine for the Eucharist. Westward of the altar, within the body of the nave, would have been placed the pulpit or *ambo* used for reading the Scriptures. Whether there were specific features provided for the monastic liturgy of this church and distinguishing it from the Cathedral we do not know.

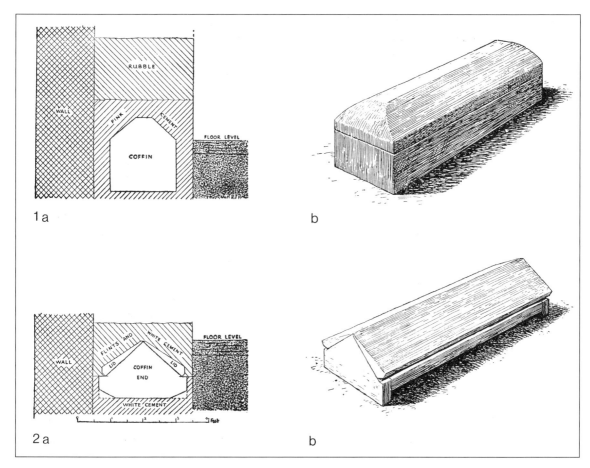

38 St Augustine's Abbey, tombs of (1) Archbishop Laurence, 619, and (2) Archbishop Justus, c. 627. Drawings show (a) sections through tombs as excavated, and (b) reconstructions of original wooden coffins, after W. St J. Hope (*Archaeologia Cantiana* 32, 1917).

The one aspect of the internal arrangements about which we can be much more definite relates to its funerary function, for not only do we have Goscelin's description of the burials as they were in the eleventh century, but archaeologists in the early twentieth century discovered some of the actual tombs – though unfortunately not that of Augustine himself. The burials of the first six archbishops took place in the porticus on the north side of the nave, and the royal burials of Æthelberht and Bertha in an equivalent position on the south. Those tombs which are still open to view are those of Archbishops Laurence (died 619), Mellitus (died

624) and Justus (died c. 627) (see **36** and **colour plate 12**). Laurence was buried in the north-east corner of the porticus against the wall (Augustine was in a similar position in the south-east corner): there a hole had been dug into the floor, into which the wooden coffin had been placed with pink mortar poured all around it; subsequently a monument of mortared rubble was built on top of this, rising about a metre above the floor (**38**). The monument was presumably decorated and had an inscription, as we know from Bede that Augustine's monument did (p. 22). The other two tombs lay to the west of the first and were generally similar in construction, but rose only a short height above the floor. The burials from the tombs were removed in the eleventh century, but they retain to this day the impression of the original wooden coffins on the mortar which surrounded them. Goscelin describes how the body of

Augustine himself was discovered within his tomb, laid out in his episcopal vestments: he also describes a sculpture of Christ in Majesty surrounded by angels which formed part of the monument above, but this may have been a much later addition (see p. 84). These monuments constitute the earliest identified church burials to survive in England, and are a unique witness to the group of missionaries who with Augustine brought Christianity to England.

If we try to relate Augustine's foundation of his new monastery in Canterbury to the wider European context, we can see that in terms of its function it had clear parallels in the Frankish world (see pp. 35–6). It was an extramural church, distinct from the Cathedral church within the city, and was intended to subsume a dual role: as a monastery, and as the funerary church of the archbishops and royal dynasty. If, however, we compare the architectural expression of this with Frankish churches of a similar function, there is a considerable gap. Frankish kings in the late sixth century had access to the skilled craftsmen and the materials necessary to build elaborate churches still in an essentially late Roman manner: columned basilicas enriched with marble decoration and gold mosaics. In Canterbury, even if financial resources were adequate, there was an absence of technical skills and of an organized masons' trade. What Augustine accomplished was therefore less ambitious and more functional. But it opened the way for the development of a distinctively English tradition of church architecture.

The flowering of the Abbey in the seventh and eighth centuries

The completion of Augustine's church by his successor Laurence was only the first step in the development of the Abbey. King Eadbald, Æthelberht's successor, added a second church, dedicated to the Virgin Mary. This stood immediately east of the first church, but nothing of it survives except the base of the west wall (and conceivably the two easternmost columns reused in the crypt of the eleventh-century

church). Further east again stands the church dedicated to St Pancras, of which there are much more substantial remains to be seen (**colour plate 13**). There is no reliable documentary evidence as to when this church was founded, but it may be significant that the cult of Pancras was fostered by Pope Honorius I (625–38), who rebuilt on a splendid scale the basilica over the martyr's shrine in Rome. The archbishop of Canterbury at this time was also named Honorius (there is no known connection), who was the last of Augustine's companions: perhaps he continued to be aware of developments in Rome and decided to foster the cult of Pancras at Canterbury.

Excavations on the site of St Pancras' took place at the beginning of the twentieth century and again in the 1970s, but the preparation of the latter for publication was delayed by the death of the excavator. None the less, it appears that the church is of at least two main Anglo-Saxon phases of construction (**39, 40**). In the earlier phase the church had a simple nave 12.8m long by 8.0m wide (42 by 26ft); to the east of this was a slightly narrower apse with a small porticus on its south side (and perhaps north as well). Between the nave and apse was a cross-wall, opened through an arcade. In the second phase the walls were substantially rebuilt on the same plan, but with the addition of porticus on the north, south and west of the nave. The walling of both periods is of reused Roman brick, and is comparable in general technique to that in the church of Sts Peter and Paul. The chancel arch wall of neither period survives without considerable later alteration, but appears to have comprised three arches carried on four columns. Sections of the columns were discovered and one remains in place with its moulded base (**41**), which is of limestone from the Paris basin: the mouldings are thought to be of early date but of Anglo-Saxon rather than Roman form, showing the influence of fifth- and sixth-century continental developments. The columns were of 0.42m (c. 1½ft) diameter, and perhaps some 4m (13ft)

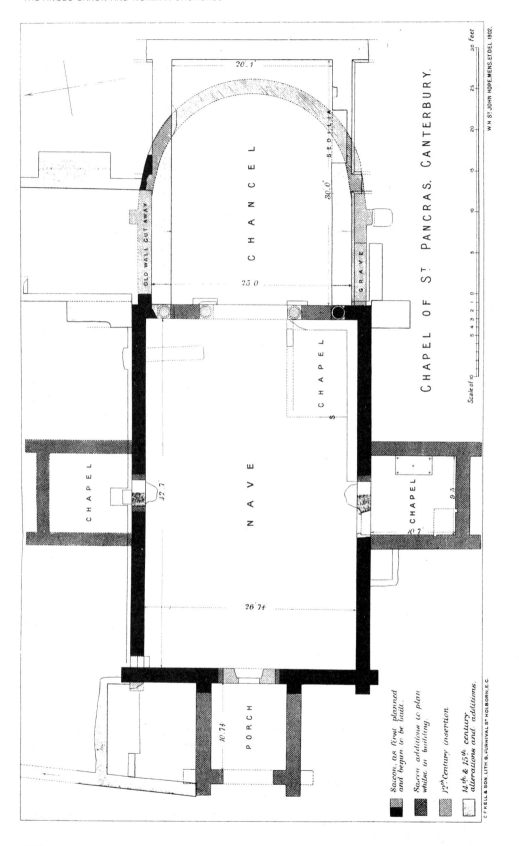

CHAPEL OF S^T PANCRAS. CANTERBURY.

W H ST.JOHN HOPE.MENS.ET DEL. 1902.

Saxon, as first planned
and begun to be built.

Saxon additions to plan
whilst in building.

12th century insertion

14th & 15th century
alterations and additions.

C.F.KELL & SON LITH 8, FURNIVAL S^T HOLBORN, E.C.

39 *(Opposite)* St Augustine's Abbey, church of St Pancras, plan by W. St J. Hope (*Archaeologia Cantiana* 25, 1902).

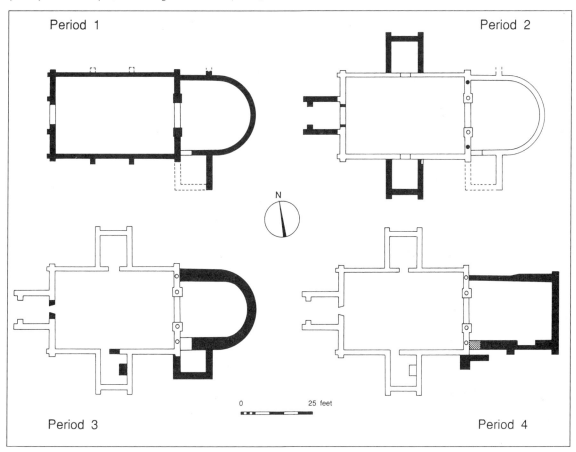

Period 1

Period 2

N

Period 3

0   25 feet

Period 4

40 St Augustine's Abbey, church of St Pancras, phased plan by F. Jenkins, 1976. His period 1 is here assigned to the second quarter of the seventh century, and period 2 to the mid-eighth (Canterbury Archaeological Trust).

41 St Augustine's Abbey, church of St Pancras, base of partly surviving column of chancel arch; seventh century? (English Heritage).

tall. The second of the building phases described above is to be dated on the basis of a burial with a coin (a late *sceat*) which was sealed by the construction levels; this suggests that the rebuilding was undertaken towards the middle of the eighth century. This would be consistent with a date for the original church in the second quarter of the seventh century. Standing within the ruins today, we may gain some reasonable idea of the scale of the nave of Augustine's first church, to which it approximates.

So far no mention has been made of the domestic buildings which must have been provided for the accommodation of the monastic community, and this is in large measure because the subject is an extremely complex one which, in the absence of further archaeological work, cannot be resolved. There is little to be seen above ground, unless the boundary wall, built of Roman brick, which leads eastward from the present cemetery gate is Anglo-Saxon and marks the original southern edge of the precinct. However, excavations in the 1920s on the north side of the church revealed evidence of a long history of domestic occupation preceding the eleventh-century rebuilding (see **34**). The earliest building in this area has always been thought to be a detached rectangular structure underlying the later refectory, and this is probably correct. Much more doubtful is the assumption that all the other buildings were no earlier than the tenth century. This assumption has been based on the premise that buildings arranged around a cloister cannot antedate the introduction of reformed Benedictine monasticism in the tenth century: but such an assumption can be self-fulfilling. St Augustine's was a major abbey with an established community through the seventh and eighth centuries, and it is difficult to accept that there were not appropriate buildings for its accommodation, especially in the time of Abbots Benedict, Hadrian and Albinus, that is, between the 660s and 730s. We know from archaeological evidence that Benedict provided very substantial domestic structures, built of masonry and with glazed windows, in the monastery which he founded later at Jarrow, and these were a worthy complement to the churches themselves. We have the evidence also of the monastery of Lorsch in Hessen, Germany, where the first monastery was built *c.* 760–7 with a fully developed claustral plan: the founders were the English missionary Boniface and his disciples. With these facts in mind it is

42 St Augustine's Abbey, capital of the Composite order, perhaps from a screen or altar canopy; date uncertain, between seventh and ninth century (English Heritage).

certainly worth asking the question as to whether some of the claustral buildings discovered in the early excavations at Canterbury go back to the seventh or eighth century or at the latest to the ninth.

During the two centuries following its foundation the church of Sts Peter and Paul itself must have undergone a process of embellishment and liturgical development, though it is difficult to reconstruct the precise nature and chronology of this. Among the finds from the site are four fragments of carved capitals of the Composite order, executed in limestone from the Paris basin (**42**). The lower part of the capitals is carved with a band of upright acanthus leaves; above this is the astragal with a zig-zag moulding; at the top the volutes are reduced to a wave pattern, with a rosette in the centre; the whole design is a very simplified version of a Roman capital. Judging by their form and the style of the carvings, they could be as early as the beginning of the seventh century or as late as the early ninth century. The capitals were originally set on column shafts with a diameter of 0.32m (*c.* 1ft), which suggests that their overall height did not exceed 3m (10ft). They did not derive, therefore, from a major structural feature, and could have come from something like an altar canopy, or a chancel screen (see **37**) like that erected by Pope Gregory in St Peter's, Rome. Such a screen could have stood on the line of an excavated foundation wall built across the east end of the nave sometime later than the original building (discussed below). That the capitals were given some prominent position is indeed suggested by the fact that they were originally painted in red ochre, Egyptian blue and a yellow pigment which, at least in one place, was the base for gilding. The artificial pigment Egyptian blue was something of a rarity in the post-Roman period, though it is known from some high-quality continental churches in the eighth and ninth centuries.

Fragments of painted wall plaster were recovered from the early excavations and at the time were thought to be Anglo-Saxon; some may be, but none can be related to the original building, and they serve mainly as a reminder that the interior of Augustine's church, if not initially at least in later centuries, could have been enriched with wall-paintings. From more recent excavations have come fragments of Anglo-Saxon window glass, coloured blue and plain, but again these are of uncertain date. Also excavated have been blue, turquoise and white glass tesserae for mosaic work, suggested to be of Roman manufacture; these were found together with other glass tesserae suggested to be of early medieval date, including gilded tesserae, and also fragments of various marbles. All these pieces could have been imported for use in mosaic work after the Norman Conquest; but we do not know for certain the origin or first use of the Roman pieces, and we should not overlook the use of mosaic work in sixth-century Frankish churches.

Some of the earlier excavators suggested that Augustine's original church had undergone an extension on the north side to accommodate further episcopal burials once the space of the original porticus had been filled up. But their supposed evidence can be interpreted in different ways, because it is unclear which archaeological features belonged to the church itself and which to the domestic buildings on its north. Bede tells us that an altar of St Gregory had been erected in the north porticus by his day (and an altar of St Martin in the south porticus), and that the

archbishops were buried in the north porticus up to the time of Theodore (died 690) and Berhtwald (died 731), but that these latter were buried in the main body of the church itself since the porticus was full. Theodore apparently lay on the north side of the nave, but we do not know the precise location of Berhtwald or his two successors. Archbishop Cuthbert (died 760) initiated a new tradition of burial within the Cathedral, and Jænberht was the last to be interred in the Abbey. Goscelin says that Jænberht asked to be buried 'in the chapter house of the brethren' rather than in the church, because of his humility: if he was indeed buried in a chapter house in 792, this is the earliest reference to the existence of such a building at the Abbey.

The church of St Mary, according to Goscelin, was also used for important burials. These included the founders King Eadbald and Queen Emma, together with their successors, including Lothar and Wihtred. They included also many of the abbots, among whom were: John, the second abbot; the famous Hadrian (died c. 709/10), apparently in a 'sarcophagus of white marble beautifully decorated'; and his successor Albinus (died 732). This information suggests that St Mary's as much as Sts Peter and Paul was intended from the start as a funerary church.

With a reasonably clear picture of the early churches of St Augustine's Abbey, it is possible to go on to ask whether they constituted a model outside Canterbury. The first witness is the church of St Mary at Reculver, founded in 669 by King Ecgberht for a community of which the priest Bassa was the first abbot. Before it was largely demolished in the nineteenth century, the church was perhaps the most impressive survival of its date in England: today it is known from the ruins, from excavations and from an important engraving (43, 44). The church stood in the centre of the former Roman shore-fort and, not surprisingly, was largely constructed of reused Roman materials. But these materials were also laid in a Roman-looking way: that is, with the stone and flint marked at regular intervals with courses of brick – rather like the

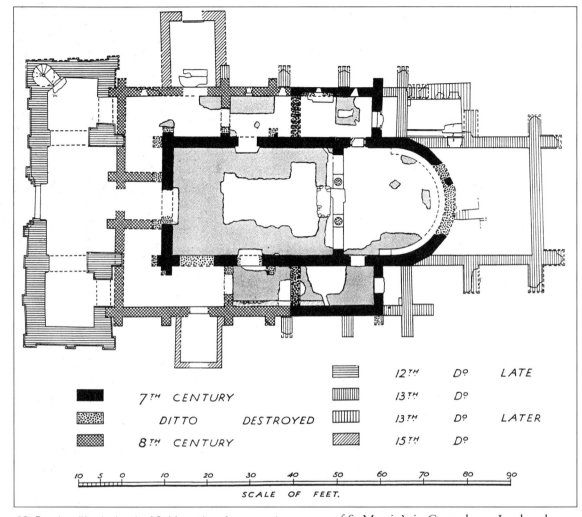

7ᵀᴴ CENTURY

DITTO DESTROYED

8ᵀᴴ CENTURY

12ᵀᴴ Dᵒ LATE

13ᵀᴴ Dᵒ

13ᵀᴴ Dᵒ LATER

15ᵀᴴ Dᵒ

10 5 0 10 20 30 40 50 60 70 80 90

SCALE OF FEET.

43 Reculver (Kent), church of St Mary, plan of excavated structures (*Archaeologia* 27, 1927).

nave of St Martin's in Canterbury. In plan the building had a simple rectangular nave, to the east of which was a polygonal apse; flanking these on north and south were single side chambers or porticus, entered from the apse. Around the inside of the apse wall was a bench for the clergy, while the altar probably stood at the east end of the nave. Between the nave and apse was a triple arcade carried on two columns, of limestone from Marquise near Boulogne, built in drums, and with simple moulded capitals and bases of a type derived from late Roman or early

44 Reculver, church of St Mary, engraving of seventh-century chancel arch during demolition (E.W. Brayley, *Delineations of the Isle of Thanet and the Cinque Ports*, London 1817) (National Monuments Record).

106

Byzantine models (the columns may be seen today in the crypt of Canterbury Cathedral). In a second period of construction the porticus were extended around the sides and west end of the nave. At a date which has been much discussed, but most probably in the early ninth century, the famous Reculver sculptured cross was erected in the nave (parts of which are also to be seen in Canterbury Cathedral).

Elsewhere more substantial parts of seventh-century buildings survive, but we do not have for them as coherent an overall picture as in the case of Reculver. Minster-in-Sheppey was founded after 664 by Queen Seaxburh, widow of King Eorconberht, and the original nave is incorporated into the present parish church. At Bradwell on Sea, which lay in the kingdom of Essex across the Thames estuary, the church of St Peter was founded by Bishop Cedd between 653 and 664, and the nave survives having been used for many years as a barn (45). A twin arch originally led from the nave to the apse, and there were porticus flanking the east end and at the west entrance.

From the evidence that has been examined, it is clear that the overall scale and conception of the original church of Sts Peter and Paul at Canterbury (and possibly the Cathedral) constituted a highly important model. Not only did this establish a tradition enduring for at least a century and a half at the Abbey itself, but it was also the formative influence, throughout the region, for the major minster churches which were the bases for Christian preaching and pastoral work in the countryside. The buildings originally created in the specific circumstances of the Augustinian mission thus became one of the major influences on the development of early church architecture in southern England.

The later Anglo-Saxon Abbey and Abbot Wulfric

Although in their early architectural development the Abbey and Cathedral were probably similar, in the ninth century they seem to have taken very different courses. At the Cathedral a major rebuilding programme was undertaken by

45 Bradwell on Sea (Essex), church of St Peter, view of nave from the north-west; seventh century (National Monuments Record).

Archbishop Wulfred (805–32), probably inspired by developments of the early Carolingian period on the Continent. A common life was enforced on the canons, and a dormitory and refectory were built for their use. Archaeological evidence has further indicated the rebuilding of the Cathedral church itself on a substantial scale, largely replacing Augustine's earlier building.

St Augustine's Abbey, in contrast, retained throughout the Anglo-Saxon period its original buildings from the time of its foundation, although these underwent a series of additions and alterations – at dates which we cannot easily determine without further archaeological research. The pattern at the Abbey was in some ways the more characteristic of late Anglo-Saxon England, where early church buildings tended to be retained in use rather than replaced on an ambitious scale to meet changing architectural fashions. The monk and historian William of Malmesbury, writing in the early twelfth century, provides a theoretical justification for such conservatism, spoken through the mouth of the last Anglo-Saxon bishop, Wulfstan of Worcester, who laments how his contemporaries were destroying the work of the saints of old. Whether such explicit attitudes about the connection between buildings and the sanctity of those who erected or used them can be traced back as far as the ninth century we cannot say; but in the case of St Augustine's Abbey the presence of the tombs of the early archbishops, kings and queens, which were one of the foundations of the church's importance, must have acted as a powerful deterrent from radical architectural schemes. This is a theme which can be traced right through the next two and a half centuries of the Abbey's history.

About the Abbey buildings in the ninth and a large part of the tenth centuries we know next to nothing from the historical sources. The first major landmark in the late Anglo-Saxon period does not come until 978, when it is recorded that Archbishop Dunstan (himself a Benedictine monk) carried out a rededication of the church of Sts Peter, Paul and Augustine. Such a rededication implies a significant reconstruction of the church, but the historians tell us nothing about the works in question. Moving on into the first quarter of the eleventh century, Goscelin tells us that Abbot Ælfmær dismantled certain arches and columns that stood over the saints' tombs (that is, the tombs of Augustine and his companions) to prepare for moving the bodies, and that he used these architectural elements to ornament the cloister. Also in Ælfmær's time there are references to the existence of an infirmary for the monks, and of a church of St Maurice and the Theban Martyrs nearby; but of the origin of these buildings we know nothing. The next abbot was Ælfstan, who *c.* 1030 removed from the ancient church of Minster-in-Thanet the relics of St Mildrith and enshrined them in front of the high altar (see p. 48).

Turning to the archaeological evidence from the Abbey site, there are several features that are likely to fall into this period between the late eighth century and the middle of the eleventh, but which cannot be more precisely assigned within it (see **34**). Reference has already been made to the foundation for a cross-wall discovered at the east end of the nave, somewhat west of the assumed position of the original wall between the nave and

apse and possibly on the line of a screen in front of the nave altar. This may imply a remodelling of the original church eastward of the liturgical division between the nave and sanctuary, possibly with the removal of the main altar from the nave to nearer the east end; such could have been the reason for the rededication in 978. More certainty may be reached on the remodelling of the west end of the building. It seems likely that the old gable wall of the nave was demolished and the nave itself extended over the site of the original west porch. A new structure in two sections was then added beyond this. The first section was an annexe to the nave, probably including a gallery at an upper level. The second section was a new porch, narrower than the nave. Some distance west of the porch, and on the same axis, was a free-standing tomb chapel in the cemetery. These modifications were comparatively modest and they contrast markedly with the elaborate new western structure added to the Cathedral in the early eleventh century, as revealed by the recent excavations.

It is very likely that some at least of the structures excavated in the cloister area and adjoining the church on its north side also belong to the late Anglo-Saxon period. Certainly from the time of Archbishop Dunstan, as the community took on a more strictly defined Benedictine character, there must have been a need for domestic offices comparable to those provided at other reformed monasteries in England in the second half of the tenth century – which adopted the plan arranged around a cloister. Other work in this area may be associated with Abbot Ælfmær's campaign. The claustral buildings discovered in the early excavations certainly belonged to at least two major phases of construction, but unfortunately it is not possible to disentangle the details without re-excavation.

Certain fragments of ornamental stonework recovered from various excavations derive from the late Anglo-Saxon Abbey, although it is difficult to be precise about their original location or date. The most important among these is a series of small turned columns with

46 St Augustine's Abbey, stone baluster shaft; late Anglo-Saxon (English Heritage).

decorative mouldings – often termed baluster shafts (**46, 47**). Such shafts were used to carry twin arches in window openings, and perhaps in a variety of other contexts. Examples closely similar to those from St Augustine's have been found at St Mary in the Castle at Dover, which is one of the major churches in Kent of the period around 1000. Other examples in their original context may be seen, for instance, in the late tenth-century church of Barton on Humber (Lincolnshire). The St Augustine's shafts could belong on their style alone to either the tenth or eleventh century. Contemporary with them is part of a monumental stone cross. Fragments of stone apparently from other colonnettes are reused in the walls of the mid-eleventh-century rotunda and must antedate this.

The final phase of the pre-Conquest Abbey's history was initiated by Abbot Wulfric II in the mid-eleventh century (see **34**). The first evidence of his documented works is a substantial donation made in 1047 to help pay for the completion of a tower which was then under construction. This tower is perhaps to be identified with the massive foundation for a free-standing structure, sited south-west of the church, towards the cemetery. Church towers were becoming increasingly popular from the middle of the eleventh century onwards and it is likely that St Augustine's was trying to catch up with the fashion, both to increase the Abbey's prestige and also, perhaps, for the practical purpose of hanging bells. Archaeological evidence has identified other mid-eleventh-century works at the west end of the Abbey church, including a small chapel with a western apse, to which a cylindrical tower was subsequently added.

The most important of Wulfric's projects, however, was one for the remodelling of the main Abbey church of Sts Peter and Paul, by joining it with a link-building to the church of St Mary further east. The plan manifests a radical intervention in the traditional pattern of the

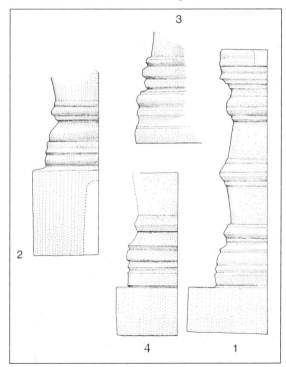

47 Late Anglo-Saxon baluster shafts: (1) to (3), St Augustine's Abbey; (4), St Mary in the Castle, Dover (English Heritage).

48 St Augustine's Abbey, view from the south-west of the crypt level of Abbot Wulfric's rotunda; mid-eleventh century (English Heritage).

buildings and Goscelin represents Wulfric as seeking the prior approval of Pope Leo IX when he attended a church council at Reims in 1049. To achieve his objective, Wulfric had to demolish the entire east end of the church of Sts Peter and Paul, and the western porticus of St Mary's; this involved disturbing the shrine of St Mildrith and many burials, for which alternative arrangements had to be made. The new work was then laid out and the construction started, but by the time of Wulfric's death in 1061 it was incomplete and work came to a stop.

The archaeological excavations in the early twentieth century uncovered the crypt level of Wulfric's building (still visible on site) and showed it to be a centrally planned structure, octagonal externally and circular internally (**48** and see **92**). It had a central rotunda 7.5m (24½ft) in diameter, defined by a ring of wedge-shaped piers; outside this was a concentric ambulatory 1.8m (6ft) wide. Circular stair turrets on the north and south provided communication between the crypt ambulatory and the upper levels of the structure. It is reasonable to suppose that there were three storeys above the crypt ambulatory, but that the central rotunda may

have been open the full height from the crypt floor to the roof (**49**). The main level of the ambulatory would have been raised above the level of the nave floor and approached up a flight of stairs; one would then have proceeded around the ambulatory to gain access to the nave of St Mary's Church on the east side. Above the ambulatory would have been a gallery; and above that again the clerestory walls would have risen above the gallery roof.

What we can only begin to guess at is how the new building was intended to be used. The new arrangement had displaced the old high altar, but it is unclear where the new high altar and the monks' choir were to stand: were they to be removed into St Mary's? Equally it is uncertain whether Wulfric had any intention of moving the shrines of the early archbishops into the new structure. One gains the impression that Wulfric had become preoccupied with an architectural idea without adequate regard for its practical consequences. Perhaps he had seen the new rotunda at the nunnery of Ottmarsheim in Alsace, very similar in conception, which Pope Leo IX had dedicated at the time of the 1049 council (**50**). Perhaps he hoped that this would provide a solution to updating his Abbey church without the need for demolishing the venerable structure erected by Augustine. But as Goscelin sharply observed: 'Kent rejoiced in the new work, although the inexperience of the workmen had made it unsuitable for monastic use.' Clearly it was unsuitable: though it was the abbot not the builders who must take responsibility.

Abbot Scolland and Master Blitherus: the Abbey church rebuilt

From the beginning of the eleventh century a change had been overtaking architecture on the Continent with the development of a new technology of construction and a new style, known today as Romanesque. The monk Goscelin came from a continental background where these changes would have been well recognized, and he himself lauded the new style: 'He destroys well

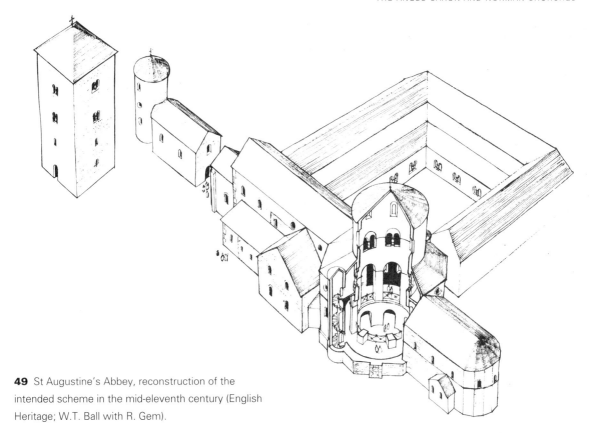

49 St Augustine's Abbey, reconstruction of the intended scheme in the mid-eleventh century (English Heritage; W.T. Ball with R. Gem).

who builds something better ... I would not allow buildings however much esteemed to stand, unless they were, according to my idea, glorious, magnificent, most lofty and spacious, filled with light and altogether beautiful.' Goscelin might almost have had St Augustine's Abbey in mind when he wrote this, and it is not surprising to find him attributing similar sentiments to Abbot Scolland: 'He was offended by the standing work which had been clumsily extended, and by the constricted plan of the structure decreed [by Abbot Wulfric] ... he was also frightened by the danger that the old monastery, consumed by long decay, might collapse.'

Scolland of Mont-Saint-Michel (Scotland as he is known in later sources) had been appointed in 1070, and when he travelled to Rome late in 1071 he discussed with Pope Alexander II his plans for rebuilding the Abbey: with papal approval he then proceeded. The relics and burials were removed from the church of St Mary, then this building together with

Wulfric's rotunda were demolished to make way for the east end of the new building. The intention was to reinstate the sanctuary of St Mary at crypt level, and to place above this the main sanctuary of Sts Peter and Paul with the shrines of Augustine and his companions; the choir of the monks would lie immediately west of these. This much of the work could be carried out without the need to demolish in advance the

50 Ottmarsheim (Haut Rhin, France), view of the church dedicated by Pope Leo IX in 1049 (R. Gem).

111

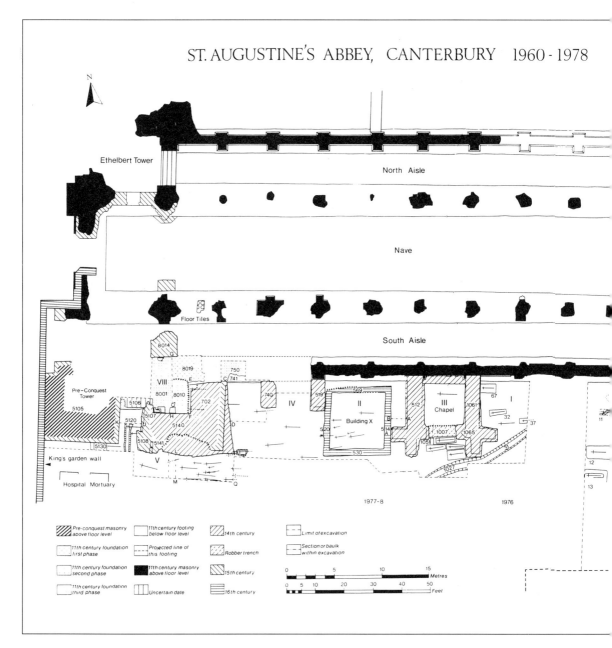

51 St Augustine's Abbey, plan of all post-Conquest phases of the church, as excavated to 1979 (English Heritage).

porticus where the archbishops' tombs lay. Scolland himself died in September 1087, when work was in progress on the new transept, and left his successor Abbot Wido to complete the crossing tower. The porticus of the archbishops was first demolished. Then in September 1091 the monuments were removed and the tombs were opened; the relics of the saints were then carried into the new building and enshrined. It thus became possible to proceed with the continuation of the new nave down to the west front, but no date is recorded for the completion of the whole church, perhaps because Goscelin was writing (he completed his account between 1098 and 1100) before this point was reached. Abbot Wido himself died in 1093 and was succeeded by Hugh de Flori, who was installed

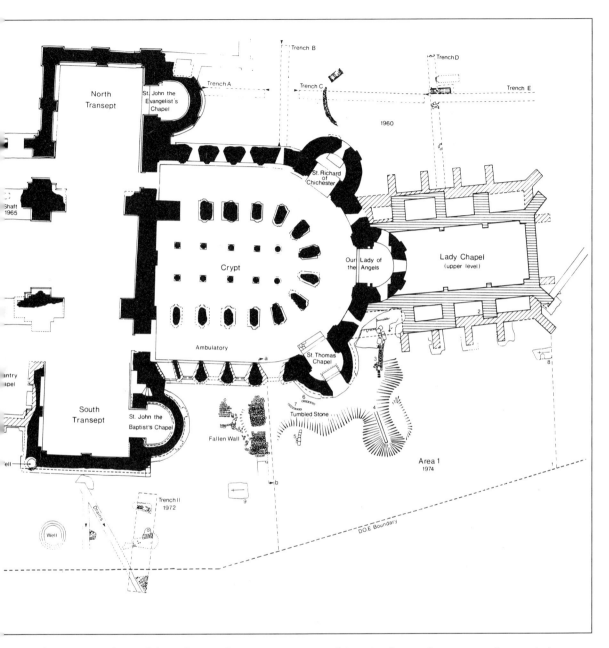

only in 1108 after a delay of several years. It was probably Abbot Hugh who brought the Romanesque church to completion in the early years of his rule.

We are uniquely well informed at St Augustine's Abbey not only about the circumstances and chronology of the early stages of the construction project, but also about the personnel involved and about the procurement of materials. There was not an architect in the modern sense who carried out the design work; rather this was the responsibility of a master mason, who would have provided the technical and artistic input to help the abbot realize his general conception. In this case the master is recorded by name as Blitherus (which suggests that he was of continental origin), and Goscelin describes him as 'the most eminent master of the craftsmen, the remarkable inaugurator of the church'. In

113

1087 Blitherus was a tenant of one of the Cathedral's properties, which suggests that he may have been working there also.

For Blitherus and Scolland to realize the project, large supplies of building materials were required, in particular good-quality freestone. Such stone was not easily available in Kent and it was convenient, therefore, to transport it by sea across the Channel from the vicinity of Caen and Boulogne, and also from the Isle of Wight. In the case of stone from the Caen quarries, requisitioning was delegated to Vitalis, who was acting as Royal Superintendent for obtaining such stone for the work of the king's palace in Westminster (see p. 60, and **11**): the abbot would pay the contracted carrier on delivery to Canterbury. At the Marquise quarry near Boulogne a different arrangement was in place. A monk with a natural aptitude in such matters was sent from Canterbury to arrange the assembly of a team of quarrymen who would receive a weekly wage. The stone was then transported in ships that may have belonged to the Abbey. In both cases the stone to be shipped was already prepared at the quarry according to whether it was to be used for plain walling or for columns, capitals, bases or other mouldings.

The terrible destruction wrought on the Abbey in the sixteenth century has left the visitor with only fragments of the great Romanesque church to see, but these are enough to appreciate its general lines (**51**). They also permit the reconstruction of much of the design by comparison with other contemporary buildings. The crypt underlay the whole east arm of the church and preserves its plan (**52**). There was a main apsidal crypt chamber, surrounded by an ambulatory passage which gave access to three semicircular chapels. The central chamber was subdivided by two rows of slender columns, with two larger columns at the east end (perhaps taken over from the Anglo-Saxon building). The columns and the main piers carried the groin vaults which covered the entire crypt. The vaults formed a platform above which the main sanctuary of the church

52 St Augustine's Abbey, view from the south-west of the crypt ruins; late eleventh century, but the arch and structure over the east chapel are modern (English Heritage).

was laid out. At this upper level the main apse and bays in front of it were probably separated from the ambulatory by an arcade carried on columnar piers. Above this arcade would have been a series of openings into a gallery surmounting the ambulatory. Higher still the main walls rose as a clerestory above the gallery roofs. The ambulatory around the apse gave access to three chapels, and part of the collapsed outer wall of the ambulatory further west was discovered in excavation. We cannot be certain of the precise details of the design, but in the reconstruction drawing offered here (**53**) the most straightforward solutions have been suggested in problematic areas: alternatives are not thereby ruled out.

It was into this new eastern arm that the relics of the early archbishops were moved in 1091. The new arrangements are described by Goscelin. The eastern chapel off the ambulatory contained the altar of the Holy Trinity, and behind this was placed the new tomb of Augustine, with Laurence and Mellitus on either side of him. The south chapel had the altar of the Holy Martyrs, and behind this the tomb of Abbot Hadrian, accounted the second major patron saint of the monastery. The north chapel had the altar of the Holy Innocents, and behind

53 St Augustine's Abbey, reconstruction of the church in the early twelfth century (J.A. Bowen with R. Gem).

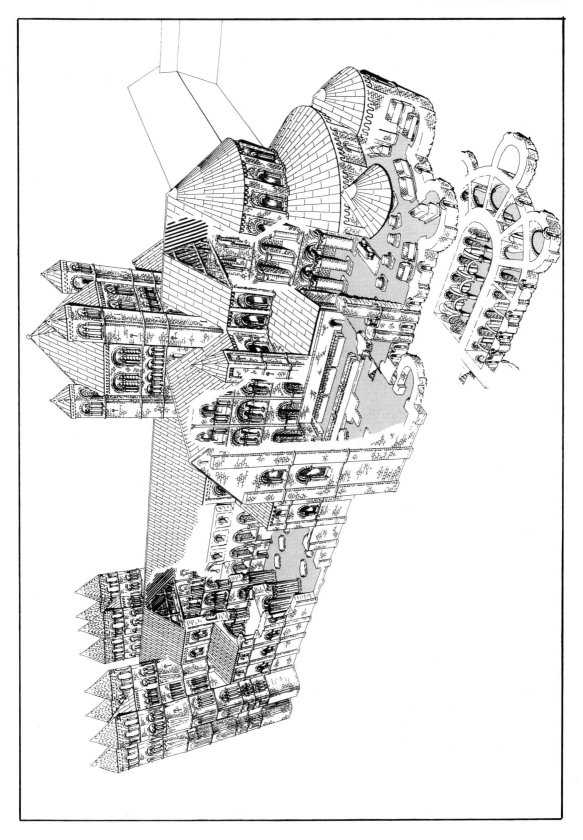

this the tomb of Abbess Mildrith. Against the ambulatory walls flanking the chapels were ranged the tombs of the other early archbishops. This arrangement differs from many other contemporary churches with important relics, where the principal shrines were placed either behind the high altar or in front of it to the side. The apse behind the high altar at St Augustine's appears in Goscelin's account and in Thomas of Elmham's drawing (see **colour plate 1**) to be blank: but it is worth asking whether this could have been the intended location of the tombs of Æthelberht, Bertha and Liudhard.

Immediately west of the crypt and main sanctuary lay the transept and crossing. The original arrangement of this area in plan is clearly seen on site today (although slightly confused by the excavating out of the earlier

55 St Augustine's Abbey, internal face of the north aisle wall; stonework eleventh century, brickwork sixteenth century (English Heritage).

crypt of Wulfric's rotunda, which had been infilled in the 1070s and lay unseen beneath the pavement). The crossing constituted as it were the heart of the monastic church, for here would have stood the stalls of the monks, where by day and night they celebrated the round of the sung office. The crossing was surmounted by a lantern tower, and to either side were the transept arms, provided each with an apsidal chapel on its east side. In the south transept were reburied some of the members of the Kentish royal house, including Hlothhere and Wihtred identified during excavation by their leaden coffin plates (**54**). From the transepts spiral stairs led to the upper parts of the building.

West of the crossing, the nave stretched for twelve bays down to the west front, where the last bays were flanked by a pair of towers. The nave piers survive only at their base, but a significant stretch of the outer wall of the north aisle stands to its full height, where it was retained in the sixteenth-century palace structure. The scars left by the aisle vaults were made good in brickwork (**55** and front cover). The wall is built largely of Caen, Marquise and Quarr stone, in the small regular blocks typical of Norman work of the last third of the eleventh century; and where some of the stone has been robbed away

54 St Augustine's Abbey, lead coffin plates from the late eleventh-century reburials of Kings Hlothhere (died 685) and Wihtred (died 725) (English Heritage).

the underlying rubble core of the wall is visible. The wall is divided into a series of bays in which can be seen the former window openings of the aisle, and the smaller windows of the gallery above (56). Between each bay is a respond formed with a series of slender colonnettes, surmounted by block-like cushion capitals. These responds carried arches across the aisle and helped support the aisle vaults. Opposite each respond was placed one of the main piers of the nave, standing on a continuous foundation wall. The piers were of compound form, combining a series of rectangular elements and colonnettes. On the east and west sides these supported the main arcades of the nave. On the face towards the nave a shaft rose right up the wall to the roof, marking the division of the elevation into bays. Following the destruction, we cannot say precisely how the gallery and clerestory levels were treated above the main arcade.

The design with twin west towers was arrived at only after other solutions had been considered, as has been shown by archaeological work. The southern half of the northern tower, as finally constructed, survived substantially until 1822 when it collapsed. There are consequently a number of illustrations of it, including a survey drawing by John Carter in 1798, and these show well the elaborate character of its ornamentation (57 and see Chapter 7). The lower parts of the tower correspond to the main height of the nave; above that it rose clear for at least two further stages, flanking the gable wall. At its external corners the tower had massive buttresses, which near their tops changed from rectangular to octagonal form, presumably to accommodate turrets. Both the main walls and the buttresses were decorated with elaborate blind arcading, and the columns, arches and surfaces within these arcades were further enriched with a variety of carved patterns. The patterns included many motifs which may be paralleled in English and Norman buildings of the decades around 1100; they also included triangular-headed 'arches' which were of Anglo-Saxon ancestry. This ornamentation

56 St Augustine's Abbey, the south-west corner of the cloister showing the north aisle wall where it is abutted by the west range (English Heritage).

must have provided the building with an exuberant façade marking the completion of the church. It is difficult to assign a precise date for this completion on the evidence of the eighteenth- and nineteenth-century illustrations, but early in the abbacy of Hugh (1108–26) seems likely, if not already in the interregnum following Wido's death c. 1093.

A number of pieces of Romanesque sculpture have been recovered from excavations and derive from different parts of the Abbey buildings. Notable among these is a stone from an archway carved with a human head and two biting animals tugging at his beard (58). The piece dates to around 1100 and is signed by the carver Robert. Unfortunately we know nothing more about the context of the piece, nor of the work of Robert. Of similar date is a capital

57 St Augustine's Abbey, north-west tower (so-called Ethelbert tower), as surveyed by John Carter 1798–9 (*Ancient Architecture of England*, 2nd edn, 1837, pl. xxx).

carved with foliage ornament and painted in blue and pink against a dark brown ground (**59**). The majority of capitals in the Romanesque church, however, were of the cushion type without carved decoration. Such

58 St Augustine's Abbey, sculptured stone voussoir with human head flanked by biting animals, signed by the carver Robert; *c.* 1100 (English Heritage).

59 St Augustine's Abbey, sculptured and painted capital with Romanesque foliage ornament; *c.* 1100 (English Heritage).

plain capitals made their first appearance in Canterbury in the 1070s, perhaps coming in with the import of Marquise stone from the hinterland of Boulogne. Other carved stones show the presence of chevron, billet and diaper ornament in the building.

The great new church designed by Abbot Scolland and Blitherus stood in the forefront of architectural developments in the Europe of its day. Its clearest links are with the workshop formed in Caen in the 1060s to construct William the Conqueror's Abbey of St Stephen (**60**), from which had derived the workshop for the rebuilding of Canterbury Cathedral, begun in 1070 by Archbishop Lanfranc, formerly abbot of Caen. From the Cathedral a workshop could then have been formed by Abbot Scolland for St Augustine's. However, St Augustine's was clearly very much more than a copy of the

60 Caen (Normandy, France), St Stephen's Abbey, interior view of the Romanesque nave looking north-west from the transept; last third of eleventh century (Courtauld Institute, Conway Library).

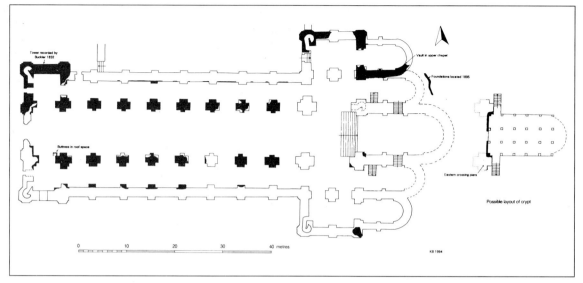

61 Canterbury Cathedral, plan of Archbishop Lanfranc's building, begun 1070 (K. Blockley and Canterbury Archaeological Trust).

design of the Cathedral (**61**). This is apparent right from the start of the work when, in contrast to the Cathedral, St Augustine's adopted the ambulatory plan for its eastern arm. According to Goscelin the practical reason for this was to combine the previous churches of Sts Peter and Paul and of St Mary, and to resolve the problems unsolved by Wulfric. But the specific models for the ambulatory plan must be sought in France, where the scheme goes back to the first half of the eleventh century. A good contemporary parallel to St Augustine's is the new east arm of the famous abbey of Saint-Benoît-sur-Loire (also known as Fleury), although this does not have so extensive a crypt (**62**). There may have been a more immediate model in Normandy itself, but we should not overlook the degree to which a master like Blitherus was capable of synthesizing earlier ideas and coming up with original new designs.

Within England the new church of St Augustine became a highly influential model – possibly even the single most important model for the subsequent development of Anglo-Norman Romanesque architecture. Even within

62 Saint-Benoît-sur-Loire (Loiret, France), St Benedict's Abbey (Fleury), interior view of the Romanesque choir and sanctuary; late eleventh century (Courtauld Institute, Conway Library, J. Austin).

Canterbury we can see that in the mid-1090s, within a few years of the completion of the new east end of the Abbey, Archbishop Anselm was demolishing the east end of Lanfranc's cathedral and replacing it with the amazingly lavish 'Glorious Choir', as it was termed by contemporaries. This new choir adopted the ambulatory plan and crypt of St Augustine's, and also the columnar piers around the main apse; the remarkable crypt still survives together with part of the outer walls of the ambulatory. The solemn splendour of the architecture and the wealth of carved decoration make this crypt one of the most memorable buildings of its date to be seen in England. Unfortunately we do not know whether Blitherus may have had any part in the development of the Cathedral design.

Outside Canterbury, a surviving building which may show the influence of the east arm of St Augustine's is the chapel of St John in the Tower of London (63). Here we see the ambulatory plan and the use of columnar piers, though the overall scheme of the chapel is rather different from a major church. The Tower was under construction in the late 1070s and 1080s under the supervision of Bishop Gundulf of Rochester, and we have seen already that the works at St Augustine's had links with the royal workshops in London: a design influence, therefore, is not implausible. But it was in the construction of great cathedral and abbey churches that the east arm of St Augustine's had most influence. It lay at the source of the current that produced the design of St Paul's Cathedral in London, Winchester Cathedral, Worcester Cathedral and Bury St Edmund's Abbey, and these in turn were key buildings in the development of Romanesque architecture in their regions.

The Romanesque church down to the fifteenth century

Even if the Abbey church had been spared at the Dissolution, it is uncertain to what extent we would still have been able to see today the design as when it was first completed in the early twelfth century. Certainly the main

63 Tower of London, White Tower, St John's Chapel, interior; late 1070s or early 1080s (English Heritage).

structure of the building remained in place: but it is likely that it had undergone considerable alteration to the surface detail that clothed it, as well as the addition of furnishings and monuments, of stained glass, paintings and sculpture, and of mosaics of tile, marble and glass. The first occasion for repair and alteration would have been a great fire in 1168 which is said to have burnt a large part of the church. A new shrine of St Augustine was erected in 1221, and there was further work to the shrine in 1300. Also we have references to the high altar of the church being rededicated in 1240 and in 1325; events which must have been associated with works of remodelling. Both in the standing fabric and from excavated evidence we can see some evidence for these changes. It appears that the ambulatory had been remodelled in the early Gothic style, involving the enlargement of the windows and construction of a new vault, the carved details of which resemble those in the present east arm of the Cathedral built following the fire of 1174. The ambulatory walls were further remodelled in the early fourteenth century. If a similar process were carried out comprehensively through the church then by 1538 it must have presented quite a different appearance from four centuries previously. Apart from such remodelling of the original building, a number of additions were made to it. Chapels were extended beyond the line of the outer walls, including chantry chapels (see pp. 131–2) and the new Lady chapel. The towers that rose over the building were also heightened for the ringing of bells and for display (p. 131); most impressive among these was perhaps the new crossing tower built *c.* 1461 to 1516, which may have competed with the Bell Harry tower of the Cathedral and may have been designed by the famous royal mason Robert Vertue.

Despite such alterations, however, the overall conception of the building continued as that of Scolland and Blitherus, and their original design remained substantially intact at least in the nave. What was no doubt more to the point to the medieval mind was that the functioning heart of the building remained unchanged in its arrangements: the monks' choir in the centre of the church, with the main sanctuary to the east, and beyond that again the shrines of the saints who were the founders and spiritual patrons of the Abbey. Still in the early fifteenth century, the famous drawing included in Thomas of Elmham's history (see **colour plate 1**) shows the essentially eleventh-century arrangement of the east end: the high altar surmounted by a beam carrying an image of Christ in Majesty, flanked by adoring angels and by relic chests; beyond we see into the ambulatory with the shrines around it – Augustine the apostle of England in the centre, and six saints on either hand; an image as it were of Christ and his apostles.

By around 1500, however, there is evidence of a plan to carry out some rearrangement of the shrine of St Augustine. At the east end of the church was constructed a large new Lady chapel (see **51**), begun on an ambitious scale, but reduced somewhat before completion; it was probably intended to replace the crypt Lady chapel and to provide a more suitable setting for the elaborate music fashionable at the time. In 1509 the chapel received the burial of Abbot John Dygon, perhaps the patron of the project; the architect again may have been Robert Vertue (designer of the Lady chapel at Westminster Abbey for Henry VII). The work must have involved the destruction of the existing eleventh-century east chapel above ground-level, and it is hard to see how the Trinity altar and the shrines of Augustine, Laurence and Mellitus could have remained in place without blocking the entrance to the new building. It seems likely, therefore, that it was the intention also to provide a grand new late Gothic setting for St Augustine's shrine in the centre, and those of his two companions to either side. But only thirty years later came the suppression of the Abbey and the destruction of its buildings and shrines – striking at the very roots of the millennium-old traditions of Canterbury.

6

The Abbey precinct, liberty and estate

Tim Tatton-Brown

The development of the monastic buildings and the Abbey precinct

The start of the construction of the new Norman Abbey church is exceptionally well documented by the monk Goscelin: much less is recorded about its completion or about the construction of the other monastic buildings (**64**). It seems likely, however, that the large new body of mostly Norman monks from the Cathedral priory, who were being installed at the Abbey during the unrest in 1087–9, must have planned and started to build the core of the claustral buildings on the north side of the Abbey church. A later source says that Abbot Hugh de Flori (1108–26) built 'from the foundation' the dormitory and chapter house. Hugh had been a Norman knight and was a rich relative of King William Rufus, and it was no doubt this abbot who at least completed all these buildings, 'at his own expense' as we are told.

The main claustral buildings

Of the Norman monastic buildings, the cellarer's hall, which ran along the west side of the cloisters, was replaced in the later thirteenth century by the abbot's lodging (**65** and see **56**). The scar for the original pitched roof of this building can still be seen at its south end. The refectory on the north side of the cloister was rebuilt and greatly enlarged on the north in the 1260s. The rubble core of the lower part of the original refectory's south wall, as well as part of the east wall of the cellarer's range can, however, still be seen in the cloister.

On the east side of the cloister the lowest part of the west wall and doorway into the chapter house is also visible. The rest of the large rectangular building (26.5m/87ft long by 10m/33ft wide internally) was, however, dug out in 1901–3 and subsequently reburied. Some photographs, and a plan that was drawn at this time, show the building with clasping buttresses on the east and a bench around the inside of the walls. On this bench were the remains of later bases and canopy fragments, as well as three more elaborate seats in the east wall. These architectural features were probably inserted in 1324–32, when we know from documentary evidence that the chapter house was rebuilt at a cost of £277.4s.8d. This remodelling exactly follows the rebuilding of the still-surviving, and even larger, chapter house at Canterbury Cathedral priory, and it is interesting to see how the architecture and building work at St Augustine's in the later Middle Ages was always in emulation of the great rival next door. As at the Cathedral, the chapter house had to be rebuilt again after an earthquake in 1382, and it is recorded that the now-vanished east window was rebuilt at this time. As in many monasteries, the chapter house was an important place of interment, and many abbots were buried here between 1124 and 1220, and again in 1346, 1386 and 1405; the later burials were no doubt after the completion of the two fourteenth-century rebuilding campaigns.

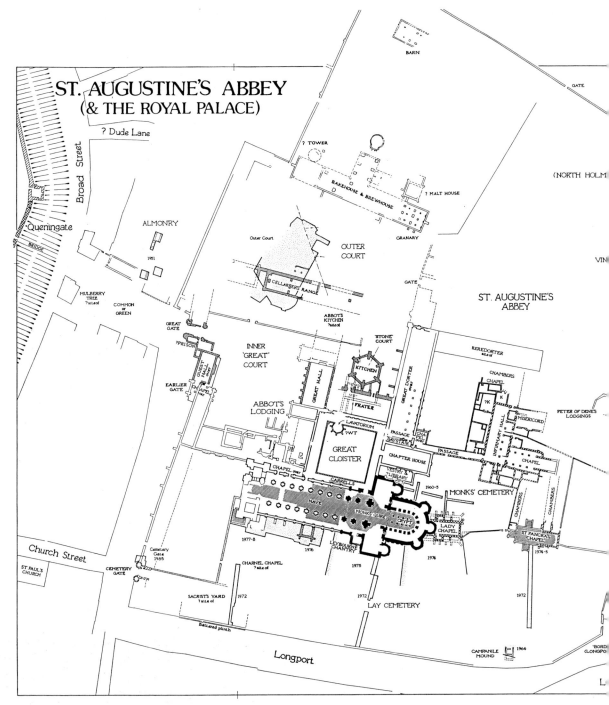

64 St Augustine's Abbey, survey of the known (standing or excavated) buildings of the medieval precinct (Canterbury Archaeological Trust).

South of the chapter house, and filling the space between it and the north transept, was another early twelfth-century building, which could only be entered from the transept. This building, which can partly still be seen today, had many cupboards in its walls, and was

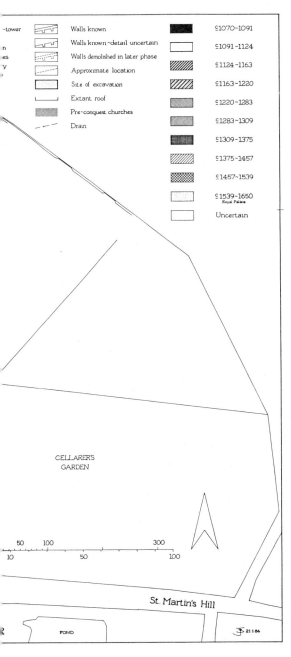

~~Lower	Walls known	£1070~1091
n	Walls known ~detail uncertain	£1091~1124
es	Walls demolished in later phase	£1124~1163
y	Approximate location	£1163~1220
	Site of excavation	£1220~1283
	Extant roof	£1283~1309
	Pre-conquest churches	£1309~1375
	Drain	£1375~1457
		£1457~1539
		£1539~1650 Royal Palace
		Uncertain

CELLARER'S
GARDEN

50   100   300
10   50   100

St. Martin's Hill

POND   £ 21186

south cloister walk. This cloister walk later contained the monks' carrells (or desks), which a late medieval document tells us occupied an area 104ft (31.7m) long by 11ft (3.4m) wide, thus taking up almost all of the width of this cloister walk.

North of the chapter house, and running northwards for over 200ft (60m) was the very large dormitory. This was also said to have been built by Abbot Hugh de Flori, and its extreme south-east corner was also uncovered in 1901–3 and subsequently reburied. Much of the large north wall of the dormitory is, however, still visible, as are three large later thirteenth-century buttresses which once supported the west wall of the dormitory. It is also worth noting that the northern part of the dormitory was retained for the royal palace after the Dissolution so that some early drawings of it do survive (see 85). It was reduced to its present shell at the end of the seventeenth century. The dormitory, as is usual with such monastic rooms, was built on a large groin-vaulted undercroft, and though only the south-east part of this was opened up in 1903, it is possible to calculate that the undercroft was three bays wide by about fourteen bays long.

65 St Augustine's Abbey, view from the site of the dormitory undercroft, looking south-west across the cloister; background right, the ruins of the west range run to the north aisle wall of the church; foreground right, site of the refectory (English Heritage).

almost certainly a treasury and vestry. On the first floor above it, there may later have been the monastic library. Earlier, many of the books were apparently kept in a cupboard, in a large niche in the wall, just beside the principal doorway into the choir from the east end of the

The internal dimensions of the dormitory were 44ft (13.4m) wide by 204ft (62.2m) long, making it the longest monastic dormitory in the country, though in area it was smaller than the huge dormitory at Canterbury Cathedral (which has internal dimensions of 78ft/23.8m by 148ft/45m). The Cathedral priory dormitory was built in the 1080s to accommodate up to 150 monks, and so by a comparison of floor-areas it seems likely that the St Augustine's dormitory was made to contain over 100 monks. None of the other great Benedictine houses in England which were also building large dormitories at this time (Westminster, Winchester, Ely, Glastonbury, Bury St Edmunds, Norwich or Rochester) exceed this, so it is clear that Abbot Hugh de Flori intended to rule over the second largest monastery in England when he was building it.

Documentary sources state that the dormitory was reroofed and leaded in 1267, and this is perhaps when the still-existing western buttresses were added. The new refectory buttressed the south-west side of the dormitory. A little later, under Abbot Nicholas Thorne (1273–83), a chapel was built in the dormitory 'with studies attached', and in 1321 a new image of the Virgin, in this chapel, was blessed by the archbishop of Armagh.

Running east from the north end of the dormitory was an equally large reredorter (the euphemism for the monks' lavatory). No part of this building is visible today, though William Stukeley shows fragments of its lower walls in a drawing of 1722. Its dimensions are, however, given in the monastic customary as 193ft long by 24ft wide (58.8 by 7.3m).

The infirmary area

South-east of the reredorter was the infirmary (see **64**). This complex of buildings was uncovered in 1903–7, but has also been covered up again, though the main walls are often visible as parch-marks in dry summers (**66**). The infirmary hall ran north–south and was eight bays long with an aisle on the east. On its south-east side was the infirmary chapel, which had two aisles ending in apses. Both the infirmary hall and the chapel were built in the early twelfth century, perhaps under Abbot Hugh II (1126–51), and in 1130 they were endowed with the revenue from the appropriate parish church of Chislet and its associated chapels (see below). The main door on the south-west side of the infirmary hall was reached by a covered passage which ran west to another passage under the southern end of the dormitory.

On the north-east side of the infirmary hall a new refectory building, called the 'miserecord', was built in the 1270s. In this refectory the monks were permitted to eat meat on certain special occasions. Adjacent to it, on the north-west of the infirmary hall, were the infirmary kitchens. Many other buildings were added around the infirmary in the later Middle Ages, including blood-letting chambers, the infirmarer's house, a prison, and various chambers for monks. Most remarkable of all, however, was the series of fine lodging-chambers built on the north-east side of the infirmary chapel in the early fourteenth century for Peter of Dene. This colourful person was a canon of York, London and Wells, and a rich ecclesiastical and civil lawyer who became a benefactor of the Abbey. (Earlier he had donated one of the still-surviving stained glass windows on the north side of the nave of York Minster in which he is depicted.) In 1322 he hurriedly asked to become a monk at St Augustine's, and was admitted, under special relaxed conditions 'on account of the tyranny of the enemies of the earl of Lancaster', that is, because King Edward II and his cronies, the earl of Pembroke and the Despensers, were threatening to arrest him and seize all his property. Eight years later, however, after the political conditions had changed, he wanted to 'return to the world', but was prevented by the Abbey from doing so. He then escaped one night by 'going through his cellar to a door which leads into the cellarer's garden, the lock of which he had previously broken, and thus he got across the wall opposite the church

66 St Augustine's Abbey, aerial view of the site in August 1995; the infirmary buildings show as parch-marks in the grass of the playing field in the foreground (National Monuments Record).

of St Martin'. He was then assisted by the rector of St Martin's, with a ladder, to climb over the main monastery wall and escape. This remarkable story, told in William Thorne's *Chronicle*, confirms for us that the cellarer's garden occupied the large area of ground immediately to the east of the infirmary complex. Ironically this garden has been occupied by the Canterbury Sessions House and prison for the last two centuries.

By the early sixteenth century the area to the south of the infirmary chapel provided the location for various chambers for senior monks.

These chambers were probably disposed in ranges running southwards towards St Pancras' chapel. It is here we might expect to find the burgeoning offices of the prior, infirmarer, sub-prior, third and fourth priors and others.

Improvements under thirteenth-century abbots

In 1260 there commenced, under Abbot Roger of Chichester (1253–73), a half-century of major building work; the Abbey was then at the height of its power and prestige. The work started in the refectory, which was completely rebuilt over the next nine years. The lowest parts of the walls of this building and the dais at its high (east) end are still visible. In 1267 the chamberlain, Adam of Kingsnorth, who must have had access to substantial private funds, provided money for many benefactions. These included the cost of the refectory gable, a new bath-house, a new chamber for the prior and '£100 for roofing the dormitory with lead'. He also gave money for a new chapel over the gate, for repairing the infirmary, and 'in aid of the changing over of the bakehouse and brewhouse', as well as many other gifts. The bath-house was perhaps one of the buildings near the infirmary, and next to it would have been the shaving-house, which was set up in 1264 with professional barbers. Previously the monks had 'shaved each other mutually in the cloister'. The western part of the new 'chapel over the gate' still survives, and its west wall with three lancets in it, and a quatrefoil above, can be seen, just to the south of the slightly later guest hall (67). Below this west gable wall of the chapel, the blocked-in arch of the earlier gateway can also just be made out.

When the refectory work was completed in 1269, a fine new octagonal *lavatorium* (washing-place) was built in the cloister opposite the refectory door. It seems to have

67 St Augustine's Abbey, west façade of the mid-thirteenth-century chapel over the gateway to the inner court; pencil drawing, 1822, by William Twopenny (British Museum – Prints and Drawings).

replaced a twelfth-century, round water-tower. This structure, whose foundations can still be seen, was finished in 1272 and cost 300 marks (£200) paid for by the abbot himself. Four years later, under a new abbot, Nicholas Thorne, the cloister itself was rebuilt 'with columns and a roof', and the refectory was whitewashed. William Thorne's *Chronicle* also tells us that 'an inner chamber for the lord abbot next to the kitchen' was built in 1276. This is the first indication we have that the abbot's lodging was at the north-west corner of the cloister.

The abbot's house and the inner and outer courts

With the accession of Thomas Fyndon as abbot in 1283, large-scale topographic changes were made (see **64**), and a completely new abbot's lodging was created in the west cloister range. This necessitated the building of a new cellarer's range on the north side of the enlarged inner court, and this in turn required a completely new outer court to be created further north, with a new brewhouse and bakehouse range on its north side. As a first stage for all this, a royal licence, granted in November 1283, allowed the abbot 'to enclose the lane between the door of the court of the Abbey and his land at Nordholm'. Then, in July 1300, the abbot and convent were licensed to enclose 150 by 80ft (45.7 by 24.4m) of land 'in the suburb of Canterbury adjoining their court for the enlargement thereof'. The culmination of all these works was the licence to crenellate the magnificent new 'great gate' of the Abbey in 1308. This exceptionally fine structure still survives on the west side of the inner court, and was perhaps built on the block of land on the west that was enclosed in 1300 (**68**).

In 1983, during the digging of foundations for a new students' union building at Christ Church College, a large section of the foundations of the late thirteenth-century cellarer's range was uncovered, and this and further excavations at Christ Church College ten years later have allowed much of the topography of the outer court area to be understood. Almost all the buildings in this area were demolished soon after the Dissolution, but the west gable wall of the brewhouse has survived, and in 1993 the foundations of the east end of this range were excavated. This part of the building was probably a granary, and part of another building was discovered to the north, which may have been a malthouse. Various drains were also discovered, running north across the outer court.

In the late thirteenth century, as we have seen, Abbot Fyndon, like many other important prelates and abbots, built himself a fine new house, almost a palace, in the west claustral range, and it was this house which was turned into the 'King's New Lodging' in 1539 and survived until the late seventeenth century. At its extreme south end was a large first-floor chapel, which abutted the north wall of the nave of the Abbey church (see **56** and **86**). A fine traceried east window for the chapel can be seen in eighteenth-century drawings, and the gable above the window survived until the second half of the nineteenth century. Sadly only the south jamb and sill of this window remain today. Beneath the chapel was a passageway (called a 'parlour') to the inner court, and something of the fine late thirteenth-century doorway from the cloister with its Purbeck marble shafts still survives. Much of the middle part of the west range, where the private chambers for the abbot (and later, for the king) were situated, has now disappeared, while the abbot's large first-floor hall was replaced by William Butterfield's new building in 1846 (see **66** and **91**). This building was, however, constructed over the remains of the original undercroft: 'the bases of its pillars and its whole general plan', Butterfield said, were uncovered. Fortunately a few seventeenth-century drawings show this building intact, with a large porch and chamber above on its north-west side (see **85**). Between 1287 and 1291, and at a cost of £414.10s.¼d, the very large new hexagonally shaped kitchen was erected immediately to the east of this entrance staircase to the abbot's hall, and after the Dissolution this

68 St Augustine's Abbey, west façade of the great gate to the inner court of the abbey, *c.* 1308; pencil drawing, 1822 & '44, by William Twopenny (British Museum – Prints and Drawings).

great kitchen was retained for use (and its roof repaired in 1543) for the King's Lodging.

On the west side of the inner court, another first-floor guest hall was built at the end of the thirteenth century, and quite exceptionally this building still retains much of its original timber 'king strut' roof (**69**). It had a kitchen beneath, and a large chimney flue survives in the back (east) wall. Immediately to the north of this hall is the great gate of the monastery which, as we have already seen, was built in the earliest years of the fourteenth century, and still stands. Beside the gateway, on the south, was the porter's lodge, and probably the Abbey prison. Outside the gate was an open space (later called a Green) which had on its west side the city wall and ditch. An ancient Roman postern gate here, called the Queningate, was still in use in the

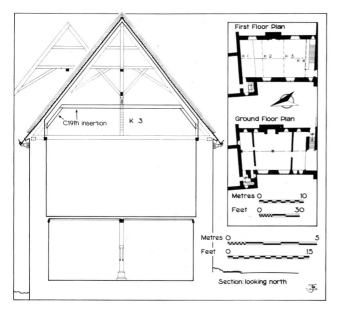

First Floor Plan

K 1   K 2   K 3   K 2

Ground Floor Plan

Metres 0 ———— 10
Feet 0 ———— 30

C19th insertion   K 3

Metres 0 ———— 5
Feet 0 ———— 15

Section: looking north

69 St Augustine's Abbey, plan and section of the late thirteenth-century first-floor guest hall, with original roof structure (Canterbury Archaeological Trust).

later Middle Ages. On the north side of the Green were St Augustine's almonry buildings – used in 1292, William Thorne tells us, by the 'poor and sick', as well as by 'scholars and sisters living here permanently' – and the stone shell of the main building survives on the street frontage. The original almonry was set up no later than 1130 when Northbourne parish church was appropriated to it. The earlier almonry buildings were situated 'before the abbey gate, for the help of pilgrims and poor men' in 1156.

The outer precinct

When Thomas Fyndon died in 1309, his successor Ralph Bourne was able to hold a huge banquet for over 6000 people at the Abbey on his return from being blessed by the pope in Avignon. During his abbacy (1309–34), all the major building work was completed and a large new outer wall was erected around the Abbey precinct (see **64**). It was certainly needed as relations between the Abbey and town were very bad at this time. In the area to the east of the Abbey buildings, as has already been shown,

a large walled garden for the cellarer was created, while to the north of the Abbey buildings a new vineyard was planted in 1320. The annual costs for looking after this vineyard, and another at the Abbey's manor of Chislet (see below), are recorded in detail in a surviving document, and it is worth noting that William Thorne records, in his *Chronicle*, that 'Abbot Ralph planted vineyards close to Nordhome' in an area that 'formerly was a den of thieves, a house of filthiness and fornication, and to it there was a common road ... in the hiding-places whereof adulteries and other such things were easily committed'. Thorne goes on to describe how the abbot thought he 'might improve this scandalous state of things', and with a royal licence 'closed the said common road, levelled up the shady holes and valleys, rooted up the thorns and brambles, cut down the bushes, surrounded it on all sides with a wall, and therein, as is to be seen to the present day [that is, the late fourteenth century], honourably planted a choice vineyard to our great advantage and honour'. In the year after the vineyard was made (1321), we are told that the abbot built his own kitchen, and a cistern 'in the stone court'. Finally the great rebuilding of the chapter house took place in 1324–32, as already mentioned.

The cemetery and bell-tower

One other area of the monastic precinct needs now to be dealt with, and that is the whole area to the south and south-east of the Abbey church. The main part of this area was taken up by the very large lay cemetery which acted as a place of burial for many of the parish churches (particularly St Augustine's churches) in Canterbury. The much smaller monks' cemetery was in the area between the infirmary and the east end of the Abbey church. This cemetery was divided off from the lay cemetery by an east–west wall running from the Lady chapel to the church of St Pancras, and part of this twelfth-century wall still remains (see **66**). The church of St Pancras is the one Anglo-Saxon church in the Abbey precinct that survived the rebuilding work after the Norman Conquest. In 1361 it was badly damaged in a storm, and left ruinous until about twenty-five years later when it was 'repaired and rebuilt' by Thomas of Ickham, the sacrist. More repairs at St Pancras' took place in 1493, and there is also mention of a 'hermit of St Pancras' at this time.

South of the church (or chapel) of St Pancras, and on a mound in the south-eastern part of the lay cemetery that is still visible, is the site of the bell-tower. The site was excavated in 1964, and this uncovered the dwarf-wall foundations of what was probably a timber-framed bell-tower. This tower, which may have been similar to the one surviving timber-framed bell-tower in Kent, at the Abbey's parish church of Brookland, in Walland Marsh (near Appledore), was perhaps superseded in the later Middle Ages by the towers on the Abbey church (as happened at Canterbury Cathedral). However, the donation of a whole series of bells by Thomas of Ickham, the sacrist at the end of the fourteenth century, is stated to have been to 'the tower above the choir' (that is, the central tower), 'the tower at the entrance to the church' (that is, the south-west tower) as well as for the 'bell-tower', and this may suggest a continued use of the detached belfry. Canterbury Cathedral priory had a similar free-standing belfry, and there was much rivalry between the two establishments over bell-ringing.

Thomas of Ickham's domain as sacrist was on the south-west side of the lay cemetery, where the sacristy was situated, and it was again this man who was a great benefactor to his own office. We are told that after the great storm 'on St Maurice's day' (in 1361), he 'repaired the grange, gates, stables and other buildings belonging to the office of the sacristan, at a total cost of £200'. He also went on to make a new cemetery gate to the west 'toward the town', which cost £466.13s.4d. This fine gateway, facing directly towards the ancient city gateway of Burgate, survives, though it was heavily restored in 1839 (see **89**). It is also worth noting

here that the lay cemetery was enlarged southwards into the large street market called Longport; this appears to have been done in the early twelfth century, for a new fair, when this main thoroughfare was moved southwards. Part of the old boundary wall, made largely of Roman bricks, has survived on the south-west, where it was reused as the north wall of the sacristy, and later as the southern boundary of the king's garden.

In 1103 Henry I granted the Abbey 'the right to hold a fair for five days in August', and a second fair was granted by King Stephen for 29 June, though these were lost in the reign of Edward I 'owing to quarrels and strife and even fights which frequently occurred in the [Abbey's] cemetery, and also on account of some heavy demands for bread and beer which the bailiffs of the town claimed in our cellars during the aforesaid fair', as William Thorne's *Chronicle* colourfully describes. However, it is also known that Edward I banned the keeping of fairs in churchyards in England in 1285.

Various late medieval and early Tudor wills give us details of some of the topographic features in the lay cemetery. So, for example, in 1497 a man asks 'to be buried in the churchyard of St Augustine's before the image of St Michael in the wall'. Another man wishes to be buried before the water conduit (now lost), while a third mentions 'a tomb of St Austen in the churchyard' (also now lost). There are also various references to the *via media* (a common footpath through the churchyard) and to the charnel chapel, which we know was built in 1287 (but not dedicated until 1299). Later wills mention a hawthorn tree and 'the image of Our Lady' beside the charnel chapel. Among the more famous people to be buried in the lay cemetery was the royal master mason Robert Vertue, who died in 1506.

Part of the cemetery was delimited on its north side by the south aisle of the Abbey church, and in the fourteenth century two chantry chapels were extended from the aisle out into the churchyard. One of these, in the angle between the aisle and the transept, was the chapel of St Anne, where Juliana de Leybourne, countess of Huntingdon, was buried in 1367.

St Augustine's and its liberty in Canterbury

The borough of Longport

Well before the Norman Conquest St Augustine's had acquired a very large triangular area of land outside the eastern city walls of Canterbury, lying between the old Roman roads leading to Richborough and Dover (**70**). This land was called the Manor or 'Borough' of Longport by the late Anglo-Saxon period, and it is carefully described in Domesday Book (1086).

70 Map of the medieval Borough of Longport belonging to St Augustine's Abbey (T. Tatton-Brown and Canterbury Archaeological Trust).

The eastern limit of Longport Borough is at the shallow valley of the Lampen Stream, and from the fifteenth century until 1974 this was also the limit of the county borough boundary of Canterbury. This limit to the city is, however, much older than this, and in Domesday Book it is defined as '1 league, 3 perches and 3 feet' from the city walls, agreeing well with distances on modern maps which show this boundary as 2.5–3km (1½–2 miles) east and south-east of the city. In 1268 an agreement was made at Westminster about legal rights within this liberty, and the boundaries were carefully defined. They remained virtually unchanged until the late nineteenth century, and are thus shown on accurately surveyed Ordnance Survey maps.

Within this area it is also possible to show that many of the topographical divisions of landholdings have remained the same for nearly

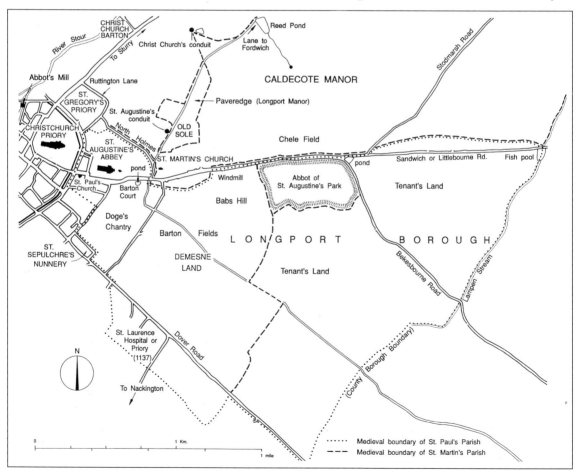

900 years, and as a result of careful research by the late James Hobbs (undertaken twenty years ago), it is possible to work backwards to the Domesday description. For example, Domesday Book says that there were 70 burgesses in Longport, while a document of 1434 lists 73 rents. After the Dissolution these urban holdings fell to the crown, and a few years later they were bought by the city corporation. The rents for these properties were thereafter collected by the city right up to the Second World War. After the devastation of the eastern parts of the city by bombing in 1942 many rents (by now trivial sums) were 'liquidated for a capital sum', but as the city archivist, the late Dr William Urry, said in the 1960s, some rents of 6s.8d (and other small sums) from holdings of the 'late dissolved abbey of St Augustine's' were still being paid to the corporation, a remarkable example of continuity.

It is possible, therefore, to show where all the main land-divisions were in the late eleventh century, and then from the late thirteenth century a more detailed map can be made as all the rents are listed for the first time in the Abbey's *Black Book* (**71**). Though the Abbey had some rents within the city walls, its main area of burgess-holdings was just outside the Abbey precincts to the south and west, in the area around the church of St Paul, whose parish had been defined in the early twelfth century as almost exactly the same area as the borough of Longport. (Only around the church itself was there a small area of the parish outside Longport Borough.) Let us now turn to look at some of these different areas.

St Paul's Church was perhaps first built and made into the Abbey's parish church in the early twelfth century. It lies just outside the cemetery gate of the Abbey on the south side of the street running down to a major gate in the city wall, called Burgate. In the 1260s, at exactly the time when the Abbey was starting its own rebuilding campaign, the church was completely reconstructed with a new nave and chancel on the north, and a much larger south aisle and chantry chapel behind it. There is even a royal licence permitting the north wall of the church

to be rebuilt 3½ft (1m) further north (that is, into the street) for a length of 60ft (18m). In 1268 the church was appropriated to the Abbey, and at the same time the new chantry at the altar of St John the Baptist was set up and richly endowed by Master Hamo Doge, the Abbey's legal adviser, who was also the friend and confidant of Abbot Roger II (Roger of Chichester). Doge, who was later buried beside the abbot in the Abbey's south transept, had a stone house not far away in 'New Street' (now called Chantry Lane), and here he had already set up the first part of his chantry in 1252. Only a small fragment of Doge's house now survives, but the parish church of St Paul still contains two fine traceried east windows and a north arcade, which date from this time.

To the south of this urban area was Retherchepe (now Dover Street), the cattle market, and just to the east of this was St Sepulchre's, a Benedictine nunnery, which was first created in the late eleventh century by the main road to Dover. Further down the road, the Abbey created the Hospital of St Lawrence in 1137 (in 3.6ha/9 acres of ground) and this was specially founded, we are told, to look after any monk who might 'incur a contagious disease, especially leprosy'. The hospital could also be used by the relatives of any monk who became destitute.

The barton

In the large area to the north of the hospital (475 acres and 1 rood according to a late thirteenth-century document – 192ha) was the barton: the demesne or home farm of the Abbey. This was based on the Barton Court, which was situated just to the south-east of the Abbey on the other side of the road (Longport) from the cellarer's garden. By the later Middle Ages there was a large pond here (called the Court Sole), and a series of great barns, granaries and other structures. Barton Court itself was situated on the west side of this farmyard complex, and it was here that the manorial and liberty courts were held, and where tenants from outlying

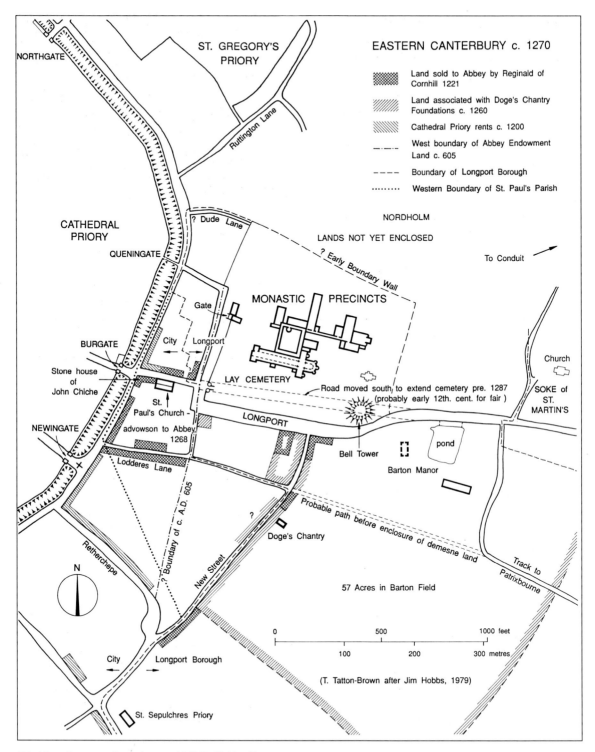

71 Map of eastern Canterbury *c.* 1270 (J. Hobbs, T. Tatton-Brown and Canterbury Archaeological Trust).

manors brought their products. Unfortunately this building was demolished in the mid-eighteenth century and replaced by the present fine house (now a school), and the barns and other farmyard buildings have also been demolished. However, the great pond, perhaps used as a fishpond, survives. South-east of this complex of buildings were the Barton fields, which covered the whole area between the Dover Road and St Martin's Hill on the north. The western slope of St Martin's Hill, and the famous church, belonged to the archbishop, but on top of the hill, and south of the road, was a windmill, and beyond it was the abbot's deer-park (now the grounds of St Martin's Hospital). On the north-east side of the park, where two lanes (to Stodmarsh, north-east, and Bekesbourne, south-east) diverge from the main road, there is another pond, and eastwards of this the Abbey owned all the land on both sides of the road as far as Fishpool Bottom (yet another pond) on the borough boundary. All this land was used by the Abbey tenants, as was the land south to the abbot's park, near Bekesbourne lane. This must be where the 28 villains and 63 bordars (smallholders) had their land in 1086. Domesday Book also tells us that they had six ploughs (there were only two on the demesne) and 17 acres (7ha) of meadow. Remarkably there was still an 18-acre meadow in this area in the seventeenth century.

The Abbey water supply

One other detached portion of St Augustine's land should also be mentioned here. This was a field, north of St Martin's Church and north-east of the Abbey precinct, called Paveridge. In this field was situated an 'old sole' (the Kentish word for a pond), and nearby was the main conduit house for the Abbey, which was fully excavated and recorded in 1988 (72). This remarkable structure, which was polygonal in plan, was built into the steep hillside on the spring-line. Just under 1km (half a mile) to the north, Canterbury Cathedral priory had built its conduit house on the same spring-line in the mid-twelfth century,

72 Canterbury, the early thirteenth-century conduit house of St Augustine's Abbey (English Heritage).

and this conduit is shown on the contemporary 'Waterworks' plan of the Cathedral. The St Augustine's conduit, which was perhaps first built in the thirteenth century, was made with a series of straight walls in its side which contained four main barrel-vaulted tunnels leading back into the hillside. These, in turn, were fed by a mass of subsidiary ducts, which brought in water from as many points in the aquifer (the water-bearing strata) as possible. The tank, and access tunnels, were repaired and rebuilt on several occasions in the post-medieval period (the conduit was also used for the king's palace), so the finer details of the medieval system are missing. However, it is likely that a lead pipe led out of the tank (no doubt with a silt-trap) on its lowest (north-west side), and this then ran down the hill and turned southwards to the Abbey precincts. As at Canterbury Cathedral priory, it perhaps led to a water-tower in the cloister, and this in turn would have connected with smaller tanks, such as in the kitchen, infirmary and abbot's lodging. Some traces of the medieval pipes, as well as many of the drains in these buildings, have been found in the excavations. There was also, as we have seen, a documented conduit in the lay cemetery.

Property in the city

Apart from all this land in the borough of Longport, the Abbey owned various other properties in the city, including the seven churches of St Mildred, All Saints, St Andrew, St Margaret, St John, St Mary de Castro and St Mary Magdalen, as well as a water-mill on the north side of the city. This is not the place to look in detail at St Augustine's urban churches, one of which (St Margaret's) was given to the Poor Priests' Hospital in 1271. We should not forget, however, that the churches were also an important part of the Abbey's estate, and several of them were very profitable to the Abbey. One church, St John-the-Poor, was, however, abandoned after the Black Death (1348–50), while another, St Mildred's, developed into a fine structure in the late Middle Ages, while still retaining traces of its late Anglo-Saxon nave. The Abbey's water-mill is also probably one of the mills mentioned in Domesday Book, but its detailed history starts in about 1129, when Abbot Hugh II 'set apart the mill of Abbotismelle for the use of the sacristy, on condition that all the corn belonging to the court of St Augustine be ground there, free and without toll. The tithe of the aforesaid mill to be paid to the almonry.' This mill was just inside the city walls on the north side of the city on one of the two branches of the River Stour. In 1257 it was attacked by the rioting citizens of Canterbury (to the sound of the boroughmoot horn) after there had been a jurisdiction dispute in the fields of Barton Manor. After the Dissolution, the city bought the mill in 1543, and repaired it in the following year. Half a century later, it was depicted for the first time on a bird's-eye-view map of the Canterbury Blackfriars, which it adjoined. The original mill was rebuilt on a large scale in 1792, and this new mill was finally burnt down in 1933.

The Abbey estates in east Kent

Domesday Book is, once again, a good starting point for seeing something of the detail of St Augustine's large rural estates. Most of these were in east Kent (see **10**), though there were some other manors in their possession that were further afield, like Plumstead in north-west Kent

73 Minster-in-Thanet (Kent), the medieval grange of the estate belonging to St Augustine's Abbey (National Monuments Record).

(now part of south-east London) or Burmarsh and Snave on Romney Marsh. The biggest estates were all, however, east or north-east of Canterbury in the very rich agricultural lands of north-east Kent (see **7**). By far the biggest and richest of them was Minster, which covered the eastern two-thirds of the Isle of Thanet. Not only was there a major centre at Minster itself, where a whole series of new stone buildings (forming a grange) was put up in the Norman period (**73**), but there were also several very rapidly developing outlying centres based on the chapels of St John the Baptist (now Margate), St Peter (Broadstairs), St Lawrence (Ramsgate) and St Nicholas (Stonar). Stonar, a seaport and quasi-town, was destroyed by the French in 1385, but from the late eleventh to the thirteenth century it was beside a vast natural haven opposite Sandwich (the second largest Anglo-Saxon and medieval town in Kent, and owned by its rival, Canterbury Cathedral priory). The three other 'chapels' in Thanet – at Margate, Broadstairs and Ramsgate – were already very large (each had a long nave and double aisles) by the mid-twelfth century, showing that they were all major population centres by this time (see **12**). The chapels only became the centres of parishes in their own right in the later thirteenth century (though still nominally 'parochial chapels' until the Reformation). At Minster itself the church was already aisled by the mid-twelfth century, but in the early thirteenth century the chancel and transepts were magnificently rebuilt, with a stone vault over the very spacious new chancel. Other granges were built in Thanet, and a particularly fine complex of thirteenth- and fourteenth-century masonry buildings still survives at Salmestone near Margate.

Apart from the eight churches in Canterbury already briefly mentioned, St Augustine's had very many other churches in Kent, and these are first listed in the late twelfth century in the Abbey's *White Book*. These cannot all be discussed here, even briefly, but it is worth noting something of their history, and this throws much light on the social and economic situation at different stages of the Abbey's history. Almost all the Abbey's fine church buildings still survive, and with the wealth of documentary evidence available, they are a particularly interesting group to study. The development of these churches can also be compared with other parish churches in east Kent owned by the archbishop and Canterbury Cathedral priory.

Immediately after the Norman Conquest the two important 'Minster' churches of Faversham and Milton (that is, head churches which had rights over a wide area in the pre-Conquest period) and their dependant chapels were given to the Abbey by William the Conqueror, and the rectory with the tithes and other revenues of these great churches were finally appropriated to the Abbey in 1345. Long before this, in about 1130, the major churches of Minster-in-Thanet (mentioned above), Chislet and Northbourne, with their chapels, were appropriated to the Abbey's sacristy, infirmary and almonry respectively. Then from the middle of the thirteenth century the long process of appropriating the Abbey's eight other rural churches was put in hand, and this was followed in the early fourteenth century by the setting up of proper vicarages there. Alongside this legal process, much rebuilding work in the churches

was also taking place, and we can take one example, Sturry (3km/2 miles north-east of Canterbury), as an illustration (**74**). Here the chancel, nave and western tower had been built in the mid-twelfth century. Then in the early thirteenth century the chancel was remodelled with some fine new windows; a contemporary vestry was added on its north-east side. A little later, in the thirteenth century, the nave walls on both sides were pierced for arcades, and simple lean-to roofs were made over the new aisles. Finally, in a more protracted process in the fourteenth century, just after the church was appropriated to the Abbey, the outer walls of first one aisle and then the other were substantially rebuilt with fine new traceried windows, parapets and double-pitched roofs.

The manor of Chislet

It is worth looking in more detail at just one of St Augustine's estates, and making an attempt to reconstruct its topography in the later thirteenth century. This can be done by using more recent materials (such as tithe maps), comparing these with the Domesday material, and also with useful thirteenth-century information from the Abbey's *Black Book*. The great manor of

74 Sturry (Kent), parish church of St Nicholas, appropriated to St Augustine's Abbey; the spire was destroyed 1812–13; watercolour, 1801, by H. Petrie (photograph in Kent Archaeological Society Library of lost original).

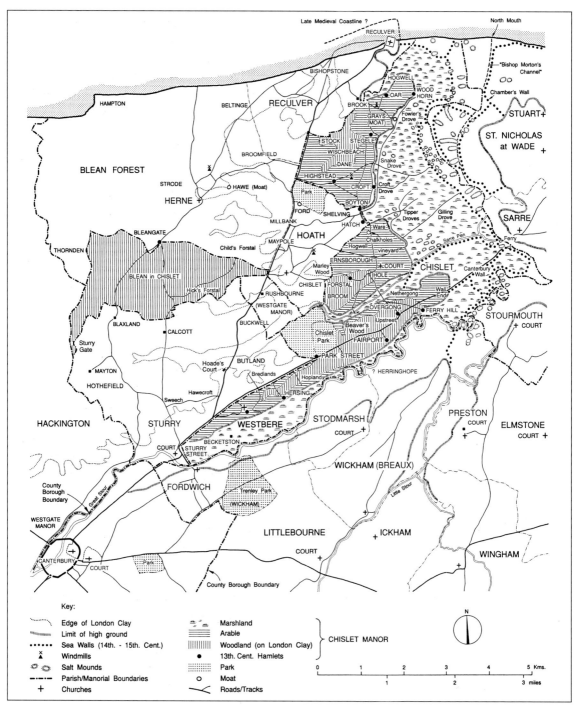

Key:

- ⋯⋯ Edge of London Clay
- ▩▩ Limit of high ground
- •••• Sea Walls (14th. - 15th. Cent.)
- ⤬ Windmills
- ⌖ Salt Mounds
- –·–·– Parish/Manorial Boundaries
- ✛ Churches

- ≈≈ Marshland
- ≡≡ Arable
- ‖‖‖ Woodland (on London Clay)
- ● 13th. Cent. Hamlets
- ⌗⌗ Park
- ○ Moat
- ✕ Roads/Tracks

CHISLET MANOR

0 1 2 3 4 5 Kms.

1 2 3 miles

75 Map of the estate of Chislet belonging to St Augustine's Abbey (T. Tatton-Brown and Canterbury Archaeological Trust).

Chislet, which in Domesday Book was of 12 sulungs (Kentish ploughlands with, very approximately, 80ha/200 acres per sulung), lies north-east of Canterbury and runs from north of Fordwich to the sea near Reculver (75). Originally it was part of a much larger district

76 Chislet (Kent), parish church of St Mary, appropriated to St Augustine's Abbey; watercolour, 1803, by H. Petrie (photograph in Kent Archaeological Society Library of lost original).

those on the modern map of Reculver and its two chapelries (only later were they parishes in their own right) of Herne and Hoath.

Turning to Chislet itself, where sadly there are no surviving Anglo-Saxon charter bounds, it is now possible to reconstruct the landscape as it developed between the time of Domesday Book (1085–6) and the later Middle Ages. The bald facts given in Domesday Book are, in summary:

There with 12 sulungs, and land for 30 ploughteams, with 5 of them being used on the demesne, and 39 ploughs used by the 72 villeins and 68 bordars on their sulungs. There was also a church worth 12 shillings and 14 serfs; 50 acres of meadow and 47 salt pans, yielding 50 loads of salt. Then there was pannage for 130 swine and 3 arpends of Vines.

This already shows the very large scale of the manor, with the 130 swine mostly, no doubt, being in the detached portion of the manor in the forest. Forty-seven salt pans is by far the largest number recorded for any manor in Kent, and there was clearly a very large industry that involved scraping up the briny mud on the eastern marshes and boiling it up in large vats for salt. Even today these mounds (many now ploughed out) can be seen in the Chislet marshes. Another unusual feature is the vineyard, one of only three in Kent recorded in Domesday Book. As we have already seen, this vineyard was still flourishing in the early fourteenth century when it was one of two being cultivated by the Abbey.

The church at Chislet that is mentioned in Domesday Book is still there (**76, 77**), at the geographic centre of the manor, right beside the manor house, Chislet Court. (In Kent the ecclesiastical manor houses are called Court Lodges.) The nave of the church still displays a late eleventh-century west wall, while to the east of the nave is a large tower built in the early twelfth century to replace the original sanctuary. This was at the time the church was appropriated to the infirmary (see above). At the end of the

that was probably called in the Anglo-Saxon period *Sturigao* (this name is given in the charter of 'AD 605', forged in the eleventh century). This district, later called the Blengate Hundred, took in all of the land north-east of Canterbury between the sea on the north, the River Stour on the south (which gave its name to the district), the tidal Wantsum Channel marshes on the east and the great forest of Blean on the west. In the later seventh century this land was divided up between the abbey of Reculver, St Augustine's Abbey (Chislet) and the abbey of Minster-in-Thanet (Sturry). The internal boundaries were not simple, however, because they were all in the eastern part of the great forest of Blean (situated on the heavy London clay) and, as the map (see 75) shows, Chislet had, right up to the twentieth century, a large detached portion of the manor in the centre of the forest, called 'Blean in Chislet'. Reculver Manor and Sturry Manor also had assarts (land cut out of forest) or 'dens' (pig-pasture in forest) in the forest, but they at least were coterminous with the older centres. By 949 when all the lands of Reculver were given to the archbishop in a contemporary charter (the abbey by then had been destroyed by the Vikings) it had boundaries that are virtually the same as

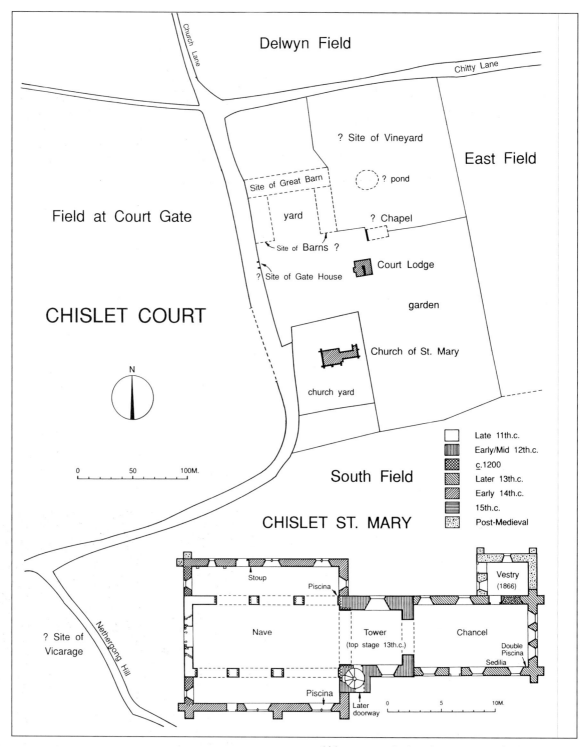

77 Chislet (Kent), plan of Chislet Court, the manorial centre of the St Augustine's Abbey estate, and (inset) plan of St Mary's Church (T. Tatton-Brown and Canterbury Archaeological Trust).

twelfth century, holes, for new arcades, were cut in the nave walls to make lean-to-aisles (showing the population was increasing), and in the thirteenth century the tower was heightened and

78 Lenham (Kent), pair of barns of *c.* 1300 belonging to the St Augustine's Abbey manor; one of the barns was burnt in 1962 (National Monuments Record).

79 Littlebourne Court (Kent), early fourteenth-century barn of the St Augustine's Abbey manor, next to the parish church (National Monuments Record).

a large new chancel (with tall lancets) was added to the east of the tower. Finally, in the early fourteenth century, the aisle walls were rebuilt with fine new traceried windows and higher, flat roofs. At about this time a large timber spire was added to the top of the tower. In 1345, just after the completion of all this work, the vicarage of Chislet was finally endowed by the Abbey, and the vicar was given a house to the south-west of the church.

The church actually stands in the south-west corner of a large rectangular area of about 6ha (14 acres) (see 77) that has Chislet Court at its centre, clearly showing that it started life, as is common in Kent, as the manorial chapel. Only in the later Middle Ages was a separate chapel for the Court Lodge built, and this new chapel was rebuilt 'on the plan of the former chapel', as William Thorne's *Chronicle* tells us in *c.* 1334. Chislet Court was rebuilt in the eighteenth century, while the chapel was turned into an oast house, but both buildings still retain fragments of their medieval masonry walls. Immediately north-west of Chislet Court there was, until it was burnt in 1925, the largest barn in Kent (of thirteen bays and *c.* 73m/240ft long). It was probably the great wheat barn, and originally had two lesser barns running south from its east and west ends (at both Lenham and Littlebourne the late medieval barns, made

for the St Augustine's Abbey manors there, still survive: **78, 79, 80**). Other buildings which have also not survived, but are documented, are the gatehouse on the west, the stables, dovecot, as well as an animal pound and a pond. East of the Court Lodge was the garden, and immediately north of it, the vineyard already mentioned.

Around this large rectangular area of Chislet Court were the four very large open arable fields of the demesne: Delwyn Field (to the north), East Field, South Field and 'Field at the Court Gate' on the other side of the road to the west.

80 Littlebourne Court (Kent), interior of the St Augustine's Abbey barn (National Monuments Record).

Remarkably all this demesne land is still owned by the Church (the Church Commissioners), having been given to the archbishop after the Dissolution. In the thirteenth century the demesne was farmed directly by the monks, but since the fourteenth century all this land has been, and is still being, leased to a tenant farmer.

Domesday Book also mentions four 'French knights' holding land in the manor, and these lands can also be located from later documentary and place-name evidence. For example, at the north end of the manor, towards Reculver, is a moated manorial site near Oar, called Grays. This must be the *tenementum domini Wm. de Grey* (tenement of Sir William de Grey) in the *Black Book*. Another knight was called William de Beauveise, and a large wood called Beaver's Wood survived until recent times in the area south of Chislet Court. A whole series of other place-names in the parish can also be related to the many tenants in the *Black Book*, and these no doubt go back to the many villeins and bordars in Domesday Book. Many of these tenants lived in small dispersed hamlets at places such as Oar, Stock, Highstead, Boyton and Croft in the north, and Broom, Ernesborough, Upstreet and Overgong in the south. Highstead, at over 30m (100ft) above sea-level, was the highest point in the manor, and here a very early windmill (erected 1208–9) was situated.

The geological evidence shows where the arable land (on lighter soils) and where the woodland (on heavy London clay soils) was situated. This again ties in with the documentary evidence. Of particular interest at Chislet is the series of marsh reclamations into the Wantsum Channel on the east. Here can still be seen the twelfth- and thirteenth-century innings and sea walls, and the sheep droves from the Court Lodge out on to the marshes. Once again the modern names for most of these droves can be directly related to names in the *Black Book*. Some of the reclaimed marshes were turned into arable land, with chalk marl being spread on the land. A large almost certainly medieval chalk pit, called

'Chalkholes', still survives just under 1km (half a mile) north of Chislet Court. It is also worth noting that the main road from Canterbury to the Isle of Thanet, via Sarre ferry, ran through the southern part of the manor. This was originally a Roman road, and on the high ground it ran through the village of Upstreet (nearby was the place of the annual fair, still called Fairport). Where the road crossed the marshes, it ran along the top of a sea wall called the Canterbury wall. In 1486 a bridge was finally built from the extreme north-east end of this wall across the Wantsum to Sarre, finally replacing the old ferry. On the eastern side of the later medieval sea walls on Chislet marshes is a mass of late medieval salt-working mounds, which by this time were used for making brine to salt herrings in the Herringhouse at Sturry. When Chislet vicarage was finally endowed in 1345, the vicars were, among other things, to have 'salt from 15 salthouses', according to Thorne's *Chronicle*.

Westbere is the one final area of the manor that should also be mentioned. The name means 'western swinepasture', and this area was in the extreme south-west corner of the manor near to Sturry. Some of this area was wooded, hence its suitability for pigs, but various hamlets grew up here, and in the early fourteenth century a fine new church was built in the village to replace the earlier chapel. Westbere now became a separate parish with its own vicar, and the prosperity of the time can still be seen in the high-quality carved tracery windows of the church and the superbly carved corbel figures supporting the chancel arch. The northern boundary of Westbere was the Roman road to Thanet, already mentioned, and to the north of this was the large deer-park belonging to the abbot. In 1537 the abbot gave it to Henry VIII, but only a year later, after the Dissolution, the park was handed over to the archbishop and disparked.

We have come a long way from St Augustine's Abbey itself, but it is in the demesne lands of the Abbey, and in the fields and hamlets of its tenants, and especially in its churches, that the physical presence of the great Abbey has survived best.

7

The Abbey site 1538–1997

Margaret Sparks

1538–1659: The destruction of the church and the use of the King's New Lodgings

The Abbey was surrendered to the king on 30 July 1538 in the chapter house by John Essex the abbot and thirty monks, about half the normal number. One of the monks had noted in his chronicle in February that year that the monks of Abingdon had been 'expulsed because of their slothfulness' with no thought that his own turn would come so soon. The abbot had hoped for protection from Thomas Cromwell, one of Henry VIII's chief ministers, as many others had done. When this seemed vain, he bargained with Sir Anthony Sentleger and Richard Layton that he might have the abbot's house at Sturry 'to receive his friends in'. Layton received the surrender, and in September thirty monks received pensions, listed according to their original names, not their names in religion, since those religious persons no longer existed.

At first there was no destruction on the Abbey site, except for the tomb of St Augustine, and probably other shrines, in September 1538 at the same time as the spoliation of St Thomas' shrine. In August the abbot was still with his household, presumably in the abbot's lodgings. He was not granted the manor of Sturry until February 1539. A papal bull indicted Henry VIII in December 1538, that he had dug up the bones of St Thomas Becket and scattered his ashes; he had spoiled St Augustine's monastery, driven out the monks and put deer in their place (an erroneous reference to the King's Park, on land mostly taken from the still existing Christ Church priory). A letter from Cardinal Pole to the Emperor Charles V said the same, with the addition that the king had destroyed St Augustine's tomb.

The applications for Abbey lands began in September 1538 and continued into the 1540s. The mayor (on behalf of the city of Canterbury) was an early applicant for the Abbey property within the walls: Canterbury citizens were in distress because of the loss of the pilgrimage trade. Plate and vestments had already been carted away. The library perhaps remained more or less complete at first. The abbot's lodgings had been earmarked for the king's use, one of many 'posting houses' which he might find useful on his journeys. In October 1539 the adaptation of the buildings round the inner or great court was begun. This work was under the direction of James Needham, Surveyor of the King's Works, whose accounts (preserved at the Bodleian Library) give details of the accommodation at the King's New Lodgings or 'the Palace'. The proposed arrival of Anne of Cleves in December set a finishing date for the work. The abbot's lodging on the east side of the court provided a great hall and a series of chambers for the king. The abbey kitchen remained in use. An old lodging on the south side was demolished to make space for chambers for the queen. On the west was the existing Fyndon gate, handsome enough for a palace, and a range of Abbey buildings converted for inner and outer great chambers. The court was made narrower by a new wall to the north which shut off the cellarer's range and the outer court. Fortunately for Needham the queen's coming was delayed by bad weather, giving fresh plaster more days to dry with the aid of charcoal braziers.

The Abbey church still stood. It was not until stone was needed for Calais and other fortifications in 1541 that the king gave orders for demolition. A fragment of another Needham account (at Longleat) shows that the work began in April 1541, with the taking down of stalls, seats, partitions and desks in the great choir and the eastern Lady chapel. Labourers were paid to carry them away – perhaps they were reused elsewhere. Floors and roofs were dismantled, the timber was then sawn up and put in the storehouse. Lead was removed from roofs, porches and steeples, and with gutters and downpipes was stored for recasting. Presumably tiles of roofs and floors were also stored. The destruction of stonework took a long time – probably no work was done in the winter. An attempt to bring down the south-west tower caused damage to the king's garden and the cemetery charnel chapel, and left a stump of masonry remaining, which was not finally removed until 1793. In October 1542 Needham's men were cleaning off stones from the fallen steeple and setting the stone in heaps, a ton at a time. This was loaded into carts for Fordwich, where it was transferred into barges for Sandwich, for shipping to Calais: the arrival of an earlier shipment was recorded in June 1541. The following spring the fallen stone was dug out from the king's garden and taken to the stone heaps, a new wall was built and the great west door space 'mured up' beside the still standing north-west tower, which remained with about half the north wall of the aisle of the nave as part of the king's palace.

A later account of George Nicholl, for 1552–3, reveals something of the way the destruction of the church had been carried out. He sold stone by the cartload to local people for

building. The source of the stone on site is usually mentioned. It seems that the eastern Lady chapel had been demolished, and the presbytery and eastern chapels. The crypt had not been filled in, as stone was dug from its walls. Parts of the south wall of the nave still stood, with stone window framing, and at least one pier from the south arcade. Floor tiles were being sold, and small marble shafts. Stone was distinguished as ashlar (large and small) and 'rubbish' or rubble. The use of the site as a quarry long continued. The lease of the palace or New Lodgings to Lord Cobham in 1564 contained a clause allowing access for the removal of stone, which was fetched by carts driven through the cemetery gate, outside the area of the New Lodgings. Robert Cecil who succeeded as tenant had a grant of stone for the building of Salisbury House in 1608, and there was still sufficient to provide the city of Canterbury with 180 loads of stone to mend the Poor Priests' Hospital (the city poorhouse) in 1621.

The King's New Lodgings, or the palace, formed a reasonably coherent set of buildings round a court, as was the usual plan for a great house at that time (81). Only the queen's lodgings on the south side had to be newly built in 1539. The former abbot's great hall was ready for use, a hall on an undercroft reached by a porch to the north with stairs and a wardrobe chamber above them. The old hexagonal kitchen was retained, with a dresser kitchen to join it to the hall. In 1543 the kitchen roof had to be releaded and in 1552 part of the hall was reroofed with new timbers. It had been built in 1294 but had been altered subsequently with a crenellated parapet towards the court.

The appearance of the New Lodgings is known from three drawings and an engraving. The Dutch artist Claude de Jonge sketched the buildings from the south-east in 1615, when the hall was having a further section of its roof repaired (82). The adjoining abbot's lodging and chapel are shown, but the queen's lodging is hidden by the Ethelbert tower. A later sketch from a nearer viewpoint to the east shows the

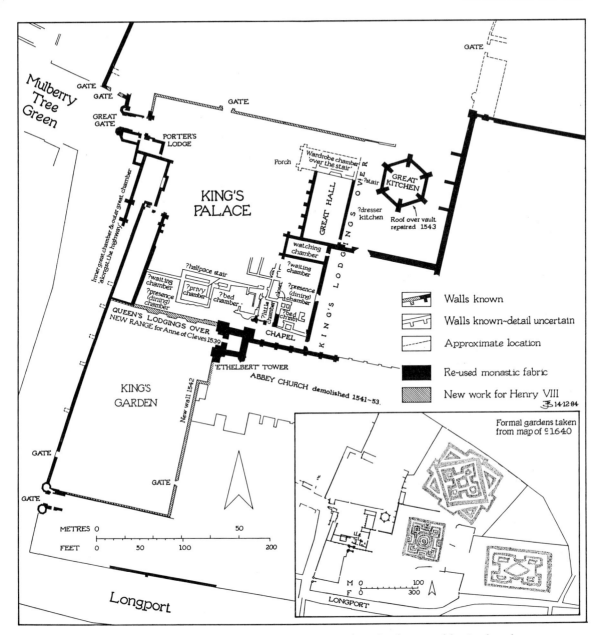

81 Plan of the King's New Lodgings or palace of Henry VIII on the site of the former palace of the abbot of St Augustine's (Canterbury Archaeological Trust).

abbot's lodging in 1627 (**83**). A general or bird's-eye view from the west was drawn by Thomas Johnson in 1655 (**84**). The west side of the hall is best shown on William Schellinks' drawing of c. 1661 from the north-west (**85**), where the porch and wardrobe chamber also appear in great detail. From this drawing it seems that the former abbot's chamber adjoining the hall to the south had been reroofed to form a continuous north–south range as far as the abbot's chapel. There were three chambers leading to the king's bedchamber, beyond which was the chapel, also on the first floor. The queen's lodgings were approached from the west, with two chambers and a bedchamber next to the chapel. This range was timber-framed on a brick and flint and stone base, with brick chimneys and brick

82 Pen and wash drawing, *'t Koster van St Augustien buyte Canterbury*, view from the north-east showing the New Lodgings, then the home of the Wotton family, 1615 (the earliest topographical view of the Abbey site), by C. de Jong (Utrecht, Centraal Museum der Gemeente Utrecht, inv. no. 11142).

83 Pen and wash drawing, *Christ Church Cathedral and St Augustine's Abbey from the South East*, 1627, by C. de Jong (Courtauld Institute, Witt Collection, no. 3560).

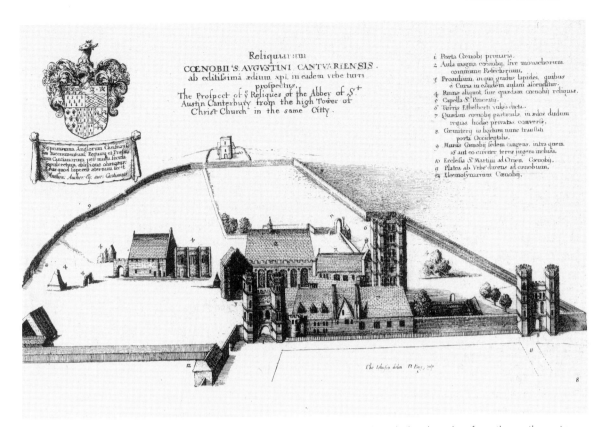

84 Bird's-eye view of St Augustine's Abbey site from top of Cathedral tower, *c.* 1655, drawn by Thomas Johnson; engraved and published by Daniel King (*The Cathedral and Conventual Churches of England and Wales*, 1656).

85 Pen and wash drawing, view from the north-west showing the New Lodgings behind its courtyard wall, *c.* 1661–5, by W. Schellinks (Vienna, Östereichisches Nationalbibliothek, Der Atlas Blaen (Van der Hem Atlas), vol. XIX, fol. 22).

gable ends. There was a timber-framed staircase 'within the court' and three bay windows to the chambers.

The queen's lodging cannot be seen on the Johnson bird's-eye view, as it is hidden behind the 'inner great chamber along the highway'. This range is shown ruined in S.H. Grimm's drawing of 1771. It appears to be of stone, and was presumably part of the Abbey guest accommodation. It butted against the Abbey 'guest chapel over the old gate'. The west gable of this is extant, reused to form the west wall of the St Augustine's College upper chapel. At the time of the New Lodgings it had an east face of brick and formed a narrow link-building with three floors and perhaps a staircase between the inner and outer great chambers. The outer chamber was the Abbey guest hall, later used as the St Augustine's College refectory. A view of the hall from the south-east, including the link-building, was drawn by B.T. Pouncy c.1780 (see 88). There are many views of the west face of the hall and the Fyndon gate beside it (for example, Francis Grose, 1768). To the south of the queen's lodging was the king's garden, which is still a garden, and beside its south-west corner 'Le Gatehouse' or the cemetery gate, still standing today as part of a house. In 1608 it narrowly escaped destruction. Robert Cecil, then tenant of the New Lodgings ('my poor lodge at Canterbury'), was using 'the ruins' as a stone quarry for his extensive building schemes elsewhere. In September the surveyor in charge reported that he had taken down the inner part of the gate, which would yield 60 or 70 loads of stone; but that he refrained from meddling with the outer part till further instructions because 'the townsmen keep a much ado'.

The royal family did not come to the New Lodgings often. Queen Mary let the site of the monastery of St Augustine and the park adjacent, to her friend and archbishop Cardinal Pole in March 1556. It is possible that they planned to return the New Lodgings to monastic use. Monks returned to Westminster in November 1556; in May 1557 Pole wrote to

the abbot of St Paul's in Rome: 'I am not indeed without hope that one of the two monasteries at my church at Canterbury may soon be restored.' Mary and Pole both died the next year, and with them the dream of a continuing Benedictine life at St Augustine's.

Under Elizabeth 'the buildings called Le Newlodginges and Le Gatehouse next to Le Newlodgings' and 'the Canterbury Parke' were let to Sir William Brooke, Lord Cobham and Frances his wife for thirty years from Michaelmas 1563, at a rent of £20 per annum, a payment of £400 and in recognition of his past services. There was a reservation for the ruined buildings of the monastery and the right of entry to remove materials, and the lessees were to maintain '200 wild beasts and deer to the use of the Crown in the Park'. Naturally the king or queen could stay in the house, should they visit Canterbury – Elizabeth came in 1573. At the time of his tenancy Brooke was Lord Warden of the Cinque Ports, Constable of Dover and Lord Lieutenant of Kent. In spite of extensive repairs in the years since 1539 more work was needed at the New Lodgings and the Dean and Chapter provided 20 oaks from Godmersham in November 1564. Brooke was a great builder and began the north and south wings at Cobham Hall about 1580. He presumably secured a further lease at Canterbury, as he still retained it on his death in March 1597. The death of his daughter Elizabeth, wife of Robert Cecil, in January 1597 'affected him much', as it did Robert Cecil himself. William Brooke's son Henry was deprived of his title and estates in 1603 for his part in a plot to establish Arabella Stuart as queen: the New Lodgings lease was taken on by Robert Cecil. But his thought and activities were elsewhere. Unlike Brooke he probably took more out from the estate in terms of stone quarrying than he added in repairs.

In these years others were taking away treasure in the form of the manuscript books from the St Augustine's Abbey library. The dispersal of the library has some relevance here, since the tenants of the New Lodgings were its nominal guardians. They appear to have allowed 'researchers' to visit it: John Joscelyn, Archbishop Matthew Parker's secretary, made notes there in 1565. John Twyne, the former St Augustine's almonry schoolmaster and later first headmaster of the King's School, knew the library well, and took books from it for himself and for others. John Wilde, a Canterbury lawyer who lived up the road in the Great House by St Martin's Church, had at least two books from St Augustine's. His grandson, also John Wilde, gave one of them to the Cathedral library perhaps about 1610 (Dean and Chapter of Canterbury, Lit. MS B.6). The impression is created that any reasonably respectable person could procure books if he wished. Henry Lord Cobham was near the end of his brief tenure at St Augustine's when he promised books to Sir Thomas Bodley and to the University of Oxford in 1602. His fall the next year prevented further negotiations. A very representative selection of important books for the history of the Abbey – registers, chronicles, customary, martyrology – came into the hands of Sir Robert Cotton, the antiquary, book collector and politician (1571–1631). He specialized in gathering together monastic books of this kind, without which the history of English religious houses could not be written.

After Robert Cecil's death in 1612 his son William sold the lease of the New Lodgings to Sir Edward Wotton of the Boughton Malherbe family. He had been Lord Lieutenant of Kent, was often sent on diplomatic journeys and held various posts at court. He was ambitious and cultivated. In his time, and that of his wife who lived until 1659, the New Lodgings were at their best as the home of a family with money and 'modern' interests. The stone ranges round the court could not compare with the brick and glass at Cobham or Hatfield, but the garden became famous. Wotton employed John Tradescant the elder, who had been at Hatfield with the Cecil family until 1615. Tradescant was in charge until 1623, with generous leave of absence for exploration abroad – to Algeria and even to

Russia. His son, also John, became a King's Scholar at the Cathedral school. It has been thought that a map of Canterbury and its environs of c. 1640 shows Tradescant's garden (**colour plate 9**) but this should not be taken too literally. The map shows three large knot-gardens and a mound, with perhaps two orchards. Experience of the cartographer's drawing of gardens in the Cathedral precinct suggests that a knot-garden was simply his symbol for any garden. The reality at Lord Wotton's estate was more sophisticated and complex. In a similar way the map shows the New Lodgings in a disconnected manner – two gatehouses, the great hall, the Ethelbert tower, a fence and range along the street and two 'houses' by the tower, perhaps to signify the king's and queen's lodgings. As can be seen from Johnson's view of 1655, the reality was very different.

The diarist Lieutenant Hammond made a visit to Canterbury in 1635. He describes the Cathedral and continues with an account of St Augustine's, where he was courteously entertained by 'a bountiful, generous and noble lady' – Margaret Wotton. He saw the Ethelbert tower; the Fyndon gate; the 'spacious and stately great Hall'; 'the round Archt Kitchin with 8 Chimneys in it'; and the ruins of the Abbey church and chapels (including St Pancras'). He comments on the removal of stone from the site. He was taken round the gardens by the head gardener (unnamed). The whole of the original walled site had been planted with orchards of delicate fruits, walks – one with lime trees – groves, mounts, 'Labirinth like wildernesses', flower gardens and fountains. 'Pretty contriv'd wooddy Mazes' are mentioned, but they were only one ingredient in a large and varied scheme. Near the house was a large fountain pool dominated by Charon with his boat and dog – guardians of Hades in Greek mythology. Stone snakes, scorpions and strange fishes directed jets of water towards the central figure. Presumably the pool was square, and on each side was a stone water nymph. One had lost an arm 'by the Royall steddy hand of our gracious Souveraigne, at his Marriage of his Royall Spouse in this City'. Charles I came in 1625 and had some days to wait for the arrival of Henrietta Maria. Ingenious waterworks were much in demand in the best gardens at that time: probably Wotton's designers took advantage of parts of the Abbey water supply which crossed the site from springs in the hillside to the north-east.

Wotton died the year after King Charles' visit, a disappointed man. He had been created Baron Wotton of Marley in 1603, but had hoped for a viscountcy. He was succeeded by his son Thomas, from his first marriage, who lived at Boughton Malherbe with his wife Mary Throckmorton – both were Catholics. Edward Wotton's widow, Margaret, continued at the New Lodgings until her death in 1659. She also was a Catholic, and of course a royalist, which caused difficulties during the Civil War. Her house was searched for arms by Colonel Sandys, probably in August 1642, and later in the war the house was attacked, goods stolen and a large painting of the Passion of Christ worth £20 was publicly burnt. Her estate was sequestrated, in the same way as those of other royalists. From the total value of £500, one-third was allowed her for her support. She gave her name to the former Mulberry Tree Green outside the Fyndon gate and thus has a lasting memorial in Canterbury, though her garden and a good deal of her house have disappeared.

1659–1791: The ruined Abbey – the historical and pictorial record

Charles II made a fleeting royal visit in May 1660 on his return from exile with his brothers James duke of York and Henry of Gloucester. The Schellinks drawing (see 85) shows the buildings at that time. The New Lodgings had become part of the Hales family estate – at some time it must have been bought from the crown. Thomas Wotton had died in 1630, leaving four daughters. The youngest, Anne, married Edward Hales, grandson and heir of Edward Hales of Tunstall. The young Edward became involved in

the Kentish rising against Parliament in 1648, lost money in trying to raise an army, and in 1651 went abroad. His wife died in 1654 but he inherited the St Augustine's estate as her share of the Wotton property. He never returned to England and died in 1683 in France. His son, also Edward, became a Catholic in 1685 but was allowed to continue as an army officer. He supported James II and went abroad with him, receiving the Jacobite title of earl of Tenterden. He also died abroad, in 1695. His elder son Edward had been killed at the battle of the Boyne in 1690. Later members of the Hales family lived at St Stephen's, Hackington, north of Canterbury, in the brick courtyard house near the church until the building in 1759 of a grand mansion, Hales Place, a little way up the hill from the church.

Thus after Lady Wotton's death the New Lodgings were no longer used as a family house. They may well have been let in several parts by the officers of the absentee landlords. On 8 September 1692 there was an earthquake. The north side of the Ethelbert tower collapsed, presumably destroying the king's lodgings and great hall, and probably the queen's lodgings as well. The 'inner great chamber along the highway' is shown ruined in 1771. The old guest hall and Fyndon gate remained habitable and from at least 1765 were let as a public house. Outside the Fyndon gate stood the almonry, always let separately, though part of the New Lodgings estate. In the old outer court area there was a house in the north-west corner – still extant as Coleridge House. (In the garden, sixteenth-century fragments of carved stonework have been preserved.) The range of bakehouse and brewhouse had been destroyed by the time of Johnson's view in 1655, and probably earlier as part of the stone quarrying operation. A small gate and house on the east side still stood in the early nineteenth century. At the south-west corner of the walled site the outer part of the cemetery gate remained used as the basis for a house put up c. 1770 by the Hales estate for letting, now called Bailey House. A well-known drawing in the series of *Antiquities or Venerable Remains ... in the County of Kent* published in 1735 by Samuel and Nathaniel Buck shows what could be seen after the earthquake, including the east window of the abbot's chapel with elaborate decorated tracery. The plate is dedicated to the 'Proprietor of the Abbey', Sir John Hales, the second son of Edward earl of Tenterden who had died in 1695.

The drawing of 1735, showing the ruined Abbey as opposed to Johnson's view of the New Lodgings, heralded a new approach to the site. A ruined abbey became a subject of curiosity for travellers and provided suitable 'views' for topographical drawings which could be engraved as plates for leather-bound volumes in gentlemen's libraries. St Augustine's Abbey site had been noticed in passing by William Lambarde (1570) as the former home of monks, a deplorable species, well swept away. William Camden (1586) was more dispassionate: he describes the site as 'buried in ruins' and quotes the epitaph of Augustine and the early archbishops. Materials for a serious study of the history of the Abbey were published in the mid-seventeenth century. William Somner, Canterbury lawyer and antiquary, devoted several pages to the Abbey in his *Antiquities of Canterbury* (1640). The Cathedral and its precinct were his chief love, but he realized the great importance of St Augustine's for early Christianity in east Kent and its later significance as an outstanding Benedictine abbey. He quoted Bede and Thorne and published the three spurious Æthelberht charters and St Augustine's privilege. In his researches he had found Thomas of Elmham's compilations towards a history of the Abbey: from the Trinity Hall manuscript he had an engraving made for his book of the drawing of the high altar and shrines (compare **colour plate 1**). Somner was on friendly terms with Roger Twysden who published Thorne's *Chronicle* in his *Historiae Anglicanae scriptores decem* (Ten authors of English [Medieval] history) (1652). Both men collaborated with William Dugdale,

the publisher if not the maker of the *Monasticon Anglicanum*, the encyclopedic work on England's monasteries before the Dissolution, that gathered together many key documents from their history and supplemented these by a series of engraved illustrations. St Augustine's is noticed in the first volume (1655), with Johnson's bird's-eye view of the New Lodgings and the high altar and shrines from Elmham. Twysden was a careful scholar, who complained to Dugdale about the absence of any qualification in the *Monasticon* about the truth of papal bulls and charters: 'there never was greater forgers ... than the monks in former times were', and he went on to instance St Augustine's.

In the mid- to later eighteenth century it was the turn for artists rather than historians to record the site. The sketches divide into two main groups – the studies of the Ethelbert tower and other ruins, and those of standing buildings still in use, especially the Fyndon gate and the guest hall. William Stukeley published the earliest of the views of the Ethelbert tower in 1722 (from the north-west). This proved a popular subject, up to the time of its fall a hundred years later (see **57**). Sometimes it was drawn from the east, as in Job Bulman's view of *c.* 1780 with the empty arch of the abbot's chapel window beside it. Two anonymous sketches of similar date are preserved in one of Richard Gough's scrapbooks in the Bodleian Library (**86**). Francis Perry's view across the site from the north shows the ruins of the abbot's hall and lodgings as well as the tower, with a gentleman in the foreground lecturing two others and pointing with his stick – an early example of the tour round St Augustine's (**87**).

The Fyndon gate seen across Lady Wootton's Green with the guest hall and the Ethelbert tower was often sketched, by Francis Grose, Job Bulman and Paul Sandby among others. J.M.W Turner did not include the gate in his view of the guest hall (**colour plate 20**) and Michael 'Angelo' Rooker painted only the Fyndon gate (1779), as a pair to his *Gatehouse at Battle Abbey*. A view of the Fyndon gate from the

86 Pen and wash drawing, view from the east of the ruins of St Augustine's Abbey, showing the west side of the cloister, the abbot's chapel and the north-west tower; eighteenth century, anonymous (Oxford, Bodleian Library, Gough Gen. Top. 61, fol. 236e).

north-east, sketched from the meadow on the site of the Abbey outer court, attracted Grose and Sandby. B.T. Pouncy made two drawings of the gate and hall from the meadow, and an unusual view of the hall from the south (**88**). Sandby drew the cemetery gate in 1786 (**89**) and published an aquatint with figures in the foreground. Since the Abbey ruins were not highly picturesque, like Lindisfarne or Croyland, it was fortunate that so many skilled artists made attractive drawings, both as a record of the buildings for the future and to prevent the Abbey and its history disappearing from contemporary mind and sight.

William Gostling (1772) remarked that 'the dimensions of the abbey church ... can hardly be traced with any degree of certainty'. Four years later the use of the walled area was described as 'a Bowling-green, Pasture grounds, Orchards, Gardens and Nurseries'. The guest hall was a public house called The Old Palace, the Fyndon gate a cockpit, later a brewery, and the monastic parlour (beneath the ruin of the abbot's chapel but still covered) was a (real) tennis court and later a fives court. Firework displays, concerts and dances were held in the Old Palace Gardens

in the summer, in provincial imitation of London pleasure gardens. The Ethelbert tower still stood, in spite of attempts in 1765 to use it for a stone quarry.

1791–1848: Sale of land and the founding of St Augustine's College

The breaking up of the site began in 1791 when the Hales family sold about 3 acres (1.2ha) on the south side of the estate, on the site of the old lay cemetery, for the building of the Kent and Canterbury Hospital 'for the sick and lame poor from any part of the County of Kent'. The Hospital opened in April 1793. It was a handsome redbrick building, in the same style as, for example, the Infirmary at Lincoln of 1776. On the adjoining site, in the angle between Longport and North Holmes Road the foundation stone of the new County Gaol and House of Correction was also laid in 1791. It was designed by George Byfield, who specialized in prisons, and at Canterbury designed the Sessions House next door. The Sessions House is a Classical stuccoed, adequately impressive building. The front of the prison towards Longport is of rusticated stonework with a suggestion of a fortress – a purpose-built prison, unlike the previous prison at the Westgate. It was opened in 1808.

87 Engraving, *North view of the Abbey of St Augustine*, *c.* 1750, by Francis Perry (*Eighteen Views of Antiquities in Kent*) (Collection Canterbury Museums ©).

Sir Edward Hales, 5th Baronet, died in 1802. He had built 'the Mansion House called Hales Place', and run the family into debt. His successor promoted an Act of Parliament the same year to allow him to sell 'part of the settled estates' to pay off his debts. The St Augustine's estate was divided into thirty-two lots and sold by auction in 1804 and 1805. As a result the St Augustine's site might easily have been lost under a maze of streets and small houses, in the same way as the St Gregory's priory site (to the north of the Cathedral) in the years after 1800. Perhaps the Abbey had too long a history to be forgotten. On 16 October 1822 early in the morning 'the inhabitants of St Paul's, Longport and Lady Wotton's Green were thrown into consternation by a tremendous noise' caused by the fall of the Ethelbert tower, which sent tons of stone into the fives court, the garden and the hospital meadow. The patients were 'exceedingly terrified'. The east face did not fall with the rest, allowing for a dramatic *View of the Ruins of Ethelbert's Tower – taken the day previous to its being utterly demolished, on the 24th of October*

88 Watercolour, view from the south-east of the former guest hall and chapel of St Augustine's Abbey, *c.* 1780, by B.T. Pouncy (Collection Canterbury Museums ©).

89 Watercolour, view from the north-west of the former cemetery gate of St Augustine's Abbey, 1786, by Paul Sandby (London, Tate Gallery, no. 1856).

1822, by George Cooper. The stone was used by the Dean and Chapter for repairs to the Cathedral nave. The stump of the south-west tower at St Augustine's had already been removed in 1793, making a clearance in the hospital meadow. The stone was sold for one shilling a cartload for mending highways. St Augustine's as a stone quarry had a long history.

However, new uses for part of the Abbey site began to be considered. The Dean and Chapter wanted more space for the King's School. In 1834 they resolved to buy the public house and its grounds, which would have been a good site for the expanding school. They were advised that it would be impossible to acquire the freehold, without an Act of Parliament, since the owner was insane, so they gave up the scheme. Others proved more persistent, though the purchase did not take place for ten years. On 13 September 1843 a letter appeared in the *English Churchman*, a High Church newspaper of that time, describing a pilgrimage to Canterbury. Robert Brett, a doctor from Stoke Newington, and a friend were staying at Ramsgate. They visited the Cathedral for Matins and were deeply impressed by the service and the building. They went to St Martin's, which was presumably in good order. Then to St Augustine's, where 'they were disgusted and horrified at the scene of sordid, revolting profanity and desecration which presented itself'. They were pleased to learn from an old man that 'the place is going to be sold, it's always changing hands, for God Almighty don't seem to prosper anybody who has it'. So the letter ended with a plea that God might incline the hearts of the Dean and Chapter 'to rescue this inheritance of their forefathers from the hands of the heathen desolator, or dispose some pious and wealthy Catholic to purchase and restore the sacred edifice'.

This letter produced a speedy result, which in effect saved the greater part of the St Augustine's site from loss of identity under streets and houses. Alexander James Beresford Hope saw Brett's letter and took up a cause which fascinated him – the rescue and reuse of a medieval holy place,

which he saw as the cradle of English Christianity. Beresford Hope (90) was the son of a wealthy Dutch merchant, of Scottish extraction, who had settled in England. He had been educated at Harrow and Trinity College, Cambridge, where he had been a keen member of the Cambridge Camden Society. A few days after the publication of Brett's letter, Beresford Hope made his first visit to Canterbury, to call upon Archdeacon Lyall in the precincts. After seeing the Cathedral he asked to see St Augustine's. Lyall said he would be very much disgusted, but he went and decided instantly that he would buy the public house and the pleasure garden when they should be for sale. He returned to London, where he instructed his lawyer to purchase the property. After this there was a pause of nine months before the property was for sale by auction. On 13 June 1844 Beresford Hope's lawyer had the site and buildings acquired for £2020 – a 470-year lease for 1½ acres. On 12 September the *English Churchman* published a note to say that the ruins had been bought by 'a very munificent churchman', and took peculiar pleasure in the fact that this had come about through a notice in its columns.

Beresford Hope was 24 at the time. He did not know what he should do with his site, but he was already planning to buy more of the dispersed plots of land to bring together what had been divided forty years before by the Hales family. He summoned William Butterfield, the Cambridge Camden Society's favourite architect, to survey the buildings for restoration. Almost immediately after the sale Beresford Hope had received a letter from Edward Coleridge, an Eton master who was leading a crusade for the founding of a missionary college. As described in a speech years later, the letter said 'Dear Hope, I see you have bought St Augustine's. Of course you are going to give it to my college.' But Beresford Hope would not be rushed, even by an extremely pushing older man. He told Coleridge he intended to devote the place to some religious purpose, though he did not yet know what it should be.

90 Alexander James Beresford Hope, rescuer of the Abbey site and co-founder of St Augustine's College in 1845 (Trustees of St Augustine's Foundation).

Coleridge had begun his campaign for 'an institution to raise up clergy for the colonies' in 1842. His friends William Broughton, bishop of Australia, and George Selwyn, bishop of New Zealand had impressed on him the desperate need for more trained clergy for colonial dioceses. Coleridge lobbied important people and raised promises of financial help from his clientele of the rich and famous. He thought he might have the college near Oxford, but he did not mind strongly where it was, so long as it could be begun without delay. He even recruited a relation, W.H. Coleridge, the retired bishop of Barbados, as first warden of the college to be founded.

In December Beresford Hope wrote to Coleridge: 'St Augustine's is yours, or rather of the Church, at once.' They formed a partnership as co-founders of the college. Coleridge was in charge of the educational and fund-raising side. Beresford Hope organized the plans and buildings with Butterfield and pursued the purchase of other plots of land. He promoted three private Acts of Parliament to obtain the freehold of his site. This was necessary because he wanted his college to be permanent and self-governing, with a proper charter and statutes, like an Oxford or Cambridge college. Although it was 'of the Church', it was not to be run by church committees. The founders had a good deal of trouble from church committees and opposition on grounds of 'Popery' in the initial stages.

Butterfield was only 30 when he began work at St Augustine's. The buildings are domestic in character: the style was set by the remaining guest hall, so the materials are flint with Caen stone dressings and red tiled roofs. The library dominates the scheme, on the site of the abbot's hall, of Kentish ragstone with Caen stone dressings and tiled roof. The design of the window tracery is taken from the fourteenth-century hall of the former archiepiscopal palace at Mayfield, Sussex. Fortunately the College chapel is also domestic in scale, like a private chapel in a courtyard house, so there was no opportunity for a large Butterfield church.

Building accounts remain with the College archives, now at the Dean and Chapter Archives in Canterbury. Plans were drawn up early in 1845 and the student accommodation was completed by December. It occupied the north side of the court, where there had been a wall and an elaborate gate to the lane beyond – both wall and gate were from the New Lodgings. The restoration of the Fyndon gate and guest hall was nearly finished at the end of 1845. In 1846 there was work on the chapel, of which the western end was medieval, and the warden's house and fellows' building, which were entirely Butterfield's design. The library and the chapel caused delays, and were not completed until early in 1848. For the first time since the beginning of the sixteenth century stone was brought to the site, from Normandy and from unspecified places in Kent for ragstone and flints. Beresford Hope paid £30,000 for the buildings and restoration, and a further £4544.18s.10d for the chapel and its fittings. The conduit (not a dovecot) in the middle of the court was given by a College benefactor, J.C. Sharpe. The library and student accommodation were sketched by L.L. Razé, the King's School drawing master (91).

The chapel was dedicated on St Peter's Day, 29 June 1848 with much ceremony by the archbishop. There was a sermon in the Cathedral and lunch at the College for 1200 people, at Beresford Hope's expense. St Peter's Day remained as a 'Founders and Benefactors Day' throughout the life of the College. The Abbey church had been dedicated to Sts Peter and Paul (whose feast day is 29 June in the church calendar). Beresford Hope liked to think that his St Augustine's College had a 'double character so that while it should be the foundation of 1848, it should also be the foundation of 596'. A similar idea exists today, whereby the New Foundation cathedrals such as Canterbury, Winchester and Durham are seen by some as the heirs and successors of the former Benedictine communities. Beresford Hope did not quite achieve this, but because of his zeal and generosity much of the site was reclaimed and the wardens and fellows of his college over almost one hundred years saw the site excavated. For this reason it is appropriate to devote space to his character and his share in founding the College.

91 Lithograph, view of the new library (on the site of the great hall of the abbot's and king's palace) and student accommodation, 1847, after a drawing by L.L. Razé (published by Henry Ward) (Collection Canterbury Museums ©).

1848–1939: St Augustine's College and excavations

Once the College was set up, the co-founders did not interfere in its organization. At first things did not go well. There were few students and the first warden, Bishop Coleridge, died after a year. The second warden, Dr Henry Bailey, created order in the College and presided over it until 1878. He was assisted by a sub-warden and one or two fellows. When the College was full there were fifty students. They studied Latin, mathematics, science, theology, and subjects useful for missionaries such as oriental languages, practical surgery and medicine, carpentry, bookbinding and printing. They played games against local schools, and were encouraged to walk, garden and assist with archaeology. Studies and outdoor activities were within a framework of chapel services – Morning and Evening Prayer daily, with Holy Communion on Sundays and Saints' days. Extra services such as Sext at midday and Compline at night (monastic offices) were added later, and the students helped in Canterbury parishes.

Throughout the College's life there were problems in recruiting sufficient students of the necessary calibre, and problems of money. The endowment of the College consisted of £30,000, a large sum in 1848, but not sufficient. The wardens and fellows were constantly issuing appeals, usually for specific objects – an oriental studies fellowship, two five courts, the repair of the gate towers, the re-laying of drains. After the 1914–18 war, when missionary zeal was not so great, there were thirty students in residence. In 1923 Warden Knight said the College cost £6000 to run: £3000 came from endowment; the other £3000 should come from the students, but many could not pay. A fund specially for fees provided £1000, and £2000 had to be found each year from grants from missionary societies or interested individuals.

It was this enthusiastic but impoverished society which carried out the excavation of the church and monastic buildings. They had no state funding and relied on subscriptions from the public and grants from the Society of Antiquaries and the Kent Archaeological Society and other bodies. Some years money had run out and there could be no archaeology. They were greatly helped by experts, such as W.H. St John Hope, the Secretary of the Society of Antiquaries, who visited and wrote letters promptly with excellent advice. St Augustine's still awaits a general survey, but in 1984 a description of the recovery of the site and a list of excavations were published in the celebratory hundredth volume of *Archaeologia Cantiana*, a tribute to the many Kent Archaeological Society officers who assisted the College.

Archaeology on the site began with Butterfield in 1845, who had the undercroft of the abbot's hall excavated so that he could obtain dimensions and devise a plan for the library. He also had permission to excavate in the hospital ground to find the piers of the nave. He was able to find the piers of the south arcade and thus determine the length of the nave, but on the north side the east end was obstructed by a wall running diagonally across the site, enclosing part of Mrs Gilbert's land – the cloister area. Beresford Hope had wanted to buy Mrs Gilbert's land since 1844, but did not obtain it until 1866. In 1867–9 the kitchen, refectory and cloister were excavated and plans made. The Kent Archaeological Society met in Canterbury in 1868. They visited St Augustine's and with them came Professor Robert Willis, who inspected the sites carefully and gave advice about the plans. Soil was returned to the site, and gardens were planted. By 1869 the College owned the land and buildings from the cemetery gate to the Fyndon gate and along to the north as far as the corner of the lane. To the south their boundary was the hospital ground. In 1882 the College bought the North Holmes estate, along North Holmes Road, once the abbey vineyard. It was a market garden with vineries and hothouses. The vendor proposed a scheme for 147 cottages on the land, so the College in some alarm paid more than they intended.

South of the North Holmes estate was the so-called Abbey Field, bounded to the south by the hospital land. Beresford Hope wanted it, as it covered the east end of the church, the chapter house and the infirmary, but the owners would not sell. After Beresford Hope's death in 1887, three new patrons for archaeology at St Augustine's came on the scene. Canon C.F. Routledge lived at St Martin's House (now destroyed) beside St Martin's Church. He was from Eton and King's College, Cambridge, and at the time was a retired Inspector of Schools. He was determined to see the Abbey Field excavated. W.H. St John Hope took command as the expert and Lord Northbourne (died 1923) gave financial backing. His position as Chairman of the Hospital Board of Management was of great significance for the eventual obtaining of the nave site. Routledge started a campaign to obtain the Abbey Field in 1893 but there was no sale until an auction in July 1900. The land was bought by trustees – Routledge, St John Hope and Francis Bennett-Goldney, the mayor of Canterbury, with the promise that when excavated it would be handed over to the College, which was done in 1915.

An excavation at St Pancras' Chapel was organized in November by St John Hope, partly so that Routledge could write to the *Times* about it and appeal for money – he described it as 'making a splash'. In 1901 excavation began in the crypt chapels and Lady chapel. As so often, it was found that treasure hunters had been there first: graves had been robbed and little was left for archaeologists. For the next two summers work moved to the slype, chapter house, dormitory and infirmary. In 1904 money had run out and in November Routledge died. There was a further season in 1907 when the chapter house and infirmary were cleared and drawn up (later covered with soil for a playing field), but there was no further work for some years. Without a devoted and capable person on site, little could be done.

This gap was filled in 1912 when Robert Ullock Potts arrived as sub-warden and bursar.

He had been at Oriel College, Oxford, and had taught in India before and after ordination. He was clear-minded, hard-working and unafraid of obstacles. He set about the completion of the excavations at the Abbey so that the 'holy ground' should be 'a source of inspiration to English-speaking peoples for all time'. His notebooks and correspondence with St John Hope are now stored with the College archives at the Dean and Chapter Archives at Canterbury: the letters show him to have been sensible and good-tempered.

In 1913 he had the wall across the nave taken down, and began discussions with the hospital about renting the nave area for excavation. He and Lord Northbourne worked together, but there were problems, especially with the hospital laundry building which was near the site of the south transept and would need to be rebuilt. (Sheets from the laundry hung out to dry can be seen in **92**.) The seasons of 1914–15 provided some of the most exciting discoveries. Previously the Romanesque Abbey church had been revealed. Now parts of the Anglo-Saxon churches beneath were found. The choir space between the transepts was excavated, and the east end of the nave as far as the rood screen. Beneath the choir and the two bays of the nave curved foundations were revealed, which were at first sight puzzling. Canon C.E. Woodruff, a Canterbury antiquarian, showed Potts the account written by the hagiographer Goscelin *c.* 1097 of the translation of St Augustine's relics in 1091. Goscelin had also described the stages of building the church, and how Abbot Wulfric built a tower, *c.* 1047, to join the Sts Peter and Paul Church to the St Mary Church (see pp. 109–10). The curved foundations were the piers for Abbot Wulfric's rotunda (**92**).

Goscelin's account was also useful to explain the burials in the St Gregory porticus. This area, north-west of the rotunda, lay under the north aisle of the nave, and had been the north porticus of the Sts Peter and Paul Church, in which the early archbishops were buried. St Augustine's tomb was not found, because it was obliterated by the sleeper wall for the north arcade of the nave, after the removal of relics in 1091. St John Hope read a paper on these discoveries to the Society of Antiquaries in 1915, which was published in *Archaeologia* the same year. Potts wrote short accounts of all his campaigns for *Archaeologia Cantiana* and they were noticed in *Occasional Papers* for the benefit of old students and local supporters. Also in 1915 a lease was obtained from the hospital for a strip of ground on the north side of the nave. Negotiations about the laundry and the other strip of land continued.

There were no further excavations during the war period, except for the grave of Abbot Roger of Chichester, in the south transept, which was discovered accidentally in June 1918. St John Hope came to see it, probably his last visit to the site, as he died the next year. His unfailing help and sound judgement, and his assistance in securing money were invaluable, and seem the more remarkable in considering how many other sites had claims on his time and interest. In 1919 an agreement was made with the hospital to build a new laundry (mostly paid for by Lord Northbourne) and lease the hospital land.

Excavations in 1920 were in the kitchen and refectory. In 1921–2 the foundations of Sts Peter and Paul Church were discovered and the nave was cleared to the west end. C.R. Peers took over St John Hope's role as consultant, with the assistance of A.W. Clapham for the Anglo-Saxon church. Potts was elected a Fellow of the Society of Antiquaries in recognition of his work in 1922, a well-deserved honour which must have pleased him greatly. Money ran out again in 1923: Warden Knight in making an appeal thought the archaeology might be completed in two years. The south aisle of the nave, south transept and a tower at the west end of the nave were uncovered in 1924, after which the Anglo-Saxon and Romanesque churches were drawn up. Peers and Clapham wrote a paper read to the Society of Antiquaries in March 1926 (published 1928) on Anglo-Saxon aspects of the site. They thought that there might be an Anglo-

Saxon cloister beneath the medieval garth, so excavations in 1928–30 were in that area. The last excavation under Potts' direction was in the north transept, where the grave of Abbot Dunster was found.

A plan was drawn up by J.G.P. Meaden, an architect with the firm of Tapper (father and son) who had long been the College architects. It was published with *Archaeologia Cantiana* for 1934. It shows the site as excavated, including St Pancras' Chapel and the infirmary, the church, the buildings round the cloister and the inner court. Potts remarked that the almonry was not included and hoped that it might be 'reunited to the rest of the ancient precinct'. He was perhaps not aware of the outer court, although one gable end still stood there, and Johnson's bird's-eye view suggests a complex of buildings.

Two further projects then occupied Potts and his friends. One was the provision of an altar for worship in the crypt. Evensong had been sung in the crypt on special days in the summer. There were consultations with Michael Tapper the architect about the restoration of the altar of St Mary and the Angels in the eastern chapel of the crypt, so that the Eucharist might be offered. Eventually the chapel was refloored, the altar restored and an arched roof set over it, as remains today. It was reconsecrated in September 1937. The altar alone is covered: those attending the service stand near it on the crypt grass.

The second project was the preservation of the ruins. Discussions were begun in 1935 with the Office of Works 'with a view to the Office taking over the guardianship of the site (we retaining the ownership as before) and spending the necessary money on its preservation'. The negotiations proved very slow, but finally a Deed of Guardianship was signed on 14 October 1938. In these same years two further pieces of land were secured. Major Love's orchard, to the north of the lane, covered the old outer court and part of the vineyard. That was bought in 1937. Eventually it became part of the site of Christ Church College and the Canterbury Archaeological Trust has carried out

92 Excavations by R.U. Potts and W. St John Hope in progress 1914, view looking west; in the foreground is the curving wall of the north side of Abbot Wulfric's octagon, between the later eleventh-century foundations of the nave arcade and north aisle wall (Society of Antiquaries, from *Archaeologia* 66, 1915).

numerous excavations there since 1983. Also in 1937 the Kent and Canterbury Hospital moved to a new site on the southern edge of the city. There was immediate interest on the part of the warden and fellows. The city wanted the site for a technical college, but building was not permitted on the old graveyard. Warden Tomlin and friends set up 'Trustees of the St Augustine's Abbey Precinct Recovery Fund' and bought the old hospital and ground in 1939. They leased it to the Council for twenty-one years to use as a temporary technical college, and proposed that the buildings should then be demolished, and after excavation a garden should be created for the enjoyment of Canterbury citizens and visitors. As a result of wartime restrictions the city continued the use of the old hospital, and it was not available for demolition until 1971.

1939–1996: Reuse of St Augustine's College buildings and further excavations

The coming of the war in 1939 in effect ended the stable life of St Augustine's College – always short of money and yet a lively and continuing community with a sense of purpose. It was indeed fortunate that the excavations were as complete as the ownership of land allowed and the arrangements for guardianship were in place

– later maintained by the Ministry of Works, the Department of the Environment and now English Heritage. By the end of 1940 most students and staff were scattered. On 31 May 1942 the College buildings were badly damaged in the extensive air raids of that night. Most of the houses on Lady Wootton's Green were destroyed.

A change in the use of the College buildings had already been discussed. In 1936 Canon W.F. France had written an article proposing a Central College for the Anglican Communion – the association of former colonial dioceses and other missionary areas which had grown to be independent Churches, under the presidency of the archbishop of Canterbury. This body also included the Episcopal Church in the USA. It was thought that students from the 'younger churches' and the others could meet and study together. The wealthier Churches would pay, especially the Church of England and the Episcopal Church in the States. The students should be housed and taught without payment.

Beresford Hope had said that his St Augustine's should be 'of the Church' but self-governing. In the end it could not escape from the Church's bureaucracy. The Church changed the use, and later could not find a use for the buildings. The idea of the Central College was taken up with enthusiasm by Archbishop Geoffrey Fisher. In 1945 France was appointed warden to see the buildings repaired and preparations made for the new college. Derelict land and the site of the almonry at Lady Wootton's Green were bought in 1946, and the house which became known as Coleridge House next door to the almonry. Apart from one small area the old St Augustine's estate was complete, as Beresford Hope had desired. In 1947 the Church of England decided against missionary colleges – missionaries were to be taught alongside other theological students. A new College charter was agreed in 1947, allowing the Central College use, and the Lambeth Conference of 1948 agreed to the proposal.

The new college did not open until 1952, with Kenneth Sansbury as warden. Canon France wrote a fund-raising pamphlet for it, optimistically entitled *The Story of an Enduring Life*. Financial problems were even more difficult than before. The Central College lived from hand to mouth on yearly collections and grants with little endowment. Land was sold: the Canterbury City Council needed land for road making and housing. The almonry was sold to them in 1959. There were negotiations with the city about housing on the North Holmes area in 1953 and 1957, which were scrapped because of a scheme to build a church teacher training college (later Christ Church College) on the site. The sale was completed in February 1961. Work on the site started in 1962, without benefit of archaeology. The first students moved on to the campus in 1963. (Coleridge House was sold to Christ Church in 1969.)

In spite of these sales of land, the financial position did not improve. Some people said the Central College was a luxury which the Anglican Communion could not afford. The archbishops met in Jerusalem in 1966 and decided that money could not be spared to cover the Central College deficit, and there would be no further grants after 1967. So the Central College closed, among recriminations. Somebody quoted bitterly 'a little patch of ground that hath in it no profit but the name'. After the Central College closed in 1967, the ordinands from King's College, London, came in 1969, for their 'theological college' year of pastoral and practical training after their studies. They were a less formal community, with wives and children coming in and out. They in turn were abolished in 1975 by a Commission on Theological Colleges, which decided that there were too many colleges, and some must close. There were further recriminations. After this the Church could find no further institutional use for the large and unmodernized buildings, so in 1976 the trustees let the buildings to the King's School which needed more space than was available in the precincts. The rent was to be used for 'educational purposes' for the Anglican Commission. This has proved to be a sensible and successful use for the old college. The trustees arranged yet another charter (1979), taking the style of the 'Trustees of St Augustine's Foundation'.

Thus in 1996 the North Holmes estate is occupied by Christ Church College of Higher Education, the King's School occupies the old St Augustine's College buildings including the Bailey House (cemetery gate). The School now owns the site (since 1993), including the Tudor garden and the playing field above the infirmary. English Heritage holds the site of the church and excavated monastic buildings in Guardianship, though the land belongs to the trustees, as does the garden alongside the prison wall. The garden on the hospital site was handed over to the city in 1977.

The hospital ground became available for excavation in 1971 and exploratory trenches were dug the next year. There were three seasons of archaeology along the south side of the church, 1974–6, directed by David Sherlock, and more work in 1977–8 on the south tower at the west end of the nave directed by Humphrey Woods. Andrew Saunders re-examined the Anglo-Saxon foundations at the west end of the nave in 1955–7 and in the kitchen area in 1960. Frank Jenkins had two seasons at St Pancras' chapel. From 1983 to August 1996 the Canterbury Archaeological Trust has excavated or carried out watching briefs on eighteen occasions in the area of the outer court, now occupied by Christ Church College. The cellarer's building on the south side and the long north range (which may include the bakehouse and brewhouse) have been identified. In 1996 the Oxford Archaeological Unit excavated in the former lay cemetery (the front yard of the hospital), in advance of the construction of a museum and visitor reception building.

A museum or some suitable place to display artefacts has long been required. The finds from the early excavations were at first displayed in a St Augustine's College museum in the undercroft of the library. In later years larger objects were on the covered steps under the library porch. In 1969 it was agreed with the trustees that larger items should go to the Department of the Environment's store at Dover Castle, and smaller items to Fortress House in London. From 1969 to 1981 there was a large hut on the site near the custodian's hut (then at the north-west corner of the playing field). The hut housed a useful and instructive display of finds and a model, which were appreciated by many visitors. In the autumn of 1981 the hut was closed, and the contents removed to Dover. It was said that the site might be closed for the winter to save paying a custodian. Fortunately this did not happen, but it was alarming for local supporters. Gradually things improved. 1988 was the millennium of the death of St Dunstan in 988. He had extended the Abbey church, and added the name of St Augustine to those of Sts Peter and Paul in its dedication in 978. For the Dunstan Year a temporary display was made on the site, and there was a new guide book. New explanatory boards were put up in the ruins, which made use of the guide book illustrations. In 1989 St Augustine's was declared a World Heritage Site, along with the Cathedral and its precinct, and with St Martin's Church. It is to be hoped that the St Augustine celebrations of 1997 and its opening of the new facilities for visitors will introduce more people to a very ancient and holy place, which through the industry of a succession of friends or devotees since the days of Beresford Hope, has been handed on to the present generation.

The kings of Kent

Susan Kelly

From Æthelberht I to Eadric

Æthelberht I (accession probably *c.* 580 x 593, died
24 February 616). Married: (a) Bertha (who
predeceased her husband); (b) Anon (the one that
Eadbald married)

Eadbald (616–40). Married: (a) his stepmother (whom
he divorced); (b) Ymme (apparently a Frank)

Eorcenberht (640 to 14 July 664). Married Seaxburh
(daughter of King Anna of the East Angles)

Ecgberht (July 664 to July 673)

Hlothhere (July 673 to 6 February 685)

Eadric (February 685 to the summer or autumn of 686)

Foreign usurpers *c.* 686–*c.* 692

Hlothhere was killed during an episode of civil war
with his nephew Eadric, who himself died soon
afterwards. There followed a brief period during
which pretenders from other kingdoms laid claim to
Kent. These included:

Mul, imposed on Kent in 686 by his brother, King
Cædwalla of Wessex, and killed by the people of Kent
in the following year. He is said to have been buried at
St Augustine's.

Swæfheard, son of King Sebbi of Essex, who gained
the kingship at some point between 1 March 687 and
28 February 688, and who died or was deposed
between July 692 and 694. He ruled jointly with
Oswine and then with Wihtred.

Oswine, who may have been sponsored by the king of
Mercia, became king in Kent at some point between
27 January 688 and 26 January 689, and he died or
was deposed after 27 January 690 and before July
692. He ruled jointly with Swæfheard.

From Wihtred to Æthelberht II

Wihtred, son of the earlier King Ecgberht and thus a
member of the Kentish royal dynasty, managed to
establish himself as king, probably in the autumn of

691. In July 692 he was ruling jointly with
Swæfheard, but by 17 July 694 he was sole ruler in
Kent. Wihtred married three times: Cynegyth,
Æthelburh and Wærburh. He died 23 April 725,
leaving the kingdom to his three sons: Æthelberht,
Eadberht and Alric. The last of these (probably half-
brother to the other two) disappears immediately from
the record. Æthelberht (II) and Eadberht (I) appear to
have divided the kingdom between them. Æthelberht
ruled east Kent until his death in 762, when he was
succeeded by Eadberht (II), probably his son.
Eadberht I ruled west Kent, and when he died in 748
he was succeeded by his son Eardwulf.

Following 762

The stability of the divided kingdom broke down after
the removal of the strong hand of Æthelberht II. There
was a rapid turnover of rulers, their areas of jurisdiction
uncertain, and some of them probably of non-Kentish
origin: Eadberht II (762–*c.* 764), Sigered (*c.* 762–*c.*
764), Eanmund (*c.* 764) and Heahberht (*c.* 765). By
765 Kent was dominated by Offa, king of Mercia. He
may at first have ruled through a local ruler, Ecgberht
(king by *c.* 765), who seems to have had ties with the
West Saxon dynasty. There is reason to believe that
Ecgberht led a successful Kentish rebellion in 776, and
ruled independently until *c.* 784 or 785; he may have
been succeeded by, or co-operated with, a certain
Ealhmund who appears as king in a document dated
784. But by 785 King Offa had crushed any remaining
Kentish independence and was ruling the kingdom
directly from Mercia. A brief rebellion broke out after
Offa's death in 796, led by 'King' Eadberht Præn,
apparently a priest (he may have been a member of the
Kentish royal dynasty forced into holy orders in order
to disqualify him from the succession). This rebellion
was brutally crushed in 798. Thereafter Kent remained
a province of the Mercian kingdom until *c.* 825, and
then a province of the West Saxon kingdom.

The abbots of St Augustine's

From the foundation to the
Norman Conquest *by Susan Kelly*

The primary sources for the dates and sequence of the Anglo-Saxon abbots are the works of the later medieval histories of the abbey: Thomas Sprott, William Thorne and Thomas of Elmham. They provide full details, but much of their information is seriously flawed and in many instances may reflect fictional reconstruction (see p. 41).

The earliest abbots

1 Peter (probably died 614)
2 John (traditional dates 607–18)
3 Ruffinianus (traditional dates 618–26)
4 Graciosus (traditional dates 626–38)
5 Petronius (traditional dates 638–54)
6 Nathanael (traditional dates 654–67)
(Vacancy 667–9)
7 Benedict Biscop (*c.* 669–70)
8 Hadrian (669 or 670 to 709 or 710)
9 Albinus (appointed 709 or 710; traditional date of death 732)
10 Nothbaldus (traditional dates 732–48)
11 Aldhun (traditional dates 748–60, but probably remained abbot until at least 762)
12 Jænberht (probably 762–4)
13 Æthelnoth (probably appointed 764; traditional date of death 787)
14 Guthheard (traditional dates 787–803)
15 Cunred (traditional dates 803–22)
16 Wernoth (traditional dates 822–44, but may have been appointed in or before 805 and still seems to have been abbot in 838)

17 Dryhtnoth (traditional dates 844–64)
18 Wynhere (traditional dates 864–6, but mentioned in two charters of 845 and so may have preceded Dryhtnoth)

The century of uncertainty *c.* 845–946

For the period between the abbacy of Wynhere and the appointment of Abbot Ælfric, supposedly in 942, the later St Augustine's historians provide a list of fifteen names. By the fifteenth century these had also been supplied with dates. But there is good reason to distrust this information and to believe that many of these names were taken from a separate source, perhaps a confraternity-list: it is very unlikely that these fifteen men were all abbots of St Augustine's and possible that none of them were:

Beahmund (866–74)
Cyneberht (874–9)
Etans (879–83)
Dægmund (883–6)
Alfred (886–94)
Ceolberht (894–902)
Beccanus (902–7)
Æthelwold (907–10)
Tilberht (910–17)
Eadred (I) (917–20)
Alhmund (920–8)
Guttulf (928–35)
Eadred (II) (935–7)
Lulling (937–9)
Beornhelm (939–42)

The late Anglo-Saxon abbots

From the tenth century onwards some independent evidence is available from abbots' attestations to land-charters, which makes it possible to check the dates given by the St Augustine's historians. It transpires that these are massively incorrect for the middle of the tenth century and slightly astray for later periods:

Wigstan (not mentioned by historians, but attests a diploma of 946 as abbot of St Augustine's)

Eadhelm (not mentioned by historians, but appears to have been abbot from *c.* 949 until *c.* 958)

Ælfric (abbot from *c.* 959; traditional date of death 971)

Æthelnoth (traditional dates 971–80)

Sigeric (? *c.* 980–? *c.* 985)

Wulfric I (? 985–1006)

Ælfmær (1006–(1023 x 1027))

Wulfric II (1045–61)

Æthelsige (1061–(1067 x 1070))

From the Norman Conquest to the Dissolution

From 1070 to 1220 based on D. Knowles, C.N.L. Brooke and V. London, *The Heads of Religious Houses in England and Wales* (Cambridge, 1972).

From 1220 to 1538 by Margaret Sparks, based on *Victoria History of the County of Kent*, 2 (1926), with cross reference to Thomas of Elmham and William Thorne, and to the *Calendars of Patent Rolls* under the year in which the king notified the pope of his approval of the election.

Dates given are of the abbot's election and death, except where indicated otherwise.

Scolland or Scotland (1070–87)

Wido or Guy (1087–*c.* 1093)

Hugh I de Flori (Fleury?) (date of election uncertain, blessed as abbot 1108, died 1126)

Hugh II of Trottiscliffe (1126–51)

Silvester (1151–61)

Clarembald (1163–73, deposed)

(Vacancy 1173–5)

Roger I (1175–1213)

Alexander (1213–20)

Hugh III (1220–4)

Robert of Battle (1224–53)

Roger II of Chichester (1253–73)

Nicholas Thorne (1273–83, resigned)

Thomas Fyndon (1283–1309)

Ralph Burne (1309–34)

Thomas Poucyn (1334–43)

William Drulege (1343–6)

John Devenish (1346–8)

Thomas Colwell (1348–75)

Michael Pecham (1375–87)

William Welde (elected 1387, blessed 1389, died 1405)

Thomas Hunden (1405–20)

Marcellus Daundelyon (1420–6)

John Hawkhurst (1427–30)

George Pensherst (1430–57)

James Sevenoke (1457–64)

William Sellyng (1464–82, resigned)

John Dunster (1482–96)

John Dygon (1487–1510)

Thomas Hampton (1510–22)

John Essex or Foche (1522–38, surrendered the Abbey to the crown)

Further reading

1 Primary sources

Augustine of Canterbury (?):
  Sermons, ed. L. Machielson 'Fragments
    patristiques non identifiés du MS
    Vat. Pal. 577', *Sacris Erudiri*, 12 (1961),
    488–539
Bede:
  *Bede's Ecclesiastical History of the English
    People*, ed. B. Colgrave and R.A.B. Mynors
    (Oxford 1969; rev. edn 1991)
Charters:
  *Charters of St Augustine's Abbey, Canterbury,
    and Minster-in-Thanet*, ed. S.E. Kelly, Anglo-
    Saxon Charters iv (London 1995)
Goscelin of Saint-Bertin:
  Historia Translationis S. Augustini, Acta
    Sanctorum Maii vi, ed. G. Henschenius and
    D. Papebroch (Antwerp 1688), 411–36
  Vita Maior S. Augustini, ed. Migne, Patrologia
    Latina, 80, columns 41–94
  Vita Minor S. Augustini, ed. Migne, Patrologia
    Latina, 150, columns 743–64
  Rollason, D.W. 'Goscelin of Canterbury's
    Account of the Translation and Miracles of
    St Mildrith (*BHL* 5961/4): and Edition with
    Notes', *Medieval Studies* xlviii (1986),
    139–210
Gregory the Great:
  Anonymous, *Vita Gregorii*, ed. and trans. B.
    Colgrave, *The Earliest Life of Gregory the
    Great* (Lawrence, Kans. 1969)
  Letters, *Registrum Epistolarum*, ed. P. Ewald
    and L.M. Hartmann, Monumenta Germanae
    Historica, Epistolae, 1 & 2 (Berlin 1887–99)
  the same, ed. D. Norberg, Corpus
    Christianorum Series Latina, CXL–CLXA
    (Tornhout 1982)
Thomas of Elmham:
  Speculum Augustinianum: Historia monasterii

  S. Augustini Cantuariensis, ed. C. Hardwick,
    Rolls Series (London 1858)
Thorne, William:
  Davis, A.H. *William Thorne's Chronicle of
    St Augustine's Abbey, Canterbury* (Oxford
    1934)
  Twysden, R. *Historiae Anglicanae scriptores
    decem* (London 1652)
Various:
  English Historical Documents, c. 500–1042, ed.
    D. Whitelock, English Historical Documents
    i, 2nd edn (London 1979)

Other primary sources (published)

Ballard, A. 'An Eleventh-century Inquisition of St
  Augustine's, Canterbury', *British Academy
  Records of the Social and Economic History of
  England and Wales* iv (1920)
Blake, E.O. (ed.) *Liber Eliensis*, Camden Society,
  3rd series 92 (1962)
Bosanquet, G. (trans.) *Eadmer's History of Recent
  Events in England* (London 1964)
Chibnall, M. (ed.) *The Ecclesiastical History of
  Orderic Vitalis*, vol. 2 (Oxford 1990)
Clover, H. and Gibson, M. (eds) *The Letters of
  Lanfranc, Archbishop of Canterbury* (Oxford
  1979)
Davis, G.R.C. *Medieval Cartularies of Great
  Britain and Ireland* (London 1958)
Davis, H.W.C. *Regesta regum Anglo-
  Normannorum, i: William I and William II*
  (Oxford 1913)
Douglas, D.C. (ed.) *The Domesday Monachorum
  of Christ Church, Canterbury*, Royal Historical
  Society (London 1944)
Douglas, D.C. and Greenaway, G.W. (eds) *English
  Historical Documents, 1042–1189* (London
  1953)
Earle, J. and Plummer, C. (eds) *Two of the Saxon*

Chronicles Parallel, 2 vols (Oxford 1892)

Erskine, R.W.H. (ed.) *Great Domesday: facsimile* (London 1986)

Farmer, D.H. *The Rule of St Benedict*, Early English Manuscripts in Facsimile, 15 (Copenhagen 1968)

Harmer, F.E. (ed.) *Anglo-Saxon Writs* (Manchester 1952)

Johnson, C. and Cronne, H.A. *Regesta regum Anglo-Normannorum, ii: Henry I* (Oxford 1956)

Knowles, D. *The Monastic Constitutions of Lanfranc* (London 1951)

Lanfranc, *Acta*, translated in *English Historical Documents*, 2, 631–5

Morgan, P. (ed.) *Domesday Book: Kent* (Chichester 1983)

Reyner, C. *Apostolatus Benedictinorum in Anglia* (Douai 1626)

Robertson, A.J. (ed.) *Anglo-Saxon Charters* (Cambridge 1956)

Rule, M. (ed.) *Eadmer's Historia novorum in Anglia*, Rolls Series (London 1884)

Sawyer, P.H. (ed.) *Anglo-Saxon Charters: an annotated list and bibliography*, British Academy (London 1968)

Stevenson, J. (trans.) *The Church Historians of England*, vol. 3, part 2 (William of Malmesbury, History of the Kings of England) (London 1854)

Stubbs, W. (ed.) *Memorials of St Dunstan, Archbishop of Canterbury*, Rolls Series (London 1874)

Stubbs, W. (ed.) *The Historical Works of Gervase of Canterbury*, 2 vols, Rolls Series (London 1879–80)

Stubbs, W. (ed.) *William of Malmesbury, De gestis regum Anglorum*, Rolls Series (London 1887)

Symons, T. *Regularis Concordia: the monastic agreement* (London 1953)

Thompson, E.M. (ed.) *Customary of the Benedictine Monasteries of St Augustine, Canterbury and St Peter, Westminster*, 2 vols (London 1902, 1904)

Turner, G.J. and Salter, H.E. (eds) *The Register of St Augustine's Abbey, Canterbury, Commonly Called The Black Book*, 2 vols, British Academy (London 1915–24)

Van Caeneghem, R.C. (ed.) *English Lawsuits from William I to Richard I*, 2 vols, Selden Society (London 1990–1)

Primary sources (unpublished – see also section 2.vii below)

British Library MS Cotton Claudius D x (The *Red Book* of St Augustine's)

British Library MS Julius D ii

Public Record Office MS E 164/27 (The *White Book* of St Augustine's)

2 Secondary sources

i. St Augustine and his times

Cameron, A. *The Mediterranean World in Late Antiquity* (London 1993)

Constable, G. *Medieval Monasticism: a select bibliography* (Toronto 1976)

Farmer, D.H. (ed.) *Benedict's Disciples* (Leominster, 2nd edn 1995)

Ferrari, G. *Early Roman Monasteries* (Rome 1957)

Herrin, J. *The Formation of Christendom* (Oxford 1987)

Hughes, K. *The Church in Early Irish Society* (London 1966)

Jones, C., Wainwright, G. and Yarnold, E. *The Study of Liturgy* (London 1980)

Jungman, J.A. *Early Liturgy to the Time of Gregory the Great* (London 1960)

Llewellyn, P. *Rome in the Dark Ages* (London 1971)

Markus, R.A., 'St Gregory the Great's Europe', *Transactions of the Royal Historical Society*, 31 (1981), 21–36

Mayr-Harting, H. *The Coming of Christianity to Anglo-Saxon England* (London, 3rd edn 1991)

Meens, R. 'Background to Augustine's Mission to England', *Anglo-Saxon England*, 23 (1994), 5–17

Meyvaert, P. 'Bede's Text of the *Libellus responsionum*', in *England Before the Conquest*, ed. P. Clemoes and K. Hughes (Cambridge 1971)

Richards, J. *The Popes and the Papacy in the Early Middle Ages* (London 1979)

Richards, J. *Consul of God: the life and times of Gregory the Great* (London 1980)

Riché, P. *Education and Culture in the Barbarian West, 6th–8th Century* (Columbia, S Carolina 1976)

Straw, C. *Gregory the Great: perfection in imperfection* (Berkeley 1988)

Wallace Hadrill, J.M. *The Frankish Church* (Oxford 1983)

Wood, I. *The Merovingian Kingdoms* (Harlow 1994)

Wood, I. 'The Mission of St Augustine of Canterbury to the English', *Speculum* 69 (1994), 1–17

ii. Anglo-Saxon history of St Augustine's Abbey

Barlow, F. 'Two Notes: Cnut's second pilgrimage and Queen Emma's disgrace in 1042', *English Historical Review* lxxiii (1958), 649–56

Barlow, F. *The English Church 1000–1066* (London and New York, 2nd edn 1979)

Bischoff, B. and Lapidge, M. (eds) *Biblical Commentaries from the Canterbury School of Theodore and Hadrian* (Cambridge 1994)

Bonner, G. (ed.) *Famulus Christi: essays in commemoration of the thirteenth centenary of the birth of the Venerable Bede* (London 1976)

Brooks, N. *The Early History of the Church of Canterbury: Christ Church from 597 to 1066* (Leicester 1984)

Brooks, N. 'Romney Marsh in the Early Middle Ages', in *Romney Marsh: evolution, occupation, reclamation*, ed. J. Eddison and C. Green, Oxford University Committee for Archaeology, Monograph no. 24 (Oxford 1988), 90–104

Brooks, N. 'The Creation and Early Structure of the Kingdom of Kent', in *The Origins of Anglo-Saxon Kingdoms*, ed. S. Bassett (London and New York 1989), 55–74

Dumville, D.N. *English Caroline Script and Monastic History: studies in Benedictinism*, AD 950–1030 (Woodbridge 1993)

Everitt, A. *Continuity and Colonization: the evolution of Kentish settlement* (Leicester 1986)

Hasted, E. *The History and Topographical Survey of the County of Kent*, 2nd edn, 12 vols (Canterbury 1797–1801)

Hunter, M. 'The Facsimiles in Thomas Elmham's History of St Augustine's', *The Library*, 5th series xxviii (1973), 215–20

Kelly, S.E. 'Trading Privileges from Eighth-century England', *Early Medieval Europe* i (1992), 3–27

Keynes, S. 'The Control of Kent in the Ninth Century', *Early Medieval Europe* ii (1993), 111–31

Knowles, D. 'Studies in Monastic History: IV – The Growth of Exemption', *Downside Review*, new series xxxi (1932), 201–31, 396–436

Krüger, K.H. *Königsgrabkirchen der Franken, Angelsachsen und Langobarden bis zur Mitte des 8. Jahrhunderts: ein historischer Katalog*, Münstersche Mittelalter-Schriften iv (Munich 1971)

Lapidge, M. 'The School of Theodore and Hadrian', *Anglo-Saxon England* xv (1986), 45–72

Lapidge, M. (ed.) *Archbishop Theodore* (Cambridge 1995)

Levison, W. *England and the Continent in the Eighth Century* (Oxford 1946)

Lewis, J. *The History and Antiquities, Ecclesiastical and Civil, of the Isle of Thanet in Kent* (London, 2nd edn 1736)

Ramsay, N., Sparks, M., Tatton-Brown, T. *St Dunstan, His Life, Times and Cult* (Woodbridge 1992)

Rollason, D.W. *The Mildrith Legend: a study in early medieval hagiography in England* (Leicester 1982)

Rollason, D.W. *Saints and Relics in Anglo-Saxon England* (Oxford 1989)

Somner, W. *The Antiquities of Canterbury* (London, 2nd edn 1703)

Tatton-Brown, T. 'The City and Diocese of Canterbury in St Dunstan's Time', in *St Dunstan, His Life, Times and Cult*, ed. N. Ramsay, M. Sparks and T. Tatton-Brown (Woodbridge 1992), 75–87

Witney, K.P. *The Jutish Forest: a study of the Weald of Kent from 450–1380 AD* (London 1976)

iii. Post-Conquest history of St Augustine's Abbey

(See 'A note on sources', p. 172, regarding this section)

a. Ecclesiastical history

Barlow, F. *The English Church, 1066–1154* (London 1979)

Blair, J. 'Introduction: from minster to parish church', in *Minsters and Parish Churches: the local church in transition, 950–1200*, ed. John Blair, Oxford University Committee for Archaeology, Monograph no. 17 (Oxford 1988), 1–19

Brett, M. *The English Church under Henry I* (London 1975)

Brett, M. 'Gundulf and the Cathedral Communities of Canterbury and Rochester', in *Canterbury and the Norman Conquest*, ed. R. Eales and R. Sharpe (London 1995), 15–25

Burton, J. *Monastic and Religious Orders in Britain, 1000–1300* (Cambridge 1994)

Eales, R. and Sharpe, R. *Canterbury and the Norman Conquest: churches, saints and scholars, 1066–1109* (London 1995)

Gibson, M. *Lanfranc of Bec* (Oxford 1978)

Knowles, D. *The Religious Orders in England*, 3 vols (Cambridge 1948–59)

Knowles, D. *The Monastic Order in England* (Cambridge 1963)

Lackner, B. *Eleventh-century Background of Cîteaux*, Cistercian Studies Series, 8 (Washington 1972)

Levison, W. *England and the Continent in the Eleventh Century* (Oxford 1946)

Southern, R.W. *Saint Anselm* (Cambridge 1990)

b. Political and social history

Bates, D. 'The Character and Career of Odo, Bishop of Bayeux (1049/50–1097)', *Speculum* 50 (1975), 1–20

Du Boulay, F.R.H. *The Lordship of Canterbury* (London 1966)

Eales, R. 'Local Loyalties in Norman England: Kent in Stephen's reign', *Anglo-Norman Studies* 8 (1986), 88–108

Eales, R. 'An Introduction to the Kent Domesday', in *The Kent Domesday*, ed. A. Williams and R.W.H. Erskine (London 1992)

Holt, J.C. 'The Origins of the Constitutional Tradition in England', in *Magna Carta and Medieval Government* (London 1985), 1–22

Hooper, N. 'Some Observations on the Navy in Late Anglo-Saxon England', *Studies in Medieval History Presented to R. Allen Brown*, ed. C. Harper-Bill, C. Holdsworth and J.L. Nelson (Woodbridge 1989), 203–13

John, E. 'The Litigation of an Exempt House: St Augustine's, Canterbury, 1182–1237', *Bulletin of the John Rylands Library* 39 (1956–7), 390–415

Keynes, S. 'The Æthelings in Normandy', *Anglo-Norman Studies* 13 (1990), 173–205

Sawyer, P.H. 'The "Original Returns" and Domesday Book', *English Historical Review* 70 (1955), 177–97

Tatton-Brown, T. *Canterbury in Domesday Book*, Canterbury Archaeological Trust, Heritage series 1 (1987)

Tatton-Brown, T. 'The Churches of Canterbury Diocese in the Eleventh Century', *Minsters and Parish-churches: the local church in transition, 950–1200*, ed. J. Blair, Oxford University Committee for Archaeology, Monograph no. 17 (1988), 105–18

Urry, W. 'The Normans in Canterbury', *Annales de Normandie* 8 (1958), 119–38

Urry, W. *Canterbury under the Angevin Kings* (London 1967)

Ward, G. 'The Lists of Saxon Churches in the Domesday Monachorum and White Book of St Augustine', *Archaeologia Cantiana* 45 (1933), 60–89

c. Literary and cultural

Barlow, F. 'Goscelin of St Bertin', in *The Life of King Edward the Confessor* (London 1962), 91–111

Brooks, N.P. and Walker, H.E. 'The Authority and Interpretation of the Bayeux Tapestry', *Anglo-Norman Studies* 1 (1979), 1–34

Campbell, J. 'Some Twelfth-century Views of the Anglo-Saxon Past', *Essays in Anglo-Saxon History* (London 1986), 208–28

Colker, M.L. 'A Hagiographical Polemic: Goscelin's *Libellus contra inanes sancte virginis Mildrethae usurpatores*', *Medieval Studies* 39 (1977), 60–108

Dumville, D.N. 'Some Aspects of Annalistic Writing at Canterbury in the Eleventh and Early Twelfth Centuries', *Peritia* 2 (1983), 23–57

Emms, R. 'The Historical Traditions of St Augustine's Abbey, Canterbury', *Canterbury and the Norman Conquest*, ed. R. Eales and R. Sharpe (London 1995), 159–68

Gransden, A. *Historical Writing in England II: c. 1307 to the early sixteenth century* (London 1982)

Leclercq, J. *The Love of Learning and the Desire for God: a study of monastic culture*, trans. C. Misrahi (New York 1961)

Rigg, A.J. *A History of Anglo-Latin Literature: 1066–1422* (Cambridge 1992)

Rollason, D.W. *The Mildrith Legend: a study in early medieval hagiography in England* (Leicester 1983)

Sharpe, R. 'Goscelin's St Augustine and St Mildreth: hagiography and liturgy in context', *Journal of Theological Studies*, new series 41 (1990), 502–16

Sharpe, R. 'The Date of St Mildreth's Translation from Minster-in-Thanet to Canterbury', *Medieval Studies* 53 (1991a), 349–54

Sharpe, R. 'Eadmer's Letter to the Monks of Glastonbury Concerning St Dunstan's Disputed Remains', *The Archaeology and History of Glastonbury Abbey*, ed. L. Abrams and J. Carley (Woodbridge 1991b), 205–15

Sharpe, R. 'The Setting of St Augustine's Translation, 1091', *Canterbury and the Norman Conquest*, ed. R. Eales and R. Sharpe (London 1995), 1–13

Tatton-Brown, T. 'The Beginnings of St Gregory's Priory and St John's Hospital in Canterbury', *Canterbury and the Norman Conquest*, ed. R. Eales and R. Sharpe (London 1995), 41–52

iv. Manuscripts and the arts

a. Sixth to ninth centuries

Alexander, J.J.G. *Insular Manuscripts 6th to the 9th Century* (London 1978)

Bayley, J. 'Evidence for Metalworking', in *Rescue Excavations at St Augustine's Abbey,*

Canterbury ed. P. Bennett (Canterbury Archaeological Trust, 2nd Monograph Series, in preparation)

Bishop, T.A.M. *English Caroline Minuscule* (Oxford 1971)

Buckton, D. 'Late 10th and 11th Century Cloisonné Enamel Brooches', *Medieval Archaeology* 30 (1986), 8–18

Budny, M. 'The Visual Arts and Crafts', in *The Cambridge Guide to the Arts in Britain*, ed. B. Ford, vol. 1, *Early Britain* (Cambridge, 2nd edn 1992), 122–78

Evison, V. 'An Enamelled Disc from Great Saxham', *Proceedings of the Suffolk Institute of Archaeology and History* 34 (1977), 1–13

Haseloff, G. *Email im frühen Mittelalter. Frühchristliche Kunst von der Spätantike bis zu den Karolingern* (Marburg 1990)

Henderson, G. *Losses and Lacunae in Early Insular Art*, University of York Medieval Monograph series (York 1982)

Hicks, M. *Archaeological Excavations at Canterbury Christ Church College: assessment report on excavations conducted between 1983–1995*, Canterbury Archaeological Trust (Canterbury 1996)

Hicks, M. and Bennett, P. 'Christ Church College', in *Canterbury's Archaeology* 18 (1993–4), 1–4

Hubert, J., Porcher, J. and Volbach, W.F. *Europe in the Dark Ages* (London 1969)

Kuhn, S.M. 'The Vespasian Psalter and the Old English Charter Hands', *Speculum* 18 (1943), 458–83

Kuhn, S.M. 'From Canterbury to Lichfield', *Speculum* 23 (1948), 591–629

Kuhn, S.M. 'Some Early Mercian Manuscripts', *The Review of English Studies*, new series 8 (1957), 355–74

Lasko, P. *Ars Sacra, 800–1200* (Newhaven and London, 2nd edn 1994)

McGurk, P. 'An Anglo-Saxon Bible Fragment of the Late Eighth Century, Royal I E.VI', *Journal of the Warburg and Courtauld Institutes* 25 (1962), 18–34

Nordenfalk, C. *Celtic and Anglo-Saxon Painting: book illumination in the British Isles 600–800* (London 1977)

Rigold, S.E. 'Six Copper-Alloy Objects from St Augustine's, Canterbury', *The Antiquaries Journal* 50 (1970), 345–7

Roach Smith, C. 'Merovingian Coins etc., Discovered at St Martin's, near Canterbury', *Numismatic Chronicle* 7 (1845), 187–91

Sherlock, D. and Woods, H. *St Augustine's Abbey:*

report on excavations, 1960–78, Kent Archaeological Society, Monograph no. 4 (Maidstone 1988)

Sisam, K. 'Canterbury, Lichfield and the Vespasian Psalter', *The Review of English Studies*, new series 7 (1956), 1–10, 113–31

Webster, L. and Backhouse, J. (eds) *The Making of England: Anglo-Saxon art and culture AD 600–900*, The British Museum (London 1991)

Wilson, D.M. *Anglo-Saxon Art from the Seventh Century to the Norman Conquest* (London 1986)

Wood, I. 'Frankish Hegemony in England', in *The Age of Sutton Hoo: the seventh century in north-western Europe*, ed. M. Carver (Woodbridge 1992), 235–41

Wormald, F. *The Miniatures in the Gospels of St Augustine* (Cambridge 1954)

Wright, D. *The Vespasian Psalter*, Early English Manuscripts in Facsimile, 14 (Copenhagen 1967)

b. Late Anglo-Saxon and post Conquest

Alexander, J.J.G. *Norman Illumination at Mont St Michel* (Oxford 1970)

Backhouse, J., Turner, D.H. and Webster, L. *The Golden Age of Anglo-Saxon Art, 966–1066*, The British Museum (London 1984)

Dodwell, C.R. *The Canterbury Schools of Illumination* (Cambridge 1954)

Dodwell, C.R. *Anglo-Saxon Art: a new perspective* (Manchester 1982)

Gameson, R. 'English Manuscript Art in the Late Eleventh Century: Canterbury and its context', in *Canterbury and the Norman Conquest*, ed. R. Eales and R. Sharpe (London 1995), 95–144

Heslop, T.A. 'The Canterbury Calendars and the Norman Conquest', in *Canterbury and the Norman Conquest*, ed. R. Eales and R. Sharpe (London 1995), 53–86

James, M.R. *The Ancient Libraries of Canterbury and Dover* (Cambridge 1903)

Kauffmann, C.M. *Romanesque Manuscripts 1066–1190* (London 1975)

Ker, N.R. *Medieval Libraries of Great Britain* (London, 2nd edn 1964)

Lapidge, M. 'Surviving Booklists from Anglo-Saxon England', in *Literature and Learning in Anglo-Saxon England: studies presented to Peter Clemoes*, ed. M. Lapidge and H. Gneuss (Cambridge 1985), 33–89

Lehmann-Brockhaus, O. *Lateinische Schriftquellen zur Kunst in England, Wales und Schottland vom Jahre 901 bis zum Jahre 1307*, 5 vols (Munich 1955–60)

Orchard, N. 'The Bosworth Psalter and St Augustine's Missal', in *Canterbury and the Norman Conquest*, ed. R. Eales and R. Sharpe (London 1995), 87–94

Rule, M. *The Missal of St Augustine's Abbey, Canterbury* (Cambridge 1896)

Sharpe, R. 'The Setting of St Augustine's Translation, 1091', in *Canterbury and the Norman Conquest*, ed. R. Eales and R. Sharpe (London 1995), 1–14

Temple, E. *Anglo-Saxon Manuscripts 900–1066* (London 1976)

Zarnecki, G. (ed.) *English Romanesque Art 1066–1200*, The Arts Council (London 1984)

v. Architecture

a. The Anglo-Saxon and Romanesque churches of St Augustine's Abbey

(For a full list of excavation reports 1844–1947 see Sparks 1985, cited in section vii below)

Blagg, T. 'Some Roman Architectural Traditions in the Early Saxon Churches of Kent', in *Collectanea Historica*, ed. A. Detsicas (Kent Archaeological Society 1981), 50–3

Blockley K. et al. *Archaeology of Canterbury, 5, Excavations in the Marlow Car Park and Surrounding Areas* (Canterbury 1995)

Blockley, K. *Excavations in the Nave and South-West Transept of Canterbury Cathedral* (Canterbury Archaeological Trust, 2nd Monograph series, 1, forthcoming 1997)

Gem, R. 'The Significance of the 11th-century Rebuilding of Christ Church and St Augustine's Abbey, Canterbury, in the Development of Romanesque Architecture', in *Medieval Art and Architecture at Canterbury before 1220*, British Archaeological Association, Conference Transactions, 5 (1982), 1–19

Gem, R. 'Canterbury and the Cushion Capital, a Commentary on Passages from Goscelin's *De miraculis Sancti Augustini*', in *Romanesque and Gothic: essays for George Zarnecki*, ed. N. Stratford (Woodbridge 1987), 83–101

Gem, R. 'Reconstructions of St Augustine's Abbey, Canterbury, in the Anglo-Saxon Period', in *St Dunstan, His Life, Times and Cult*, ed. N. Ramsay, M. Sparks and T. Tatton-Brown (Woodbridge 1992), 57–73

Jenkins, F. 'St Martin's Church, Canterbury: a survey of the earliest structural features', *Medieval Archaeology* 9 (1965), 11–15

Jenkins, F. 'Preliminary Report on the Excavation at the Church of St Pancras at Canterbury', *Canterbury Archaeology* (1975/6), 4–5

McAleer, P. 'The Ethelbert Tower of St Augustine's Abbey, Canterbury', *Journal of the British Archaeological Association* 140 (1987), 88–111

Parsons, D. (ed.) *Stone Quarrying and Building in England, AD 43–1525* (Chichester 1990)

Peers, C.R. and Clapham, A.W. 'St Augustine's Abbey Church, Canterbury, Before the Norman Conquest', *Archaeologia* 77 (1928), 201–18

Potts, R.V. 'The Plan of St Augustine's Abbey, Canterbury', with 'A Note on the Layout of the Cloisters' by A.W. Clapham, *Archaeologia Cantiana* 46 (1934), 179–94

Routledge, C.F. 'St Martin's Church, Canterbury', *Archaeologia Cantiana* 22 (1897), 1–28

St John Hope, W.H. 'Excavations at St Austin's Abbey, Canterbury: the Chapel of St Pancras', *Archaeologia Cantiana* 25 (1902), 222–37

St John Hope, W.H. 'Recent Discoveries in the Abbey Church of St Austin of Canterbury', *Archaeologia* 66 (1915), 377–400 (also published in *Archaeologia Cantiana* 32 (1917), 1–26)

Saunders, A.D. 'Excavations in the Church of St Augustine's Abbey, Canterbury, 1955–58', *Medieval Archaeology* 20 (1978), 25–63

Sherlock, D. and Woods, H. *St Augustine's Abbey, Report on Excavations, 1960–78*, Kent Archaeological Society, Monograph series 4 (Maidstone 1988)

Sparks, M. (ed.) *The Parish of St Martin and St Paul*, Canterbury (Canterbury 1980)

b. General architecture, sixth to twelfth centuries

Clapham, A. *English Romanesque Architecture*, 2 vols (Oxford 1930, repr. 1964)

Duval, N. (ed.) *Naissance des arts chrétiens: atlas des monuments paléochrétiens de la France* (Paris 1991)

Fernie, E. *The Architecture of the Anglo-Saxons* (London 1983)

Gem, R. 'Architecture', in *Cambridge Cultural History of Britain*, 1, *Early Britain*, ed. B. Ford (Cambridge, 2nd edn 1992)

Gem, R. 'Architecture of the Anglo-Saxon Church, 735 to 870: from Archbishop Ecgberht to Archbishop Ceolnoth', *Journal of the British Archaeological Association* 146 (1993), 29–66

Heitz, C. *La France pré-romane* (Paris 1987)

Krautheimer, R. *Early Christian and Byzantine Architecture* (Harmondsworth, 2nd edn 1975)

Krautheimer, R. *Rome, Profile of a City, 312–1308* (Princeton 1980)

Kubach, H.E. *Romanesque Architecture* (New York 1975)

Musset, L. *Normandie romane, la Basse Normandie*, Zodiaque series, La Nuit des Temps (1987)

Vergnole, E. *L'Art roman en France: architecture, sculpture, peinture* (Paris 1994)

vi. The Abbey precinct, liberty and estate

(See also sections 2.ii, iii and v preceding)

Bennett, P. 'Rescue Excavations in the Outer Court of St Augustine's Abbey 1983–4', *Archaeologia Cantiana* 103 (1986), 99–117

Cotton, C. 'A Contemporary List of the Benefactions of Thomas Ickham, *c.* 1415', *Archaeologia Cantiana* 37 (1925), 152–9

Evans, S. 'Excavations at St Augustine's Abbey, Canterbury', *Archaeologia Cantiana* 26 (1904), 1–8

Hamilton Thompson, A. 'A Descriptive Note on Sir W.H. St John Hope's Plan of the Infirmary of St Austin's Abbey', *Archaeologia Cantiana* 46 (1934), 123–218

Hussey, A. 'Further Notes from Kentish Wills', *Archaeologia Cantiana* 31 (1915), 118

McIntosh, K.H. (ed.) *Sturry, the Changing Scene* (Ramsgate 1972)

McIntosh, K.H. (ed.) *Fordwich, the Lost Port* (Ramsgate 1975)

McIntosh, K.H. (ed.) *Chislet and Westbere, Villages of the Stour Lathe* (Ramsgate 1979)

Munby, J., Sparks, M. and Tatton-Brown, T. 'Crown-post and King-strut Roofs in SE England', *Medieval Architecture* 37 (1983), 123–35

Rady, J. 'Excavations at St Martin's Hill, Canterbury', *Archaeologia Cantiana* 104 (1987), 123–218

Routledge, C.F. 'Excavations at St Austin's Abbey, Canterbury', *Archaeologia Cantiana* 25 (1902), 238–43

Somner, W. *The Antiquities of Canterbury* (Canterbury 1640); 2nd edn by N. Battely (London 1703)

Sparks, M. (ed.) *The Parish of St Martin and St Paul* (Canterbury 1980)

Tatton-Brown, T. 'Three Great Benedictine Houses in Kent: their buildings and topography', *Archaeologia Cantiana* 100 (1984), 179–85

Tatton-Brown, T. 'The Buildings and Topography of St Augustine's Abbey, Canterbury', *Journal of the British Archaeological Association* 144 (1991), 61–91

Tatton-Brown, T. 'The City and Diocese of Canterbury in St Dunstan's time', in *St Dunstan, His Life, Times and Cult*, ed. N. Ramsay, M. Sparks and T. Tatton-Brown (Woodbridge 1992), 75–88

vii. The Abbey site 1538–1997

Primary and secondary sources

St Augustine's College, Archives, unpublished: Dean and Chapter Archives, Canterbury (for references to papers used, see Sparks 1985 below)

Allan, M. *The Tradescants* (London 1964)

Clark, A. (ed.) *The Life and Times of Anthony Wood*, 3 (Oxford 1894), 401 (for reference to the earthquake in 1692)

Colvin, H.M. (ed.) *The History of the King's Works*, IV, pt. ii (London, 1982), 59–63

Legg, E.W. (ed.) 'A Relation of a Short Survey of the Western Counties Made by a Lt. of the Military Company in Norwich in 1635', *Camden Miscellany* XVI (3rd series, London 1936)

Needham, J. Accounts of King's New Lodging, unpublished: Bodleian MS Rawlinson D 799 (1539); MS Rawlinson D 781 (1542–3); British Library Add. MS 10109 (1543) and Longleat MS XXX (1541–5). Pages from Rawlinson D 781 have been published by Humphrey Woods, in M. Sparks (ed.) *The Parish of St Martin and St Paul, Canterbury* (Canterbury 1980), 76–8

Nichols, J.S. (ed.) 'Narratives of the Days of the Reformation', Camden Society 77 (London 1860)

Pole, R. (Cardinal) Letter on the re-introduction of monks to Canterbury, *Calendar of State Papers Venetian* VI (1861), no. 904

Sherlock, D. 'The Account of George Nycholl for St Augustine's 1552–1553', *Archaeologia Cantiana* 99 (1984), 25–46

Sparks, M. 'The Recovery and Excavation of the St Augustine's Abbey Site, 1844–1947', *Archaeologia Cantiana* 100 (1985), with references for excavation reports. Brief notes of excavated sites since 1983 are in the Canterbury Archaeological Trust *Annual Reports*

Tatton-Brown, T. 'The Buildings and Topography of St Augustine's Abbey, Canterbury', *Journal of the British Archaeological Association* 146 (1991), 61–91

Watson, A.G. 'John Twyne', *The Library* 8 (1986), 132–51

A note on sources relating to the post-Conquest history

(Full references are given in section 1 (pp. 165–6), or in section 2 as cited below.)

The starting-point for an investigation of St Augustine's lands and tenants is Domesday Book (Erskine 1986, Morgan 1983; 2.iii.b: Eales 1992) and the texts related to it. Two are published, the *Domesday Monachorum* of Christ Church (Douglas 1944) and the *Excerpta*, one of the three texts from the *White Book* of St Augustine's (Ballard 1920). Additional details are to be found in the two unpublished texts in the *White Book*, the *Noticia terrarum sancti Augustini* and the *Brevis recapitulacio solingorum* (2.iii.b: Sawyer 1955). All three texts have been updated in the twelfth century, as has the *White Book*'s list of minsters and dependent churches belonging to St Augustine's (analysed in 2.iii.b: Tatton-Brown 1988).

Of the Abbey's four cartularies, only the *Black Book* has been published (Turner and Salter 1915–24) and this contains the least amount of early material, though it is still of use for the understanding of the Anglo-Norman endowment. Both the *White Book* and BL Cotton Julius D ii contain much early material, including charters of Abbots Scolland and Hugh I and II, an early list of knights' fees, a memorandum on lands lost after the Conquest and much else, all of which would repay much more detailed analysis than has been possible in chapter 3; indeed a full description, or better still publication of both manuscripts, and the *Red Book* of St Augustine's (BL MS Cotton Claudius D x) is much to be desired. Fortunately the pre-Conquest charters of St Augustine's have been published by Dr Kelly, whose introduction discusses both the contents of the unpublished cartularies, and the relationship between them (Kelly 1995). An edition of the early Christ Church cartulary is in hand by Professor Robin Fleming; notice of it in chapter 3 is based on a lecture given by Professor Fleming at the Institute of Historical Research on 28 February 1996. The pre-Conquest disputes between the two communities are printed with translations in Robertson 1956, and the post-Conquest cases, also with translations, in van Caeneghem 1990–1.

There are a few notices of St Augustine's in the general histories of the Anglo-Norman period, notably Eadmer's *Historia Novorum* (Rule 1884, partially translated in Bosanquet 1964), Orderic Vitalis' *Historia Ecclesiastica* (Chibnall 1990, with parallel Latin text and translation) and William of Malmesbury's *De gestis regum Anglorum* (Stubbs 1887, translated Stevenson 1854), a modern edition of which, with parallel translation, is being prepared by Oxford Medieval Texts. The Lives of St Dunstan by Osbern and Eadmer give some details relating to the late eleventh century; both of these, and Eadmer's letter to the monks of Glastonbury, are printed in Stubbs 1874. The works of Gervase of Canterbury are edited by Stubbs 1879–80. The *Acta Lanfranci*, appended to the 'A' text of the *Anglo-Saxon Chronicle*, is printed in Earle and Plummer 1892, i, 287–92, and translated in Douglas and Greenaway 1953, 631–5.

An edition of Goscelin's Lives of the Canterbury saints is being prepared by Richard Sharpe. Goscelin's *Translatio* of St Mildrith has been printed and discussed by Rollason 1986. For the content and significance of Goscelin's works, chapter 4 relies on 2.iii.c: Colker 1977, Rollason 1983 and Sharpe 1991a, 1995. There is an account of Goscelin's career in 2.iii.c: Barlow 1962 and of that of his contemporary, Reginald of Canterbury, in Rigg 1992. Thomas Sprott's Chronicle is as yet unprinted from the manuscripts in the British Library and Lambeth Palace (BL Cotton Tiberius A ix, Lambeth Palace MS 419). The Latin text of William Thorne's Chronicle was printed in Sir Roger Twysden's *Historiae Anglicanae scriptores decem* of 1652, but chapter 4 has used the translation of Davis 1934. Elmham's work, the *Speculum Augustinianum*, is printed by Hardwick 1858 and discussed in 2.iii.c: Gransden 1982. There is a study of the historical traditions of St Augustine's in 2.iii.c: Emms 1995, more favourable than the assessment in 2.iii.a: Brett 1975 or 2.iii.b: John 1956–7; the latter deals with the long jurisdictional dispute between St Augustine's and the archbishops of Canterbury.

Index

(Page numbers in **bold** refer to illustrations)

The Authors

Dr Richard Gem has researched and published widely in the field of Anglo-Saxon and Norman architecture. He is currently Secretary of the Cathedrals Fabric Commission for England.

David Farmer was until his retirement Reader in History at Reading University and was at one time a Benedictine monk. He is author among other works of the Oxford Dictionary of Saints.

Sandy Heslop and *John Mitchell* both teach in the School of World Art and Museology at the University of East Anglia. The former is a specialist in Anglo-Saxon and Norman art; the latter in early medieval art in Italy. Both have published widely in their fields.

Dr Susan Kelly has recently published her research on the Anglo-Saxon charters of St Augustine's Abbey, which has made a major contribution to its early history. She is a research associate with the British Academy.

Margaret Sparks has made a special study of St Augustine's Abbey over many years and has published a guide to the site. She is also consultant historian to the Dean and Chapter of Canterbury.

Tim Tatton-Brown is an archaeologist and architectural historian specializing in the study of major medieval buildings. He has worked on the medieval topography and buildings of Kent for many years.

Dr Ann Williams is a specialist in late Anglo-Saxon and early Norman history. She has recently published a book on the survival of English families and nationality following the Conquest.

This volume is part of a major series, jointly conceived for English Heritage and Batsford, under the general editorship of Dr Stephen Johnson at English Heritage.

Titles in the series:

Sites
Avebury Caroline Malone
Danebury Barry Cunliffe
Dover Castle Jonathan Coad
Flag Fen: Prehistoric Fenland Centre Francis Pryor
Fountains Abbey Glyn Coppack
Glastonbury Philip Rahtz
Hadrian's Wall Stephen Johnson
Housesteads James Crow
Ironbridge Gorge Catherine Clark
Lindisfarne Deirdre O'Sullivan and Robert Young
Maiden Castle Niall M. Sharples
Roman Bath Barry Cunliffe
Roman London Gustav Milne
Roman York Patrick Ottaway
St Augustine's Abbey, Canterbury Richard Gem et al.
Stonehenge Julian Richards
Tintagel Charles Thomas
The Tower of London Geoffrey Parnell
Viking Age York Richard Hall
Wharram Percy: Deserted Medieval Village Maurice Beresford and John Hurst

Periods
Anglo-Saxon England Martin Welch
Bronze Age Britain Michael Parker Pearson
Industrial England Michael Stratton and Barrie Trinder
Iron Age Britain Barry Cunliffe
Roman Britain Martin Millett
Viking Age England Julian D. Richards
Forthcoming
Norman England Trevor Rowley
Stone Age Britain Nicholas Barton

Subjects
Abbeys and Priories Glyn Coppack
Canals Nigel Crowe
Castles Tom McNeill
Channel Defences Andrew Saunders
Church Archaeology Warwick Rodwell
Life in Roman Britain Joan Alcock
Prehistoric Settlements Robert Bewley
Roman Towns in Britain Guy de la Bédoyère
Roman Villas and the Countryside Guy de la Bédoyère
Shrines and Sacrifice Ann Woodward
Victorian Churches James Stevens Curl
Forthcoming
Roman Forts in Britain Paul Bidwell
Ships and Shipwrecks Peter Marsden

Towns
Canterbury Marjorie Lyle
Chester Peter Carrington
Durham Martin Roberts
Norwich Brian Ayers
Winchester Tom Beaumont James
York Richard Hall

Landscapes through time
Dartmoor Sandy Gerrard
Peak District John Barnatt and Ken Smith
Forthcoming
Yorkshire Dales Robert White